A NEW HISTORY OF IRELAND

Also by R. Dudley Edwards:
Church and State in Tudor Ireland

R. Dudley Edwards

A
NEW HISTORY OF
IRELAND

Gill and Macmillan

First published in 1972

Gill and Macmillan Limited
2 Belvedere Place
Dublin 1
and in London through association with the
Macmillan
Group of Publishing Companies

Jacket designed by Hilliard Hayden

7171 0580 6

Printing history
10 9 8 7 6 5 4 3 2 1

Printed and bound in the Republic of Ireland by
the Book Printing Division of
Smurfit Print and Packaging Limited, Dublin

To my wife

Contents

Contents

Preface

THIS is an attempt to present Ireland as an historical entity
from the time of its first emergence in written documentation.
Early geographers, historians, navigators, travellers and
other writers from the Mediterranean, referred to Ireland
as one of two islands close to the north-west of their world.
Occasionally these writers tell us something of the inhabitants of these islands. They distinguished different communities, by name and characteristics, so that it would
appear that various groups might exist concurrently and
that some of them spread overseas from Ireland to Britain
or to the coast of the European continent. As some of these
writers are known only from later quotations, we are not
always sure whether in fact the people and places to which
they refer are of an earlier or a later period. Early writings
in Ireland are equally imprecise, coloured perhaps more by
the period in which they were reproduced than by that of
their original authors. St Patrick's autobiographical frag-
ments, for instance, are known to us only from ninth-century
texts which may not preserve the distinctions which he
made in the fifth century. In the absence of other material
contemporary with him, we cannot be sure that he intended
to convey separate ethnic distinctions when he referred to
people in Ireland sometimes as Hiberionaci, sometimes as
Scotti.

Nowadays, the idea of an Irish community suggests the
modern concept of a nation. The community's most obvious
individual characteristic, language, is no more indicative in

Ireland today, however, than in the United States of America. But there can have been only two alternative meanings of the term 'Irish' when it is first encountered: the inhabitants of Ireland, or the people who spoke Irish.

This history attempts to present the events connected with the inhabitants of Ireland, or from Ireland, without any conscious selection to establish any thesis. The author is, however, aware of a strong disposition in himself to stress the community in relation to the island. In this he has, he believes, been pre-conditioned by the evidence which has stressed the unity of the people in one tradition or another. The early Christian writers may have made more of this oneness than would have been obvious to those of their contemporaries who, for example, felt themselves more to be men of Connacht than men of Eireann; just as to modern Americans we are more European, or even more British, than Irish, except perhaps on St Patrick's Day, or when we speak of Ireland or our Irish ancestors.

Thus this history may seem to overstress changing ideas, particularly those which link the community with contemporary Europe or America. This, however, must be noted in an Ireland which is divided politically and where the close association with Britain is more emphasised in one area. It is also to be remembered, however, that the mutual exclusiveness of the international state system of modern times has often made impassable national barriers which in the past were sometimes not even apparent. Thus the modern community of Ireland has been built up from the varying traditions of Gaelic Celts and Latin Christians, of Scandinavians and church reformers, of Cambro-Normans and canon lawyers. Henry viii had to accept it that only by establishing himself as 'king' instead of 'lord' of Ireland could he hope to secure the love, the fear and the loyalty of the Irish, and counteract their allegiance to the pope or to some traditional claimant to the Gaelic kingship. Thus it is the foreigners who have proclaimed the entity of 'Ireland', even if the historians are obliged to delimit the nation-consciousness of its various communities. The historians too, must call in question the would-be participators in political activity when they claim to set bounds to 'the march of the nation'. The history of Ireland is part of the history of mankind.

R. Dudley Edwards
5 April 1971

I

Celtic, Latin and Scandinavian Ireland

IRELAND'S situation, as the outermost of two large islands to the west of the European mainland, has exposed her to many influences in time. The earliest period of her history can be denoted by three terms, Celtic, Latin and Scandinavian, each of them associated with the language of successive groups which settled in Ireland. From the Celtic tongue is descended Irish and Scots Gaelic as well as Welsh, Cornish and Breton (the language of migrants from Britain to France some fifteen hundred years ago.) But the ancient Irish, who preserved many recollections of themselves, were unaware that they had any connection with the Welsh or with the speakers of languages other than Gaelic which existed in Britain. From some of their origin stories it is clear that they believed themselves to be the descendants of a people from Spain, called after a leader named Mil. This, at least, is what we learn from accounts written in the seventh century A.D. and later, during the period in which sufficient contemporary writing exists to enable us to call it historic. Our firm knowledge of pre-historic Ireland, the period before the seventh century A.D., is largely derived from the accounts of foreign historians and geographers as well as from the discoveries of modern archaeology.

Archaeologists now distinguish successive strata of primitive human activity by reference to different weapons and materials. About six thousand years before Christ, an ice-cap which had extended over much of north-west Europe began to recede, and some evidence suggests that there were

residents in Ireland at that time. While it is not certain that
this was in the old stone age, in the time of palaeolithic man,
it is generally accepted that, in the middle stone age,
neolithic men were to be found in Ireland. Their weapons
of stone were sharp, but unpolished. Some three thousand
years later neolithic men, who polished their weapons, are
known to have existed in Ireland.

At a later stage, weapons of stone were replaced by those
of copper and bronze and, finally, with the coming of iron,
man reached the age which is still with us, in which his
dominance over metal has had such a remarkable effect
upon the animal world and on vegetation, as well as on
human beings.

The isolation of Ireland from her neighbours in these
ancient times is emphasised by our lack of knowledge about
where its inhabitants came from. Clearly, until the disap-
pearance of the glacial mass in the ice age, the island was
uninhabited. Archaeologists connect palaeolithic man with
the northern areas of Europe, from Iceland to the Baltic
and even as far as the Central Plain of Europe. In later
neolithic times, archaeologists draw connections between
Ireland and southerly areas as far as the Mediterranean and
beyond. The links are seen in the great stone monuments
or megaliths which survive from the north-west coast of
Ireland to Stonehenge in south-west England, and thence
to various sites in the Mediterranean.

The writing of history as we know it began some 2,500
years ago with authors like Herodotus, who gave an account
of the ancient Greek world. Later writers who used Latin, the
language of the Romans, described the world they conquered, from the Greeks in the Mediterranean to the Celts
on the Atlantic Ocean. Such writers, like Caesar in the
first century B.C. and Tacitus in the first century A.D.,
were mainly concerned with Roman problems, and their
comments on perimeter areas like Ireland were incidental
and often second-hand, and must be treated accordingly.
Thus the classical historians are not sufficiently precise to

enable us to feel satisfied that they can add much to our knowledge of pre-historic Ireland. It is necessary to be extremely critical in studying them as they confuse ancient peoples and contradict one another, but perhaps their chief advantage for us lies in their clear unawareness of any significant boundaries between national territories. The earliest classical writers refer to islands off the west coast of Europe as 'the tin islands', to which traders went to secure this ingredient, essential in the making of bronze. Who were these traders? Were they Celts? The data seems to afford no certain answer.

Some writers treat of the Celts as a warrior people in central Europe, whose martial exploits terrified the Greeks, and, even more so, the Romans, whose capital they sacked in the fourth century B.C. These Celts afterwards populated the areas roughly corresponding to the modern countries of Switzerland, France, Spain, Belgium, Britain and Ireland. But the Celts were confused with the Iberians, whom they displaced in Spain, and with the Germans and the Ligurians at the mouth of the river Rhone. These misapprehensions should put us on our guard against accepting stories of these ancient peoples as if they applied to the ancient inhabitants of Ireland. Perhaps the greatest characteristic of the Celts was their individual military organisation. With their horses and chariots of war they were able to achieve victory over their enemies. At a later date they became less able to combine and stand up to disciplined forces; and after their conquest in Gaul by the soldiers of Caesar they ceased to be independent except in the outlying areas of Europe. In Ireland they successfully imposed their own culture on the defeated pre-Celtic peoples. They would also appear to have identified themselves with existing traditions of worship, to judge from their continued associations with such sacred monuments or megaliths as those of the Boyne Valley, which are now dated back to 3000 B.C.

After the conversion of the Roman Empire to Christianity, many writers sought to reconcile the history of the pagan world with their own concept of the Christian way of life. Under the influence of these classical writers, the early Christian inhabitants of Ireland sought to put on record the Irish oral tradition of the past, within the Christian framework of writers like St Isidore of Seville. By the beginning of the eighth century Irish historians had become involved in the prevailing European studies in chronology, which ultimately succeeded in dating events by reference to the life of Christ. Origin stories of Irish tribes were synchronised with decisive dates in world history. Successive generations in turn readjusted the synchronisms to earlier events, until Irish history was dated back before 2000 B.C. Accordingly the early Christian writers in Ireland underplayed the paganism of ancient Ireland and overstressed any links with Christianity and with the history of the pre-Christian Jews which they believed they detected in the old stories. The Ireland which they presented is therefore largely unreal, but they did look at it from within, while the classical writers had regarded it more remotely.

To the Romans, close connections between Ireland and Britain were very evident. In the later part of the first century A.D., when Roman Britain was governed by Agricola, we are informed by Tacitus, who was his son-in-law, that the conquest of Ireland was planned in order to terminate the sense of independence which still survived among conquered Britons. The project was sufficiently real for the governor to retain an exiled Irish ruler as a potential focus of a Roman alliance, should the invasion follow. Agricola apparently considered that one legion, and friendly allies, would adequately hold the country.

As it turned out, Roman influence in Celtic Ireland was to be confined to commercial activities and Christian missions. Of the first the evidence is archaeological, consisting mainly of coin hoards. Perhaps there were some pre-Christian linguistic borrowings of commercial and military terms. With the success of the Christian missions we are introduced to the Gaelic descendants of the Celtic

Irish of proto-historic times, a period extending from the end of the fourth into the seventh century.

What was this Gaelic Ireland, which the Romans did not conquer and which we first know of from Roman Christian missionaries? Can we view it as a society in terms of politics, economics and culture generally? Linguistically, it was a country inhabited by people who spoke Irish but who, until the substantial infiltration of Roman Christianity, were unaccustomed to writing and preferred to rely on the magic of the spoken word. Modern historical research entitles us to affirm that Ireland was divided politically and socially into about 150 communities. The political and social unit was known as the *tuath* and was ruled traditionally by a *rí* or king who was supreme leader in war, and represented his people, over whom he may once have been also judge and priest, in peace. There were groups of these communities or *tuatha*, sometimes denoted as *mór thuatha*. Occasionally the leader of such a confederacy was designated as *ruirí*, or, in the case of a large-scale confederacy headed by a dominant dynasty, *rí ruirech*. One traditional group of *tuatha* was the *cúige*, when five such confederacies were dominant long enough to establish the 'fifth' as a technical term, so that subsequent writers sought to perpetuate a 'pentarchy'. Inevitably these became equated in later times with the ecclesiastical 'province', a term imported from the Roman Empire's civil divisions. These, however, were fixed administrative units, territorially defined, unlike the Irish confederacies which expanded and contracted with the fluctuating fortunes of the dominant dynasties. By the seventh century A.D. the five-fold division had been replaced by seven or eight main groups. The more important kings of these were sometimes called high king (*ard rí*), a title which later tended to be confined to kings of all Ireland, (*ard rí Eireann*), although we learn of a high king in west Munster in the ninth century and in Ulster in the fourteenth. But the high kingship of Ireland was a late development, which subsequent historians tended to project backwards into

mythological times. It is important to remember that none
of these higher functionaries could, except by conquest,
displace the king of the *tuath*, usurp his jurisdiction or impose
any additional restrictions leading to centralisation of the
kind enforced by imperial Rome. In the Irish hierarchy of
kings a limited and personal relationship operated upwards
and downwards, and varied with individuals and with their
power.

The organisation of Celtic society in Ireland remained
essentially military, and the Celts were very slow to organise
large political communities. The Irish high king was exalted
in status, but his jurisdiction, in theory at least, did not go
beyond the individual *tuath* over which he ruled. Such a
constricted system was very difficult to understand by anyone
accustomed to the Roman system, with its concept of the
emperor, the sovereign ruler, whose authority transcended
that of all subordinates and whose very will was law. Under
the Irish system, the law enforced itself in the *tuath*, and
sanctions operated by the observance of customs in which
the individual families acted collectively. In the Roman
system, the ruler or his official enforced the law; in the Irish,
the community applied the law as defined by the ruler in
accordance with immemorial tradition (*seanchas*).

Socially, Ireland might be described as a collection of
local communities, in each of which there were three groups
of people. A professional element (*aos dána*) shared advisory
powers with the king, as well as functions connected with
sacred occasions, solemn feasts, the ascertainment and
proclamation of the law, the dignity of the rulers, and the
safeguarding of the health of the people. All these functions
were differentiation of activities which in archaic times were
monopolised in the *tuath* by the king, but which he subsequently shared with the druid (*draoi*), the poet (*fili*),
the physician, the judge (*breitheamh*) and the historian
(*seanchaidhe*). Apart from the professional element, the rest
of the population was divided between the free (*saor aicme*)
and the unfree (*daor aicme*). The free enjoyed the possession

of cattle, of the produce of the land, and other elements of wealth. The unfree included the enslaved descendants of defeated peoples and of an increasing number of prisoners kidnapped from the decaying Roman Empire. Economically this was a static, self-sufficient, agricultural society, in which there was little opportunity to build up capital. This did not mean that there were not contrasting periods of plenty and of scarcity. For agriculture, the seventh century would appear to have been prosperous and the second half of the eighth century disastrous.

Undoubtedly the possession of large flocks of cattle and many serfs might appear to make room for development. So conservative had Ireland become, however, that it failed to develop any administrative system or to countenance the growth of the power of the prince as in Roman law, or as this developed in Wales under the influence of the neighbouring Anglo-Saxon kings. With the passage of time the militarist emphasis of Celtic society in Ireland was accentuated and clients became more dependent on their masters. The precise rights of the free people (*neimhead*, 'hallowed') in contrast to the unfree, were laid down in great detail in a series of tracts on custom and legal tradition known as the Brehon Laws.

The free families within a *tuath* exercised full responsibility for the activity of their members. The laws provided a means of compounding for offences between persons in accordance with a carefully graded system for the satisfaction of injuries and the payment of compensatory fines. These varied in accordance with the social status of the injured party and his family. To say that such a system operated automatically may appear to be rather theoretical. When, however, we remember that the system provided an alternative to the vendetta or to chronic warfare, it can be appreciated how in fact it could operate within the jurisdiction of a community unlikely to exceed five thousand persons (the total Irish population being perhaps about half a million). Thus warfare was largely confined to political

relations between the *tuatha*. The individual freeman asserted
himself as an adult by demonstrating his martial powers, as
one of the companions of a young ruler or as a challenger
to a reigning king. As the wealth of the country was largely
in cattle, for a thousand years the Irish warrior class tended
to show their strength in cattle-raids from one *tuath* to
another. By the seventh century, perhaps under the influence
of Christianity, the warrior class had become a thing of the
past, of song and of story, except in so far as they were
affected by the rivalries of kings in individual *tuatha*, who
might strive to win prestige, or even perhaps to dominate
their fellow kings and establish a sphere of influence beyond
that which their fathers had enjoyed. In the same period,
again perhaps under Christian influence, individual unfree
persons may have been emancipated with the consent of
their masters.

At the time that Ireland comes into documented history,
a number of warlike kings are on record because of their
success in destroying old conglomerations of kingdoms.
With the descendants of Nial of the Nine Hostages, the
Uí Néill, as they came to be called, we come upon a new
phenomenon right at the beginning of recorded history.
The victories of the Uí Néill, not merely over the Ulaidh,
or the men of Ulster, but over the northern half of the
country as a whole, led to the growth of a new legend which
gave the Uí Néill the status of high kings of all Ireland and
broke up permanently the old tribal organisation of society.
When it came to the period in which the record was being
written down, the Uí Néill and their political achievement
had become such a central fact that the historians concerned
themselves to adjust their pedigrees to the new situation
and all recollection of a different tradition passed into
oblivion. Thus the Uí Néill came to acquire almost an
ecclesiastical sanction for their genealogical pretensions.

The culture of ancient Ireland in certain spheres was very
rich, notably in matters concerned with speech and with
story. In the period after Christianity became extended

fairly widely over the country as a whole, the ancient origin stories were written down, and in successive generations became more influenced by the historical books of the Old Testament and even by the legends of classical Greece and Rome. The introduction of written knowledge appears to have been accompanied by a diversification of professional activities: the *seanchaidhe* became concerned with history, the *breitheamh* with law. The universal 'learned man' had begun to specialise. In these circumstances, it is important for us to remember that the whole approach of the pre-Christian Irish to fact was different from what it was in the Roman system and what it is to us. Men of magic exercised power by speech, and it was only gradually that the written word became accepted outside the the area of religious activities and a speech-dominated people adjusted themselves to the written gospel as it was known in the Roman Empire of the fourth century. Ultimately an ecclesiastical sanction was given to ancient oral traditions, but only after these had been represented in writing, shorn of their more dangerous pagan elements implying recognition of the continued existence of Celtic gods.

Thus apart from what we know with certainty about St Patrick in the fifth century, the early history of Christianity in Ireland, perhaps a hundred years before, is shrouded in mystery.

St Patrick we know about because his own writings have been preserved, but otherwise we know little of the beginnings of Christianity in Ireland. The trade connections and cultural contacts between Roman Britain and Ireland apparently brought the gospel to groups in the east and south. At the beginning of the fifth century, the Roman Empire became seriously threatened in the west and was obliged from the year A.D. 410 to abandon its British province in a vain attempt to prevent the Goths and Vandals from taking over modern France, the Iberian peninsula and north Africa. Linguistically, at the time of its abandonment by Rome, Britain was divided into a more latinised area south of a line from the river Severn to Yorkshire, where Roman civilisation extended over the whole area, and, in contrast, an area north and west where Roman usages were confined to the military encampments.

It is clear enough that despite the disasters which terminated the political rule of Rome the traditions of her civilisation survived when political power passed elsewhere. Christianity was sufficiently organised to enable contact to be maintained between the capital and the former provinces, though the connections were only occasional, being largely confined to times of crisis. One of these was the spread from Britain of a heresy associated with the name of Pelagius, which is chiefly remembered because of the part taken in eradicating it by the supporters of the campaign of St Augustine of Hippo. Pelagius, who had fled from Rome before its fall to Alaric the Goth, had expounded the view that man is capable of attaining salvation by the use of his own natural virtues. This, to Augustine, was a denial of the necessity for relying on the graces conveyed through the supernatural merits of Christ. The western Church sided with Augustine, and in the year 429, St Germanus of Auxerre visited Britain in a missionary campaign against the Pelagian heretics. Pope Celestine 1 dispatched another missionary, Palladius, to deal with the same heresy among the Scots (as the Romans called the Irish of Ireland and north Britain) who believed in Christ. Of Palladius among the Scots we know nothing more, but it would appear that his sphere of activity was different from that of St Patrick, whose mission was to the pagan Irish. These would not have been infected with the heresy.

It seems reasonably certain that Patrick had been a member of a family in Roman service in the less latinised part of Britain. He had been captured by Irish raiders and for six years herded pigs in some remote area, among the woods and mountains in the north or north-west of Ireland. In the autobiographical fragment which he calls his Confession, Patrick tells us how God spoke to him, a slave suffering from cold and want, and promised him protection. He escaped home to his parents in Britain. Later on he felt inspired to return to Ireland as a Christian missionary. In a dream he saw a letter inscribed 'the voice of the Irish' (*Vox Hiberionacum*); and as he read he heard the voices of people, near the western sea, who cried out: 'We pray thee holy youth, to come and again walk among us.' And Patrick adds: 'I was pierced to the heart and could read no more, and thereupon I awoke.'

St Patrick was moved to return to Ireland to win the people to the worship of the true God. In his narrative he is very emphatic that he considers his own human attributes totally inadequate to achieve anything, and that his success in winning many Irish souls to the Christian belief was entirely due to God. He insists that he himself was but 'a sinner, one of the most rustic, one of the least of all the faithful, most contemptible to many.' Learning did not come easily to him. In spite of his enthusiasm and determination, he failed to satisfy his religious superiors; to his dismay he was considered too rural and ill-equipped. Indeed his writings show him to have been unaccustomed to Latin; his language is structurally similar to that of a person who thought in a Celtic tongue. Patrick, however, does more than assert his own orthodoxy by denying any suggestion of contamination by Pelagianism. He is, in fact, concerned to attribute his escape, his missionary vocation, his return to Ireland and his survival on the mission to the direct intervention of the Almighty. Sometimes, he tells us, this occurred in visions he saw in his sleep; on other occasions, it was through various actions of God, such as changing the minds of men who had rejected him for the Irish mission because of his inadequate education, or saving his life when he was threatened by hostile persons in Ireland.

Out of the whole narrative there emerges the positive impression of a very remarkable personality recording in his old age the evidence of divine favour in bringing about a successful mission and winning over to Christianity substantial numbers of people over a great part of the island. Patrick is not writing history: he rarely describes specific people, or particular places or events. It is easy to infer, though wrongly, that his achievement was to evangelise the country as a whole. This, we know, had not been completed by the sixth century, and the final victory of Christianity over druidism probably did not take place before the middle of the seventh century. We do not know with certainty anything about Patrick's death, and even the traditions of his burial are divided. But this remarkable personality so influenced those who came in contact with him that the legends became widespread and linked him to many places, and indeed to countries, which have no contemporary records to suggest that he was connected with them in any way.

Genealogies of the Corca Laoighdhe (in south-west Cork) claim they were the first Irish Christians. Their maritime situation, and later associations with the south-west coast of Britain and with south-west continental ports, would tend to corroborate this, at least as regards their being among the earliest peoples open to Roman influence through visiting traders. Early Christian tradition in Ireland is associated with some half-dozen saints whose activities are located in the east and south, including Ibar of Beggary Island (Wexford), Ciaran of Saighir (Offaly), Declan of Ardmore (Waterford), and Abban of Moyarney (Wexford) and Killabban (Leix), and insists that their work began before Patrick. Of Palladius there appears to be no ancient tradition.

It would seem, then, that Patrick, who may very well have worked with the Ulaidh in the north and with the Uí Néill in the west and in the central plain, was in fact the apostle of the pagan Irish. Of the details we know very little, apart from his own writings, which place him in the era of naval raids by Irish and British war leaders, one of whom, Coroticus, he denounces for capturing and killing Irish converts of Patrick's. There is no contemporary documentation for fifth-century Ireland. We cannot be certain of Patrick's exact dates. As Pope Celestine, who appointed Palladius, died in 431, it has been customary to attribute the beginning of the mission of Patrick to the year 432. But others have argued for a date some thirty years later. As Patrick does not mention contemporaries by name, we cannot be sure of the dates attributed in later writings to the activities of fifth-century Irish kings.

It is not until the late sixth century that we enter on the firm ground of contemporary documentation in Irish history. By that time the Christian Church in Ireland, undoubtedly shaped on the pattern of the Roman Empire in the west by Patrick, Palladius and their contemporaries, had become assimilated to the Irish social system. The original episcopal system linked to individual *tuatha* had become outmoded by a monastic order politically linked to the overkings.

Monasticism had come to the western Roman Empire in the late fourth century, when it is associated with St Martin of Tours. Like Patrick, Martin's rusticity made him unwelcome among the more sophisticated urban clergy. In one sense, the movement led by St Germanus of Auxerre was anti-monastic, as it stressed the futility of the perfectionism favoured by the hermits and monks. Perhaps St Patrick's education can be linked to the Auxerre region as later sources alleged. Perhaps too the episcopal foundations in the north midlands, allegedly of Auxilius (at Killashee), of Iserninus (at Kilcullen), and of Secundinus (at Dunshaughlin) were made by missionaries from the same area in Gaul. Certainly the church in Ireland in the fifth century had no particular monastic bias, but with the collapse of the Roman administrative system in western Europe before the onslaught of the Goths, the Saxons and the Franks, Christianity in Britain and Ireland came to depend upon contacts with the Rhone valley, where monasticism had developed as an intellectual and social movement, notably in the island of Lerins near Provence.

In Britain the same century which witnessed the with-drawal of the Roman garrisons also experienced the raids and subsequent settlements of the Saxons and Angles. They destroyed in great part the Roman way of life in what we now know as England. It was in Wales and the western countries that Christianity survived, as well as in modern Brittany which was settled about this time from Britain. Monasticism seems to have proved the successful method of organising Christianity outside the former Roman Empire, and British saints like David appear to have been educated from the Rhone valley and thus to have communicated monasticism to Ireland. Perhaps the north British monastery of Candida Casa, founded by St Ninian in the late fourth century and traditionally the formative influence on certain north of Ireland saints like Finnian of Moville, Eoghan of Ard Straw and Tigernach of Clones, provided colleagues for Patrick's mission. There are traces too of a group of British saints in the Boyne area whom later writers may have added to Patrick's group as the legend about him grew.

The Roman Church had been developed in a centralised empire which contrasted with the Irish policy, with its multiplicity of independent *tuatha*. The earliest church regulations in Ireland aimed at preserving the bishop's independence of the king, too successfully perhaps to enable the Roman jurisdictional system to be assimilated in Ireland. Instead the Irish, including the kings, endowed their saints with gifts of lands which could be integrated into the social system and which grew imperceptibly, like the changing political alliances, into groups of houses without any pro-visions dissociating the foundations from the people. Thus the saints displaced the bishops in popular estimation. Concurrent with the coming of Christianity to Ireland there took place the political revolution which established the Uí Néill domination from Connacht over west and central Ulster, and north Leinster. The predominating fact in the dawn of written Irish history was that St Colmcille of the Uí Néill who was at the head of the most influential monastic group in the north, ruled from his foundation on the island of Iona off the coast of the Scottish territory which had been settled from Ireland.

More than a century later the Venerable Bede, in his *Ecclesiastical History of the English Nation,* pays tribute to the missionary enthusiasm of the Irish saints whose foundations had spread from Iona to Lindisfarne off the east coast of Northumbria. It was this enthusiasm which broke down the rigid and exclusive jurisdictional system of the Roman dioceses, since the saints who founded groups of monasteries became the heroes of cults, comparable to such mythological creations as Cuchulain and Oisin whose votaries were not confined to one *tuath* or one age. This enabled the clergy of Ireland to be accorded a professional status such as that enjoyed by the poets, without respect to whether they were attached to Ciaran of Clonmacnoise or Patrick of Armagh. They were of course associated with a different political system in the northern half of the country, brought about by the Uí Néill displacement of the older groups in the north and north midlands.

It is difficult for us to trace this development. Just as political victors tried to eradicate all signs of the earlier situation, the ecclesiastical victors in the struggle between the traditionalists and the Roman modernists tried to rewrite the history of the early period of the Church in Ireland as if all had been moderns and Romans. The reformers, to use a later term, became identified with the strengthening of the powers of the kings, though they did not attempt to reimpose the system of episcopal jurisdiction. They preferred, when secular influence increased, to attempt a more purified system like that of the *Céli Dé* (Culdees).

The reformers were not, however, able to weaken the reputation of the great religious communities even where the *co-arb* or successor of a monastic foundation was a layman, which many of them were, in the eigth century. Such lay superiors were often selected from one family which had become custodians of ecclesiastical lands and properties. At Armagh, for example, the successors of St Patrick identified themselves with the reform movement so far as to bring themselves into line with Roman usage on the dating of Easter and the method of ecclesiastical tonsure, but they successfully resisted the re-establishment of the system of episcopal jurisdiction until the twelfth century. There is evidence that this was also the attitude of the successors of St Brigid at Kildare and of St Ciaran at Clonmacnoise. Reforming congregations such as the *Céli Dé* were established but had only a partial success.

The golden age of Irish monasticism extended for most of the sixth century into the first quarter of the seventh. It was a period remarkable for the artistic achievements of the writers and illuminators of liturgical books, the craftsmen who fashioned sacred objects and the builders of religious houses. The study of chronology became important because of the need to date Easter and the other variable feasts of the Church, and as a result the annalists of north-eastern monasteries began formally to record historic events. There was also an attempt to compile definitive biographies of Patrick, Brigid and other saints. In general it can be said that the schools of learning which emerged in the new monasteries adopted Latin culture, in art as much as in literature.

Side by side with this development, an indigenous literature in Irish was also growing. It is particularly associated with St Colmcille, who was esteemed as a great patron of the *filidh*, the professional literary class of pre-Christian Ireland. His reputation as a poet is evidenced by a considerable body of hymns and other material ascribed to him in succeeding centuries. While Colmcille was thus credited with many writings which may well have been the work of less gifted men, the fact that he was one of the Uí Néill, the ruling northern family, undoubtedly gave prestige to Irish literary development in Latin communities. The seventh century saw the beginnings of devotional poetry in Irish, an indication that the oral facility had not been entirely lost by the transfer to writing.

Writing on secular subjects also became common; the prolific sagas of the old literary tradition of Ireland were elaborated under the influence of pagan classical authors such as Virgil. But the Christian Latin influence in these sagas is also clear; they were compiled in the period when churchmen in Ireland were no longer preoccupied with professional writings and the copying of liturgical works.

Thus, Latin learning and its written system profoundly modified and partly christianised early Gaelic learning, which had depended so largely on oral transmission. However, not all the remnants of pagan customs were eradicated, and old traditions persisted among a people with long memories. Christianity, as it extended over the Roman Empire, and into its border provinces such as Britain, was essentially an urban phenomenon. Outside the centres of Roman civilisation, belief in the gods of the Celts and other peoples remained very strong. Although the introduction of writing into Ireland replaced the druids by the *filidh*, the supernatural powers of the professional class could still be employed, by means of satire, to denounce and punish those negligent of ancient tradition. In addition, the fact that Christianity and alphabetical writing were simultaneously communicated to Ireland gave some supernatural sanction to the archaism of its Celtic society.

In Britain, the century which witnessed the withdrawal of Roman garrisons also saw the invasions of the Anglo-Saxons who destroyed the Roman way of life in much of what is now eastern England. So bitter was the fighting and so savage the destruction that the Christians of Britain, driven into northern and western parts and into Wales, did not share the desire of missionaries in Gaul and Rome to win over the Anglo-Saxons to the gospel.

But towards the end of the sixth century, the Church at Rome reached some understanding with the barbarian peoples which enabled it to sponsor missions among them.

In this effort to convert the Anglo-Saxons, Pope St Gregory won some co-operation from the Franks, who had turned to Christianity after their conquest of much of Gaul. Roman Benedictine monks under St Augustine of Canterbury tried out Gregory's plan in Britain, but their work had unbroken effect only at Canterbury and in south-eastern parts.

In northern Britain the missionary work was largely in the hands of Irish monks from Colmcille's foundation on Iona. Through Colmcille, the Uí Néill and the Dál Riada, the first Irish colonisers in Scotland, made an alliance which lasted for over fifty years, so providing the peaceful atmosphere necessary for the spread of Christianity.

From Iona, Colmcille's disciples christianised the Irish settlers in Argyle and gradually the Picts of Scotland and the Anglo-Saxons of Northumbria. By the end of the sixth century Christianity had again become a force in Britain. Inevitably, however, because of inadequate communications with Rome, a wholly different system of organisation existed in the Irish and Welsh spheres of influence, in contrast to the newer Roman missions centred at Canterbury. The latter were organised episcopally and maintained more up-to-date methods of calculating the date of Easter, the greatest Christian feast of the year. The loyalty of the Welsh and Irish to their more antiquated festival system led to serious differences with the Canterbury monks and, ultimately, to the withering of the Celtic missions. The Irish withdrew from the island of Lindisfarne from which they had christianised Northumbria. To Bede, who in other respects was so fulsome in his praise of Irish monks in this area, the failure of these to accept the directions of Roman missionaries put them in danger of hell fire. Eventually the Northumbrians and the other Anglo-Saxon peoples accepted Roman methods as decreed by the Synod of Whitby in 664, but it took another century before the Welsh and Cornish agreed to submit. As for the Irish, so strong was the influence of Colmcille and his tradition on Iona that his ninth successor, Adomnán, was only able to secure acceptance of the Roman system after a very difficult campaign during which he was temporarily exiled from the island. But by the end of the seventh century, the monasteries founded by Colmcille or his disciples, both in Scotland and in the northern half of Ireland, were prepared to accept the Roman system.

In Munster and in other southern parts of Ireland, the Roman system had been adopted about two generations earlier, but there is evidence that rival communities existed there, favouring either the older or the newer system. Both eagerly sought to win supporters not merely from among the living but also, and which was perhaps more important, by appealing to the memory of their great founders. Although the Synod of Whitby led to the re-establishment of the diocesan system in England, which had disappeared after the withdrawal of the Roman soldiers, the episcopal system of jurisdiction was not introduced in Ireland for another five hundred years. The great monasteries continued to dominate religious life in the country, even if they had settled their differences with Rome over the calculation of Easter and the method of tonsuring the clergy.

There was another area where the influence of Irish Christianity was significant for a century or two after the destruction of the Roman Empire in the west. On the mainland of Europe, especially between the Rhine and the Seine, a substantial number of Irish monks were active as hermits or as missionaries from one place to another. Outstanding among these missionaries was St Columbanus, who made his foundations in Burgundy, in the Rhone valley and subsequently in parts of modern Switzerland. Columbanus, a man of sixty when he reached this area, was fired by an enthusiasm for winning souls and for achieving reforms which made him virtually irresistible, that is until he was confronted by powerful vested interests. To the single-minded Columbanus, the goodwill of the Frankish rulers and their clergy was a wholly inadequate deterrent when he became aware that the royal race behaved as though it above the Christian law. There followed denunciations he local rulers and their clergy. When an effort was de to show that Columbanus failed to observe Roman law concerning Easter and the Roman jurisdictional system, he attacked the learning of his opponents and appealed against them to the Pope, Gregory the Great. Later he wrote to Pope Boniface iv urging that he clear himself of the suspicion of heresy by a declaration of faith before a Church synod. Inevitably there were few to favour Columbanus when he was driven out of the Burgundian kingdom. The Benedictine monastic rules favoured by Rome came to be preferred to the more austere system of Columbanus. Thereafter the enthusiasm of the Irish gave way and, while they were long remembered, their foundations were assimilated into the local system and so conformed more closely with the methods adopted in Rome.

In addition, the extension of monastic development from Ireland must have been disrupted by mortality, invasion, and by a series of great plagues, from about the end of the seventh century, which decimated western society. The Scandinavian raiders who dominated the coast line of Europe during the ninth century also pillaged the monasteries. For a short period, Irish scholars found refuge with Frankish patrons. But even these scholars seem to have vanished from the scene once Christian Ireland, and its Latin culture, became more laicised in facing up to the Viking invaders from Scandinavia.

The eighth-century Scandinavian attacks on western Europe represent the last great invasion from the north which drastically transformed the Roman Empire of the west. The Scandinavians profoundly altered the trend of history for approximately five centuries, penetrating into the east from the Baltic and the Black Sea, paralysing the new Roman Empire of the Frankish ruler, Charles the Great, and leaving a permanent mark on Anglo-Saxon England during the ninth century. Finally one hundred years later, under the influence of French civilisation, they established the duchy of Normandy.

The Scandinavian raiders were originally interested in loot. In Ireland they concentrated particularly on the monasteries, which had become extremely wealthy in precious metals, the donations of enthusiastic converts. The Northmen, as they were usually called, inevitably terrified the peaceful inhabitants of the monasteries who described their attacks so vividly that for many generations it was difficult to believe that anything good came to Ireland as a consequence of the Scandinavian wars.

Our own familiarity with twentieth-century aerial warfare, and with the way in which apparently peaceable people can become involved in it, has made it possible to look at the northern invasions in a different light. Groups of people who had little liking for one another were thrown together in the face of common peril as warfare became part of their daily lives. Under the impact of war, monks and men of religion were willing to countenance the ancient pagan cultures of Ireland, the stories of gods and heroes of old and the ferocity and brutality of their deeds. Isolated monasteries could hardly hope to survive the destructive raids of the Northmen; those which joined together were better able to withstand attack.

Early ninth-century Ireland had not suffered any major invasion for more than five hundred years. The fact that the neighbouring island of Britain had been under constant attack from the Romans, from the Anglo-Saxons, as well as from the pagan Irish, had created a different mentality in the two islands. Towards the end of the eighth century, it might be said of Ireland that the fusion of Latin and Gaelic traditions had been so successful that over those parts of the country where Christianity's impact had been substantial the primitive warfare of the descendants of the Celts had virtually disappeared. It is true that conflicts still arose, and that political alliances continued to bring about a resort to battle, particularly in those areas where Christian influences had been only superficial. But kings and nobles had become possessors of great flocks of cattle and people were primarily concerned with farming.

It must be stressed that this was the world of Colmcille as depicted by Adomnán; and even in that world there could be battles, as, for example, the conflict noted in the Annals of Ulster for 760 A.D. between the communities of Cluain and of Birr. In general there would appear to have been a substantial improvement in agriculture from the fifth to the seventh century, suggesting that a self-sufficient economy of some degree of affluence had replaced the more primitive nomadic system of earlier times. It may very well be that this was followed by a regression in consequence of the stresses and storms of the second half of the eighth century, in which bad weather conditions and destruction of crops led to famine and plague. The period's end coincided with the beginning of the Scandinavian raids.

It has often been said that Christianity had done much to soften the Romans, causing them to abandon those martial virtues which had kept together the greatest unit of civilisation the world had ever known. Allowing for the obvious difference, monastic Ireland had certainly affected its martial people in the same way. Even the poets no longer enjoyed the prestige of an earlier day and it has been claimed that, were it not for the intervention of St Colmcille, this element of the population which concerned itself with recording and glorifying the military attributes of its patrons would scarcely have survived. Clearly the early Christians had little sympathy with the traditions of pagan Ireland, but through the Scandinavian invasions which commenced late in the eighth century relations between Irish and Latin culture became more integrated.

The first raids of the Vikings, as those Scandinavians who looted overseas were called in their home country, created a lasting resentment between them and the intellectual and religious elements of Irish society. Their visits were recorded as disastrous and the beginning of a new barbarism. The capacity of their ships to invest the country's rivers and coasts paralysed the monastic system. As natural sailors, the Vikings made full use of their military superiority over the communities where defence forces were inadequately organised, with the exception of a few who were sufficiently secularised to resist successfully.

The first Scandinavian attacks were followed by the establishment of permanent military camps. From these strategic points it was possible for them to raid across the Irish Sea to Britain. Military bands, of mixed Irish and Viking origin, apparently became involved in these wars at an early date.

The third stage in the Scandinavian impact, in the course of the ninth century, was the making of permanent settlements, some of which persist to our own day at Dublin, Wexford, Waterford, Cork and Limerick. These coastal settlements quickly grew into towns and centres of trade, and the Scandinavians themselves adapted to Irish conditions. Urbanisation was the great contribution of the Norse to Ireland. Within two centuries they had also become subordinated to the more powerful Irish kings, and most of them had adopted Christianity, although they maintained their overseas ecclesiastical connections, particularly with England.

But civilised life had sustained serious reverses from which some of the centres of learning and religion did not recover. In the political sphere, the less martial *tuatha* weakened under the impact of the more aggressive. A good illustration is the development of Dal gCais, a minor state in Munster to the west of the lower reaches of the river Shannon. Under its king, Brian Boru, it carried on ceaseless warfare with both the Limerick Vikings and its Irish neighbours, particularly the kings of Cashel. Brian Boru succeeded in taking over Cashel and dominating Munster as a whole. He imposed his influence on Leinster and Dublin, and obliged the high king Maelsheachlain to concede precedence to him. In displacing Maelsheachlain he brought to an end the high kingship of the Ulster Uí Néill, which had lasted almost undisputed for three hundred years.

It was not unusual for Vikings to be in alliance with one Irish kingdom against another: intermarriage between the new peoples and older inhabitants became common enough, particularly among the ruling classes. By the end of the tenth century the Scandinavian settlements had been practically absorbed into the Irish body politic. It was against foreign forces of Scandinavians assembled at Dublin that Brian Boru fought the famous battle of Clontarf in 1014; and Brian's victory, which cost him his life, was not followed by any displacement of the existing Viking kingdoms in Ireland. The Gaelic kings managed to contain the Norse, restricting their settlements to areas around the coastal towns they had founded.

In the century after the battle of Clontarf there was some growth in political centralisation in Ireland, on what we today would call a provincial level, similar to the amalgamation of kingdoms in England and France. The absence of any form of central government had made it difficult for the Scandinavians to dominate the country as a whole. Though the chief kings gained in power from the reinforcement of military characteristics, the Irish reaction to the Vikings remained for long at a local level and no centralised system of administration emerged. The Viking challenge had left Brian Boru's own forces so diminished that on his death at the moment of victory much of his centralising initiative was dissipated. His descendants and the royal families of Leinster and Connacht fought continuously for the chief kingship until the O'Connors of Connacht appear to have secured it without challenge by the time the Normans came to Ireland about 150 years later.

The high kingship itself remained essentially a primacy of honour, chiefly of value in battle. Only by tribute, hostages and some military support could the high king exercise any influence over the provincial and other kings. Furthermore, he could not transmit his personal primacy to his successor.

As in England and in the Scandinavian world, military prowess only occasionally passed from father to son in sufficient degree for the inheritor to continue enjoying his father's hard-won pre-eminence. Developments in Ireland thus had their counterpart in western Europe, where a persistent state of war consolidated feudalism. This was a self-contained system, a political and social hierarchy which linked various landowners to a common lord on a military basis and which effectively protected a community under a landowner from external attack. In Ireland, however, the lord, still known as the king, was not necessarily accorded full political jurisdiction corresponding to his proprietary right. The persistence of segmentary opposition was a phenomenon indicative of recurrence of particularism. Thus the lord might have to share his power with a rival or brook an opponent in one particular area. Such rivals came from the same or rival dynasties. Thus heredity existed, but primogeniture did not. A lord succeeded by winning over a group of key subordinates rather than by the acclaim of the community.

The growth of political amalgamations was paralleled by a movement for the reform of the Church. The earlier reform movement re-emerged in Ireland once closer relations were again established between it and its neighbour after the Norman conquest of England in 1066. The Normans who came to England from France had become allies of the reforming popes. Having adopted the religion and manners of their Frankish hosts, these descendants of Scandinavian settlers became both intrepid fighters for French military and cultural traditions and the armoured shock troops of the reformed papacy. They took to the crusades with enthusiasm, and, in the name of reform, won papal blessing for their incursions to Britain in the eleventh century and to Ireland in the twelfth.

The atmosphere in Europe in the eleventh century had undoubtedly much to do with reform. Superstition played its part, as the fear of plague and death, the lack of scientific explanation for unexpected natural phenomena, the sense of doom attendant upon the defeats of Christian armies in the crusades, the widespread belief that the end of the world was imminent, all gave rise to popular religious pilgrimages and to a desire for reform. Temporal authorities too appear to have strengthened their own positions by promulgating reforms and winning the approval of eminent churchmen. New upstart families which established their authority sought to link themselves with remote, but respectable, antecedents. Brian Boru, in setting himself up as high king in Ireland, had been careful to identify himself with the primacy of Armagh, and the high kings who came after him, from his own Munster or from rival provinces, always accorded pre-eminence to the successor of St Patrick.

Vikings accentuated substantially the secularisation of Christian society in Ireland. Earlier efforts to secure the immunity from warfare of religious and of non-combatants became less relevant in an age which constantly experienced looting raids and the pillage and slaughter of whole communities. Tendencies to restrict ecclesiastical property and offices to particular families became more marked, and even the coarbs, successors of the great saintly founders at Armagh, Bangor and other monasteries came to include men who had never taken holy orders.

The papacy itself in the middle of the eleventh century had become the prize of Roman families, so that the very centre of Christendom needed reform. This it was given by the German emperors, who, however, as temporal masters, showed little concern for the Church *per se*. This situation in Rome puts into perspective the usurpation of the church of Armagh by secular families. They considered it more important that the successor of St Patrick should enjoy a generally-recognised primacy than that the spiritual activities of the great monasteries be modernised in accordance with European reforming ideas. Reform in this situation was not easy. As long as questions of prestige, disputes over the high kingship or struggles between the patrons of great monasteries took priority, the very notion of reform might never arise.

In Ireland, therefore, controversy over reform became intertwined with the resolution of political issues. Mutual distrust between Irish and Norse—which was partly economic in motivation—was evident in what appears as a collective plan by the Scandinavians to gain immunity from the Irish ecclesiastical system. In spite of marital connections between Norse and Gaelic rulers, the Dublin Norse attempted to link themselves ecclesiastically with England. Their associations overseas led the Ostmen, as the Norse in Ireland had come to be called, to regard the whole of north-west Europe as a unit. Northern Britain and Ireland were parts of it; a Norse king of Dublin, for example, could aspire to become king of York. After the Norman conquest of England, the Irish Ostmen turned to the chief Anglo-Norman archbishop at Canterbury for the consecration of their bishops. Bishops from Dublin and other Ostman towns undertook to become his suffragans. Indeed, it was Archbishop Lanfranc of Canterbury, the protégé of William the Conqueror, who took the lead in urging the chief Irish kings to sponsor ecclesiastical and moral reforms.

Church reform in Ireland during the eleventh century largely centred on the need to reaffirm the primacy of bishops. This involved the subordination of the great monasteries to a diocesan system of church jurisdiction, and the connections of many of the older monasteries with more parts of the country than one gave rise to considerable difficulties in securing acceptance for the new system. In Ireland at the end of the eleventh century the reform party became active and was supported by Muirceartach Ó Briain, high king 'with opposition'. His request to Archbishop Anselm of Canterbury to consecrate a bishop at Waterford was supported by bishops in Dublin, Meath and Leinster. But the ambitions of Canterbury were restrained by the visits of papal legates from time to time. They helped to strengthen the connections with Rome and weakened the expansionist tendencies of Canterbury, so that Irish bishops in Norse towns ceased to take oaths of obedience to English archbishops.

The synod of Rath Breasail in 1111 proposed to establish a diocesan system of twelve suffragan bishops, under archbishops at Armagh and Cashel, and made it clear that reform in Ireland would be associated directly with the papacy. However, it took another forty years of negotiations before the connection of Dublin and the other Norse towns with Canterbury was fully severed and the Ostmen brought finally into the Irish ecclesiastical system.

The reform movement in Ireland in the middle of the twelfth century was dominated by St Malachy, whose influence was decisive and lasting. The great St Bernard of Clairvaux, in his life of St Malachy, described those who opposed the reforms of his friend in Ireland as sinners against the light, and he implied that the successors of St Patrick at Armagh had abandoned all religious practices. But we must make allowances for exaggeration in the account Bernard gives of Malachy's life, since Bernard was writing for the simple purpose of edification and promoting church reform. At the same time, it is clear enough that concurrent with the Scandinavian impact, the spontaneous enthusiasm of the first Irish monks had given way to the more moderate virtues of scholars, administrators and security men. Irish monasteries in this atmosphere began to replace, record and collect lives of their founders, but these biographical writings bear close resemblance to the lives of warlike chiefs and political rivals. This greater emphasis on the worldly successes of churchmen and saints was undoubtedly associated with the secularisation of monasteries which St Bernard found so lamentable. The extension of Christianity throughout the country had not been accomplished without a vulgarisation of its spiritual aims, and the stress on miracles in a wide variety of activities shows the extent to which ancient pagan heroes had been replaced by hero-saints with an equal reputation for securing supernatural support in their struggles against the forces of evil and also against the fame of their own saintly rivals.

Great collections of literature, profane as well as sacred, were thus preserved in the monasteries. Among their treasures were the ancient Saga of Fionn MacCumhaill, and the Ulster Saga of Cuchulain, *Táin Bó Cuailnge* (the Cattle Raid of Cooley). In addition, the survival of a great body of topographical writings made it possible to link different localities with the more widely known of the great saints and heroes. The old stories were passed on in a form very obviously influenced by the assumptions of Christianity. Indeed their authors sought ecclesiastical sanction for them, if only to protect the stories from destruction by church reformers, who were inclined to dismiss them as profane and possibly evil. But such learning as the scholars aired only serves to indicate the low level which intellectual life had reached. The victory of these reformers was only achieved when they eventually succeeded in excluding secular interests, literary as well as political, from the monasteries. Thus the Church became dissociated from the traditional learning of the people; and secular learning, including the provision of historical ancestry for the new royal and professional families, developed outside its former centres. Reform ultimately broke the alliance between the monasteries and Gaelic culture.

It was St Malachy who devised the compromise by which the new episcopal system proved viable in Ireland. Malachy had been called from his monastery at Bangor in succession to the bishopric of Connor and the archbishopric of Armagh, but political rivalries forced him out of each office for a time. Yet the position of the reform party was maintained. Malachy arranged with the local political ruling family, with whom he was concerned as Abbot of Bangor, that they abandon their monopoly of church appointments. They were however guaranteed the fruits of church lands, on condition that they agreed to contribute a fixed proportion to the support of the bishop and clergy, in much the same way as minor kings supported overkings.

In Europe in the twelfth century it was largely due to St Bernard's inspiration that the triumphant reorganisation of the Church continued around the foundation of new religious orders like the Cistercians. After the establishment of the first Cistercian houses in Ireland in the 1140s, reform of the older monasteries quickly got under way. Malachy's personal prestige attracted the Cistercians and other foreign religious orders to Ireland, though many monks returned to Clairvaux at the first opportunity, disillusioned with the Irish. Malachy himself died while visiting Bernard at Clairvaux in 1148. Before his death he had secured papal confirmation for an Irish archiepiscopate independent of Canterbury. This arrangement was sanctioned by the papal legate at the Synod of Kells in 1152; and archbishoprics were created in Dublin and Tuam in addition to those already approved for Armagh and Cashel. Two years later, the consecration of a new Cistercian monastery at Mellifont in the presence of the high king appeared to guarantee permanence to reform.

In the eleventh and twelfth centuries the popes made use of temporal rulers to press reluctant churchmen to adopt further Roman usages and strengthen diocesan jurisdiction. They appealed to secular authorities to promulgate laws restricting the incidence of war, such as giving immunity to women and to clerics, and imposing sanctions for the non-observance of Sunday as a holy day. Similarly in Ireland during the previous two centuries, it was largely by pressure from temporal authorities that Rome had successfully induced monastic communities to abandon their outmoded usages particularly regarding the dating of Easter.

The effective reformation of the clergy in Ireland in the twelfth century seemed to require even closer links with the papacy, if needs be at the price of replacing native secular rulers by the Anglo-Norman kings of England. At a time when St Bernard had inspired the second crusade from Europe in 1147, Pope Adrian IV had felt justified in giving crusader rights in Ireland to Henry II of England; and the papal title 'Lord of Ireland' was conferred on several kings. The popes had allied with the Normans in order to remain independent of the German emperor, and put no obstacles in the way of Norman ambitions in England and Ireland if these could be associated with the papal policy of reform.

The Irish kings were lavish in their grants of land to the Church and to the new religious orders, but from Rome's point of view it was the Normans who proved most successful eventually, since they extended within their sphere of influence in Ireland the parochial and the diocesan system. This was organised feudally, on the basis of the landed revolution brought to these islands from Normandy. Norman kings of England, and later of Ireland, became in theory owners of their new territories in the manner of the ancient Romans: they granted subordinate offices and great estates to their chief followers. But the feudal knights were too vigorous to countenance the growth of royal absolutism and the new legal system was qualified by frequent appeals to the sword until a new Europe began to emerge in the fifteenth century. A civil war was fought among the descendants of William I in England within a century of the Conqueror's victory at Hastings. Commenting on the reality beneath the nominally Christian life, the Anglo-Saxon chronicle reported men as saying openly that Christ and his saints were asleep.

Under Henry II, from 1154, there was some restoration of order. But there arose a clash between the authority of the pope and that of the king. Renewed study of Roman law provoked conflicts between churchmen and secular rulers, each concerned to secure their own absolute power. The popes, for their part, based their claims on canon law, which was developed out of the imperial Roman code. In the course of the dispute, some of Henry II's knights murdered the Archbishop of Canterbury, Thomas Becket. The king, with good reason, deplored the murder and did penance for it, but he continued to set limits to the claims of the pope in England. The king maintained laws restricting the clergy, imposed in the constitutions of Clarendon in 1164, which made the Anglo-Norman church dependent for its endowment upon the state. Thus it was that the successors of the first Norman allies of the popes aspired to an authority within the Church greater than that exerted by any emperor. This the popes could hardly have foreseen.

As far as pre-Norman Ireland was concerned, the absence of a parochial system sustained by the payment of tithes might appear to feudal Europe to have justified the intervention of Henry II in the name of reform. The tithe system as it developed in twelfth-century Europe and in the Norman dominions had been fully integrated with feudal society and with the beginnings of a capitalist economy. The self-sufficient economy which still persisted over much of Ireland was unlikely to make the Church affluent there. Norman Ireland was to replace it by a tithe system which gave the clergy enough capital to live a better ordered and a more well-to-do way of life, comparable with that in England and not far below the level of France. It tended, however, to restrict episcopal office to those notable as administrators and not as saints.

In addition, the rise of towns in the Scandinavian areas, the introduction of a Danish coinage from England and the extensive purchasing of slaves from the Bristol market encouraged Bristol merchants to extend their activities to Ireland. It was to his Bristol subjects that Henry II was to hand over the city of Dublin after the Norman invasion. Thus, although a minor dispute over the ambitions of a provincial Leinster king was the pretext for Anglo-Norman intervention in Ireland, the Normans were bound to come once they attempted to round off their dominions and take in trading-places with which they, their city merchants and the Irish Ostmen had become associated.

2

Gaelic and Norman Ireland, 1169–1399

In the year 1166, after his defeat by the high king Rory O'Conor, Dermot MacMurrough was deprived of his kingdom of Leinster and driven out of Ireland. He took refuge with the Augustinian monks at Bristol, and with the consent of Henry II, the Angevin King of England, negotiated the assistance of several Norman knights in Wales, asking them to effect his restoration in Leinster. Should the enterprise succeed, Dermot promised to one of his new allies, Richard Fitzgilbert, Earl of Pembroke, who was better known as Strongbow, the hand of his daughter and the right of succession in his own kingdom. Thus it was Dermot who brought the first Norman forces back with him to Ireland, and he was restored to his kingdom in 1167. Two years later a larger force landed, with Strongbow at their head. They stormed Waterford and conquered Leinster as a whole, and on the death of MacMurrough in May 1171, Strongbow succeeded to the King of Leinster. This form of inheritance, common enough in England, was as yet unknown in Ireland.

The high king, Rory O'Conor, had vainly tried to defeat the Normans. His high kingship had been an energetic, military one, and for a moment, after MacMurrough's death, O'Conor seemed to have won widespread support against the invaders. But an unexpected sortie by the Normans dissipated his army before Dublin and the high king withdrew, never again to command such an all-Ireland host.

To Henry II, Strongbow's success also constituted something of a threat. Henry decided to visit Ireland to prevent the establishment of independent Norman lordships there, and when he did so in October 1171 he received the submission of the Norman *conquistadores*. But in addition, in virtue of his claim to be lord of Ireland, he sanctioned the granting of territories to Strongbow in Leinster and to Hugh de Lacy in Meath. Some of the Irish kings also submitted, Notably O'Brien of Thomond and MacCarthy of Desmond, since they were anxious to put limits to the new conquests. Their action, as it turned out, marked the end of the conflicts for the high kingship between Irish kings. Henry also took the Scandinavian towns of Dublin, Wexford and Waterford under his protection, received the leading churchmen, and was recognised by a church synod at Cashel as lawful ruler of Ireland and patron of the reform movement. The synod added that in future the usages of the Church in Ireland should be identical with those in England.

Although an even greater foreign body than the Scandinavians was now present in Ireland, to the traditional annalists the community had undergone little obvious change, except in one respect: the system of autonomous states began to involve foreign lords with ambitions to replace existing Gaelic kings with their own dynasties. All the same, the community of Ireland must not be looked on simply as an outlying area of the realm of England, nor its history written simply from the standpoint of the invaders, since the absence of any administrative bureaucratic system in pre-Norman Ireland meant that things went on much as before.

Four ecclesiastical provinces had already been imposed by a supranational authority, that of the pope, a fact which underlines the absence of a recognised unity of authority in civil as well as in church affairs in Ireland. The new dioceses, which were related to the reorganisation of minor kingdoms, and the whole episcopal system of jurisdiction, were com-

pletely at variance with native practice. Even the authority
of the successor of St Patrick at Armagh was called into
question, and under pressure from the reformers Armagh
was obliged to share its pre-eminence first with one archbishop at Cashel and subsequently with two more at Tuam
and Dublin.

Politically, twelfth-century society in Ireland was far from
static. Meath and Munster were partitioned in the course
of wars between different kings, and the revived *cúigí* broke
up. Successive outstanding kings sought to defeat their rivals
by pitting one against another. Dermot MacMurrough had
followed the sort of career associated with a crude character
of a very crude age. He successfully extended his influence
from his minor dynastic kingdom to take in the whole of
Leinster, but he fell because he had been the ally of the
Uí Néill high king who was defeated by O'Conor of
Connacht. With the aid of such allies as O'Rourke of
Breifni, the new high king then seemed to be on the point
of breaking up every potential combination of rulers,
including MacMurrough, which might displace him. And
it was only because he obtained allies abroad that
MacMurrough won enough strength to challenge O'Conor
at the highest level. After his death, and Strongbow's
succession in Leinster, Henry II, like O'Conor, had to
prevent any Norman or Gaelic ruler from becoming a
threat to him as a potential high king in Ireland.

Churchmen in Ireland acted as reconcilers between these
conflicting interests. Through the intercession of the Archbishop of Tuam in 1175 they reached an agreement with
Henry II at Windsor and accepted Henry's lordship.
O'Conor's authority as King of Connacht was recognised,
but his title as high king was quietly abandoned. In this
way the Gaelic kingship of all Ireland came to an end. But
the position was made easier for the former high king. He
became responsible for collecting from the other kings a
tribute for their foreign lord who, for this purpose, undertook
to put his forces at O'Conor's disposal. Thus, in a nominal

sense, O'Conor remained king over the other kings of Ireland, although he disclaimed all authority over areas which Henry in future would rule directly. These included the Norman lordships such as Meath and Leinster, and the port towns such as Dublin and Cork. To churchmen like the Archbishops of Dublin and Tuam, the whole arrangement might have appeared to promise peace, and might well have done so had O'Brien and other Irish kings not subsequently revolted against O'Conor. The agreement at Windsor was a frank recognition by Henry of the limitations of his new lordship, which in any case meant very little to him. It was also a virtual admission that he did not propose to set up any formal structure of administration. Instead, his intention was to use Strongbow and other grantees in Ireland as his representatives, although this obliged him to play off one against the other.

Rory O'Conor had accepted the feudal relationship of lord and vassal. He took the Plantagenet king as his *dominus* and swore to be his *homo*. However, when the Irish kings of the north and of the south ceased to recognise the authority of the former high king and rebelled against him, Henry could plausibly argue that he must make new, realistic arrangements independently of O'Conor, and give *ex post facto* approval to the unauthorised enterprises of his liegemen in Ireland. One of them, John de Courcy, had conquered much of Ulaidh in the north-east. For Henry to have refused recognition to de Courcy's conquests would have meant risking the establishment of an independent lordship in an area traditionally connected with the Isle of Man and highland Scotland, over which the English king had no control.

Thus at a council at Oxford in 1177, two years after the Windsor agreement, Henry sanctioned further Norman conquests in Ireland. Ambitious schemes, such as de Courcy's, to replace and supplant Irish kings, secured limited approval from him. O'Conor's authority in Munster was treated as if it had been abrogated. Indeed, there was no point in preserving the Windsor arrangements if O'Conor had constantly to call for aid from the king's men in Dublin. The Normans in Ireland were thirsting for spoil, and Henry could not afford to discourage them to such an extent that they might decide to leave his sphere of influence and set themselves up as captains of mercenary armies for Irish kings, whom they could aspire to succeed just as Strongbow had done in Leinster. Thus the Oxford policy was realistic, if ethically doubtful, and perhaps even a little conservative. The need to restrict, or control, Anglo-Norman ambitions was to determine what policy English kings would adopt with regard to Ireland. At Oxford the Munster kingdoms of Thomond and Desmond were granted to Anglo-Norman adventurers, with the exception of the cities of Limerick and Cork which were reserved to the crown.

A lasting settlement might have brought peace, but the attempted displacement of the Munster kings proved a failure. Even the more effective first conquerors did not survive for long. Hugh de Lacy was assassinated in Meath, in circumstances which suggest that he had failed to reach any accommodation with the defeated Irish rulers.

The Irish policy of successive English kings was invariably subordinated to the interests of their community as a whole, and to that of England in particular. When Henry II made his youngest son, John, Lord of Ireland, he clearly had in mind the possibility that this title might be dissociated from the crown of England; and this might well have been the outcome had John not ultimately succeeded his father. The king's representatives in Dublin had no policy except a day-to-day one. They did not identify with the Irish community, and the Anglo-Normans who already lived under English common law were regarded as an outlying group in the community of England. The principal functions of the king's representative in Ireland were simply to maintain uniformity of law with England and to secure for his master the obedience of his great Anglo-Norman subjects in Ireland and their aid in times of crisis.

4

During Henry 11's reign there was established in Dublin the nucleus of the administration which was to last for seven-and-a-half centuries and create a tradition more influential in the Ireland of today than is often appreciated. At first this was a centralised military and financial authority, but gradually it developed judicial and local organs as well. In the long run it led to regular meetings of conciliar and parliamentary bodies, bringing Ireland into line with constitutional developments elsewhere in western Europe. Despite its limitations, the Anglo-Norman kings' government in Ireland was to play a decisive part in the emergence of the idea of a self-sufficient state. To this extent the Anglo-Norman king appeared, particularly to churchmen, to offer a solution to the endless conflicts for the high kingship and thus to assist materially the extension of church reform. The weakness of the king's position, however, was that he was obliged to rely on relatively insignificant persons to exercise his power, or hand over nearly all his authority in Ireland to one or other of his great, but self-seeking, Anglo-Norman lords. At first Henry 11 had only those of Leinster and Munster to turn to, but before his death in 1189 further Norman lordships had been established in Ulster and Munster.

After an abortive Norman attempt on Connacht in 1177, shortly after the Windsor agreement, but without royal sanction, the western kingdom was not subject to further interference. This at least was the position until the temporary abdication of Rory O'Conor in favour of his son in 1183, and then it was Rory himself who invited the Normans to the province two years later when he attempted to resume his rule. Since his son would not agree, Rory sought the aid of Donal O'Brien of Thomond and some of the foreigners in Munster. He then made temporary terms with his son. This was the first time that the Normans appeared in Connacht as mercenaries, but they came more frequently in the succeeding fifteen years. The change coincided with the arrival of Prince John in Ireland. Elsewhere in the country it was noticeable how Normans were making their first appearances among the forces of the Irish and against their own, partly because of their resentment of royal-favoured courtiers at the expense of soldiers and their dissatisfaction with the conservatism of the Oxford policy.

Henry II had died in 1189 and his eldest son who succeeded him, the crusader Richard I, left much of his affairs, including Ireland, to his brother John. John replaced de Courcy as his justiciar in Ireland, after the latter's defeat by the united armies of Connacht and Thomond in a new attack on the western kingdom. John gave his assent to a speculative grant of Connacht to William de Burgh, a minor grantee who had become a strong influence in north Munster and had married a daughter of Donal O'Brien of Thomond. It was perhaps in an effort to thwart de Burgh in north Munster, where there were already rival Norman claimants, that John was prepared to favour him in Connacht, temporarily at least, if only to see that the tribute provided for in his father's agreements with Rory O'Conor was restored. But the Anglo-Norman conquest of Connacht was not achieved until a generation later by William de Burgh's son, Richard, and only after complicated wars and negotiations with Irish rivals for the western kingdom.

John became King of England in 1199, and within two years he changed his policy with regard to de Burgh. The king decided to support the claims of Cathal Crobhdhearg, brother of Rory O'Conor. De Burgh was ordered out of Connacht and summoned to court. After complex negotiations, which had not been concluded before de Burgh's death in 1206, Crobhdhearg accepted one-third of the province as a feudal lordship from John, paying to the king an annual tribute for the remainder. This solution continued to operate until Crobhdhearg's death in 1224, although for a moment in 1215, when John gave conflicting grants to Richard de Burgh and to Crobhdhearg on the same day, it appeared as if the king was in two minds about the whole situation.

John's unpredictability is an important factor in these intricate events. His jealousy of the greater barons led him to make such rapid changes of plan that he seems to have followed no policy other than that which the whims of the moment might dictate. It was partly because of this lack of policy that in 1215 he was compelled to agree to Magna Charta at Runnymede. The Great Charter of Liberties, as Magna Charta has been traditionally described, was a declaration of customary rights and privileges, recognising the community's age-old participation in government as against the centralising authority of the monarchy. Specifically, the king declared his intention to honour and preserve the people, in their various groupings in the community, in the control of their property and in their traditional liberties and freedoms. In this recital the Church was accorded priority and certain towns were also named.

It became customary, with minor variations, to reissue Magna Charta from time to time and at the beginning of the reign of each of John's successors. In Ireland under Henry III the administration's reference books recorded, with parliamentary statutes, a version of Magna Charta in which Irish towns were substituted for English. This document was known as the Great Charter of Ireland, 'Magna Charta Hiberniae'. After a lapse in the later Middle Ages there was a revival of interest in Magna Charta in the seventeenth century, when central government and absolute monarchy were again an issue under the Stuart sovereigns, particularly with regard to taxation.

King John has been judged more favourably by historians for his supposed accomplishments in Ireland than for what he did in England. But, in fact, the reaction to his unpredictable and tyrannical government was not dissimilar among his great followers anywhere, and his alleged significance as a major contributor to the development of Anglo-Irish government and English institutions in Ireland would not have occurred to his contemporaries. By the end of the first quarter of the thirteenth century, the English monarchy in Ireland had become weakened by the great Norman lords, who collectively prevented the central administration in Dublin from becoming more absolute. Under King John, the principality of de Courcy in northeast Ireland had been subordinated to the crown and transferred to the younger Hugh de Lacy, Lord of Meath. The expansion of Anglo-Norman power in the succeeding three generations, however, was largely due to the superior strength of the great lords vis-à-vis the monarchy. They were sufficiently powerful to deny to the Irish in general the rights of English law, and this gradually led to the division of the country into mutually exclusive areas, largely organised on a military basis.

The monarchy, however, was not without substantial influence. It was able to use its power over the Church to secure the appointment of reliable administrators among important prelates. These men imposed some limits on the great lords and extended English influence even into the relatively independent Irish areas. It was, on the whole, well served by a series of remarkable viceroys, many of whom were churchmen, through whose agency it became customary to have regular meetings of the colony, known as great councils and later as parliaments. The crown also exercised considerable, though diminishing, power over the towns, until they grew into virtually independent entities. But it was not able to prevent Anglo-Norman lords from converting the Irish on their estates into serfs. The king's court could offer an impartial judicial enquiry between conflicting subjects and could even impose the beginnings of a criminal jurisdiction to restrict violence between them, but for most purposes it had no right to intervene between a lord and his Irishman (*Hibernicus*), whose rights could only be judged in the manorial court of his Anglo-Norman lord. In theory the historic provincial kingly families were entitled to access to the foreign lords' courts, but in practice this right was often ignored.

Dynastic needs meant that John's successor, Henry III, had to put the defence of his French possessions before the conquest of Ireland. This matter was never of sufficient importance to him to be worth a serious attempt. He virtually handed over his authority in every province to the most outstanding hereditary lord prepared to give him nominal allegiance. The changes wrought by these foreign lords in Ireland in the twelfth and thirteenth centuries were affected by their fortunes elsewhere, and the loss of Anglo-Norman possessions in France by 1216 accentuated their tendency to develop English traditions in Ireland. In England, too, resentment against royal favourites who enjoyed French titles reflected a sharpening sense of English-ness in the community of the realm.

The existence of a community in Ireland among the French and English-speaking followers of the king did not give them any sense of self-sufficiency. Nearly two hundred and fifty years later English officials in Ireland, anxious to protect themselves against dismissal during the Wars of the Roses, stressed the self-sufficiency of English institutions in Ireland, but it is not until this later period that references to Magna Charta Hiberniae suggest the emergence of a separate community among the king's men in Ireland. It is important to note that even then such officials did not think of themselves in relation to Ireland as a whole: they were never prepared to come to terms with the Irish, whom they always regarded as inferior, dangerous, barbarous and intolerable.

The weakness of the English monarchy in Ireland during the thirteenth century is well illustrated by acts passed in great councils and parliaments, in which the Irish outside the areas of English jurisdiction were described as the king's enemies. Councils and parliaments became concerned to legislate for a collective policy in dealing with an Irish menace and the Dublin administration tried, with limited success, to gain control from the great lords over the right to make war, instead of merely seeing that local defence forces were organised to contain Irish raids. By the beginning of the fourteenth century about two-thirds of the country was under English power, or at least the power of Anglo-Norman lords, but thereafter the area diminished by more than one half.

Was racism the prominent characteristic of Ireland after the Norman invasion? In the first flush of victory, Norman conquerors showed little such tendencies. Intermarriage was common and frequently minor Norman war leaders were willing to be employed by rival Irish kings. Norman conquerors could even be found fighting one another. The first signs of racial hostility might possibly be detected in the installation of the de Burghs in Connacht in 1227. It was, however, at a later date, after the stalemate which precluded the Anglo-Normans from gaining more than two-thirds of medieval Ireland, and particularly as the colonists began to drain out of the country, that there emerged a sense of siege in which the language of racism was employed. But as far as the king of England was concerned in the thirteenth century, there was never more than qualified approval for the conquests of new areas which might well be used against the monarchy in its next moment of need. The requirements of the king's complex relations with his barons, rather than racism, governed his Irish policy in the thirteenth century.

The mid-thirteenth century saw the beginnings of an Irish rally which clearly revealed the growth of an indigenous effort to contain the English. Ultimately the Irish set bounds to the Norman conquest. In 1261 MacCarthy of Desmond successfully terminated at Callan the attempt of local Normans, in alliance with the viceroy, to extend their sphere of influence. Almost simultaneously in the north, O'Neill was defeated at Down, but the occasion was principally significant since it was followed by the first of a series of agreements among Gaelic chiefs to re-establish an Irish high kingship. Too much emphasis must not be put on these events, but they did indicate that belief in Norman invincibility no longer applied. In Scotland foreign methods and men were employed to effect change at one time; much the same could be said of Ireland where it was a leader from Norway, and later one from Scotland, who secured the endorsement of the northern kings. When Robert Bruce won the independence of Scotland after the battle of Bannockburn in 1315, his brother Edward was invited to Ireland, where he was crowned high king. Edward Bruce nearly succeeded in destroying the English lordships in Ireland. He failed to do so, but he did put an end to the royal policy of exploiting Norman areas of influence there. Instead the king permitted the development of Anglo-Norman lordships on which the future was to rest, and this marked the real beginning of their colonial mentality in the Middle Ages.

To coincide with Edward Bruce's invasion, the Gaelic princes sent a remonstrance to the pope explaining why they had taken up arms against the English and invited Bruce to rule Ireland. Their collective statement is an indication of their deep resentment at being exploited by the English, who denied them access to the king's courts and excluded Irishmen from church benefices in the Anglo-Norman sphere of influence. The rebels' remonstrance was primarily prompted by papal support for the government of King Edward II, but the defeat and death of Edward Bruce at the battle of Faughart, near Dundalk, in 1318, as well as the innate conservatism of the papacy, precluded its acceptance. However the pope did resist pressure from English ecclesiastics to excommunicate those Irish who had withdrawn their allegiance from the English king and also to stigmatise as heretics those who preached that it was lawful to rebel against him. Earlier in the Middle Ages the right to renounce a feudal lord, the solemn act by which a vassal publicly dissociated himself from his relationship with his lord, could be availed of in practice. But from the twelfth century onwards, Europe became more and more accustomed to absolute ideas of sovereignty, originating partly from the eastern Roman Empire, which became central to the conflict of empire and papacy in the west. The powers of emperor were also claimed by kings, such as the Plantagenets in England. The Plantagenets were neither willing to continue recognising a vassal's right to disavow allegiance, nor to acknowledge the claims of conquered or semi-conquered peoples to a measure of self-government. Under Edward ii this policy provoked resistance in Scotland and Wales as well as in Ireland, at the very time when the weakness of the central monarchy was so apparent. But in Ireland, the failure to complete the conquest meant that the incipient colony secured a degree of self-government, at the expense of more accommodating arrangements which might have been made between the king and the autonomous Gaelic states. This development was to make it impossible in the long run to bring together Gaelic and Anglo-Norman communities, at least until a new situation was created by the Reformation.

Historians have generally, and probably correctly, argued that the Bruce invasion was the main reason for the decline of the English in Ireland in the later Middle Ages. The argument is largely based on the extensive destruction which took place throughout the central plain of Ireland during the war with Bruce, and the subsequent failure to maintain a unified policy against the Irish. Bruce's expedition was followed by three-quarters of a century in which local interests predominated in Ireland. The English king was too weak to exercise any significant influence and henceforth Anglo-Norman lords were encouraged in their own ambitions. Successful local commanders were frequently rewarded with hereditary titles. Bermingham was created Earl of Louth, Fitzgerald Earl of Desmond, Butler Earl of Ormond and another Fitzgerald was made Earl of Kildare. In another sphere altogether, local Anglo-Norman or Anglo-Irish lords, as we can now describe them, successfully impeded a projected heresy hunt at Kilkenny by insisting against the recently appointed English bishop of Ossory that heresy was unheard of in the Irish tradition. Criminal proceedings were brought against the Earl of Desmond in 1331 in a momentary recovery of royal power, but they were not pursued—an indication of the limitations inherent in any attempt to subordinate the great Anglo-Irish lords. It was, however, in Connacht that the weakness of English government was perhaps most fully exposed.

In 1333, less than twenty years after Edward Bruce's defeat, there occurred the murder of the Brown Earl of Ulster. His death extinguished the main line of the greatest Anglo-Norman lordship in Ireland, whose title, together with that of the lordship of Connacht, had been held for nearly a century by the de Burgh, or Burke, family. Edward iii's government decided to marry the de Burgh heiress to the Duke of Clarence, a younger son of the king, in order to bring back to the crown this remarkable group of lordships, which were concentrated in one family and included half the lordship of Meath. The government was able to arrange for the payment of rents and the carrying out of the lord's responsibilities within the Meath area, but the position was very different in Connacht. There a complete break was virtually made with the government when a collateral family took over the estates and 'went Irish', abandoning the name of de Burgh for that of MacWilliam. Within a short time their hibernicisation was complete, as far as the English government was concerned, though an examination of appointments made locally by the pope would suggest that the Norman way of life was maintained. But in such areas the king's writ ceased to run, and the government was gradually forced to concede *de facto* recognition to persons whose title was denied in English law and to invest them with local administrative authority, if only to maintain the mere fabric of royal jurisdiction.

The position in Ulster from an English point of view was, if anything, even more disastrous. Outside of the town of Carrickfergus, the whole province passed out of the English sphere of influence. The Mandeville family, suspected of involvement in the murder of the Brown Earl in 1333, transformed their name into that of MacQuillan. Throughout the rest of the province, Gaelic lords reasserted themselves as independent kings, and from this date began the significant autonomy of the O'Neills in mid-Ulster and of the O'Donnells in the west. In all parts of the island Gaelic ruling families, some of them new, consolidated their power, particularly by employing Scots mercenary forces. The government seems to have learnt little from its own lack of wisdom in applying to the letter rules for the descent of land. Clarence and his descendants made several efforts to recover their inheritance, but ultimately, two centuries later, Henry VIII had to concede the claims of the usurpers' descendants. Perhaps it would be rash to attribute wisdom gained by experience as the reason for avoiding harsh dealings with offenders like the criminous Earl of Desmond, who was restored to favour in 1351.

The king's administrators in Ireland favoured the development of a parliament on English lines, but parliament in Ireland became increasingly preoccupied with questions of revenue. Possibly the greatest reason, however, for the neglect of the English colony in Ireland or rather for its being permitted to run its own affairs in the middle of the fourteenth century, was the outbreak of the Hundred Years' War between England and France, which once more turned the king's attention to spectacular dynastic warfare on the continent.

Population figures in medieval Ireland are difficult to establish exactly, but a substantial rise in the population of the independent Irish states appears to have taken place concurrently with increasing migration to England from the area ruled by the king. Apart from questionable statistics connected with papal appointments, it is difficult to draw any firm conclusion, but it does seem clear that a population increase was a contributory factor in the rise and successful military enterprises of the O'Neills and O'Donnells in the north, and of the O'Briens and MacCarthys in the south-west. There was also a substantial expansion of the activities of learned professional families, which were always extremely sensitive to the existence of generous and well-to-do patrons. Once more it is difficult to pin down this development with any precision, since much of the literary material which has survived is available only in late medieval texts. There is reason to believe, however, that the richness of learned writings at the end of the fourteenth century and early in the fifteenth was a quite recent development. In an effort to add to their own prestige and that of their patrons, the historians of the O'Donnells—notably the O'Clearys— would appear to have provided themselves with fictional data going back to the beginning of the thirteenth century. However questionable this material may be for the earlier date, it is clearly indicative of a substantial cultural develop-ment during the later period. Briefly, to judge from the literary output of professional families, the community of Ireland was in a flourishing state before 1400, and it con-tinued to regard the enterprises of the King of England and his adherents as of little consequence.

The position of the contemporary Irish Church is also important. Wherever the English administration could still operate effectively, appointments to church benefices were reserved as rewards for Englishmen and some of the Anglo-Irish, usually from among those faithful administrators, the civil servants. In the ecclesiastical provinces of Armagh and Tuam after about 1330, few positions interested English officials except the highest. A somewhat similar state of affairs existed among the religious orders. The reform movement seems to have bogged down before the middle of the thirteenth century. In 1228 the Cistercian houses in Ireland were visited, and the general chapter of the order in France were told appalling stories of how Cistercianism had broken down among a people allegedly unfit to be members of that austere order. The visitors' condemnation would appear to have been due to their dissatisfaction with the failure of Irish monks to produce an exact replica of the French Cistercian way of life. An attempt was made to put an end to their barbarous influences by combining houses in areas where the less primitive Anglo-Norman monasteries could prevail. Ironically, the fault of the Irish monks seems to have been their preference to remain closer to nature than civilised men from urban France, however austere, could tolerate. In such circumstances the Cistercians were divided between Irish and English spheres, and, it must be noted, the forces of division in this instance had apparently little to do with the politics of the conquest. Yet this division did not happen in Wales.

Of other religious orders and congregations in medieval Ireland it can be said that, in general, military orders were favoured in the English sphere of influence and begging friars in the Irish. The military orders were brought to Ireland by those returning from crusades and pilgrimages, two forms of Christian activity much favoured by the Normans. The military orders proved a valuable prop to the English colony in the days when it began to shrink and became depopulated. In the fifteenth century these orders made military contributions to the defence of the English Pale, as the king's area of influence came to be called, and helped to maintain an English and international identity where the Irish appeared to threaten the very existence of the king's government. The Franciscans and other orders of friars, accustomed to some more modest properties than the preservation of austerity demanded of the Cistercians, were very successful in Gaelic Ireland. In particular, the interest in nature of these disciples of St Francis seems to have established close relationship between the religious and the secular poets of Gaelic society from the thirteenth century onwards.

Some idea of the original contribution thus made to literature would be familiar to readers of *The Irish Tradition* by Robin Flower and of the studies in medieval Irish literature for the last half century. They are a valuable illustration of the reality of the medieval Irish community, and of its contacts with contemporary Europe. The Irish language as such, however, became very inflexible from the time of the Norman invasion. This is a phenomenon which is not easily explained, but it would appear to suggest that the Gaelic way of life had a very limited capacity for adjusting to a cosmopolitan society. In the realm of historical writing, for example, no new developments took place in annalistic work between the eleventh and the sixteenth centuries.

This, perhaps, was in part dictated by a desire among annalists to remain detached in their work, something which was no longer considered necessary in contemporary England, where the great chroniclers had developed a more sophisticated and popular method of writing history. The persistence of cold war conditions in Ireland, as well as the Gaelic tradition of playing down the affairs of the Anglo-Irish as being of less importance, offers further possible explanation for this lack of fresh development in literature. In the English sphere of influence some ecclesiastical annals and even minor chronicles emerged during the same period, but the very paucity of this material, and the extent to which it too declined, underscores the case for looking on the colony as essentially an outpost of England. Furthermore, its days appeared to be numbered in the fifteenth century.

The perilous state of the colony had decided Edward iii to send his son, the Duke of Clarence, as viceroy or justiciar to Ireland, in what became his most famous attempt to recover his wife's estate in Connacht. In 1366 a parliament held by Clarence at Kilkenny enacted statutes to hold the Irish enemy at bay and protect the declining colony. The statutes were again and again appealed to in the subsequent war between the races which had just begun. They were a tacit abandonment of the English claim to conquest and a panic attempt to set limits to endless Gaelic infiltration. The Statutes of Kilkenny enacted that Irishmen be excluded from all church offices within the Pale, heavy penalties being imposed on those who contravened the regulations. The king's subjects were directed to abandon controversial distinctions between those among them who were English by birth and those who could be considered English only by descent. The English, and also the Irish living among them, were ordered under pain of outlawry to use only the language, customs, fashions, mode of riding and apparel of the English and to eschew all things Irish. Particular attention was paid to such travelling elements of the population as poets and entertainers. Above all, it was decreed a traitorous matter, for judgment of life and limb, to give war gear to the Irish or to enter into any alliance by marriage or otherwise with them. However this particular statute had little effect and could rarely be enforced. Two years later, in 1368, the Irish parliament passed a statute of absenteeism, to which the king gave his approval only after lengthy consideration. To protect the beleagured colony, absentee owners were to provide resident defence forces, and in the event of their failing to do so, the king was empowered to resume their Irish lands. But since the king's own family were among the many involved, nothing so drastic was attempted in practice, except at rare intervals. However, the fact that a hundred years later the Earl of Desmond could be executed for defying these laws is proof that they had not fallen entirely into disuse. In enactments such as those at Kilkenny there was little doubt that the king's justiciars were giving way to the frantic alarm of resident Anglo-Normans and of townsmen, fearful of their exposed positions.

In Ireland, as in contemporary Europe, the growth of towns was encouraged by privileges and incorporation. The first Normans appear to have wanted to found many more towns than the few early foundations which survived and won parliamentary representation by the fifteenth century. But the early struggles between the king and the great Anglo-Norman lords must have adversely affected urban developments. Towns such as Dublin were highly individualistic, and their growth was probably at the expense of the smaller communities. These towns soon adopted a fortress mentality vis-à-vis the Irish outside their walls.

At the end of the fourteenth century Richard II made two expeditions to Ireland, in what was the last effort of an English king to recover the medieval colony by a great display of arms. But in reality this was an attempt to employ a more statesmanlike policy. The Statutes of Kilkenny could not be ignored, but the occasion in 1394 of the first visit to Ireland of an English king since those of John nearly two centuries earlier was used to proclaim good relations with the independent Irish lords, the hibernicised Anglo-Irish and the doubtfully loyal great earls. Most of the ruling Gaelic and Anglo-Irish lords submitted with every gesture of deference and humility, as the record would have it. The king's visit was thus a spectacular success. Sworn statements of allegiance were secured from all and sundry, which justified lawyers in later generations in pressing for the confiscation of the lands of those who had by then defaulted. However, it is probably more correct to suggest that nothing more was involved in these submissions than the traditional Irish acknowledgment of a superior to a king. This would have been particularly true of independent rulers who had no previous experience of the implications of surrender in feudal Europe. Of even greater significance was the proposed arrangement for the future organisation of the Irish government. Each province was to be regarded as an administrative entity, and an effort was made to bring the more prominent absentees into government by obtaining recognition from those who submitted for the authority of the predominant Anglo-Irish lord as well as for that of the king. Two centuries later a similar organisation was favoured by the Elizabethans. The province, then, remained the effective unit; a clear indication that the central administration in Ireland was totally incapable of maintaining itself without the support of the king's government from England and of the existing local powers.

But Richard II's scheme was unrealistic. In Leinster the powerful Art MacMurrough Kavanagh, having sworn to the Duke of Norfolk, Marshall of England and Lord of Carlow, was then expected to migrate and make way for new English colonists, carving out for himself a new estate from the lands of rebel Irish. Richard's second visit in 1399 was conceived in anger because the agreements made during his first visit had been broken after his return to England. His cousin Mortimer, Earl of Ulster, had been killed in one of the encounters that followed in Carlow. However, on this second occasion Richard only stayed two months in Ireland, since it was there that he learned of the treason against him in England, which quickly led to his deposition and the succession of his cousin, Henry of Lancaster, who reigned as Henry IV.

Concurrently, the system of autonomous states, built around the great Irish lordships, was re-established in the north, west and south. In various areas Anglo-Irish lords and towns did develop relationships with Irish, but there was little incentive to political centralisation.

The thirteenth and fourteenth centuries in Europe had seen the development of high levels in cultural, intellectual, religious and social development. Very little of this impinged on contemporary Ireland or on its Anglo-Norman colony. Conditions of chronic warfare were accompanied by a sense of cultural frustration. Some vague imitations of European developments manifested themselves in literature, as we have seen, but the rise of European universities saw no parallel in Ireland except in one or two abortive proposals. The English influence on the Church created a comparable situation. With the organisation of the military orders, such as the Knights of St John, regular clergy and semi-military communities were located at strategic points to restrict a Gaelic resurgence. Within the walled towns some degree of civilised life was possible, but in military conditions, particularly in the Gaelic spheres, a poorer civilisation inevitably prevailed.

5

Over all this there hung the sense of past greatness. As the Anglo-Irish colony weakened and shrivelled, it looked more hopelessly to the future, more fearfully at the Irish enemy beyond the gates, although it shared with the Gaelic resurgence a nostalgic recollection of its antecedents, to which creative achievement had made only a negligible contribution. As the fifteenth century dawned, some vague intimations might be discerned in the revival of cultural festivals, but it was no more than an occasional and rarely an original stirring. The glory of the Island of Saints and Scholars was a thing of the past.

3

Ireland and the English dynastic nation state, 1399–1603

In fifteenth-century England the power of the monarchy diminished, partly because its efforts to conquer France involved such a heavy drain on its resources. The Lancastrian kings (1399–1461) contrasted with the Plantagenets (1154–1399) in the weakness of the crown and the corresponding strength of the greater lords. This situation culminated in the civil war known as the Wars of the Roses, out of which emerged the rival dynasty of York (1461–85). The Yorkist kings, however, were also weak, and it was left to the Tudors (1485–1603) to reverse the tendency and pull down the great landed houses which aspired to overcome the crown or maintain their own quasi-monarchical powers.

In Ireland the weakness of the Lancastrians witnessed the continued emergence of two groups of independent dynasties, Gaelic and English respectively. The dominant Gaelic rulers were O'Neill in the north, O'Donnell, O'Conor and O'Brien in the west, MacCarthy and O'Sullivan in the south and MacMurrough Kavanagh in the east. The dominant English, or Anglo-Irish, were the Burkes of the west, but no longer of the north, the Fitzgeralds of Desmond in the south, the Butlers of Ormond in the south-east and the Fitzgeralds of Kildare in the east. To these might be added the virtually independent towns, notably Galway and Limerick in the west, Cork and Waterford in the south, Carlingford, Drogheda and Wexford in the east, and Carrickfergus in the north-east. Only Dublin and its environs obeyed the king's writ. By the end of the sixteenth century the Tudors had effectively superimposed their power on all these areas and the modern British-dominated Ireland had emerged.

It is important to emphasise the strength of certain outstanding Gaelic lordships in Ireland. Where they were connected with a neighbouring town they seem to have been particularly effective in dominating local Anglo-Irish lords, or at least in restricting their expansion. Thus, MacCarthy, in alliance with the city of Cork, could easily keep Fitzgerald of Desmond at bay. Similarly O'Brien, when he controlled Limerick, could contain MacWilliam Burke. But the latter, with the assistance of Galway city, tended to dominate the Gaelic O'Kellys and O'Connors in territories nearer the Shannon. In the north, where there was no outstanding town, O'Neill, by using Lough Foyle at Derry, and O'Donnell, by intimidating O'Connor's Sligo, preserved their external contacts, their sea-trades with Dublin, and also apparently their connections with the Scottish Highlands for the importation of mercenary troops. A flourishing urban development can also be detected in the fifteenth century. This, however, provoked a movement away from the independent lordships. Townsmen, particularly in the east, were so fearful of the Irish that they played an important part in inciting the revival of effective English government from Dublin, though their effort was not to be successful for well over a century.

Yet the fifteenth and sixteenth centuries did witness a change in the relations of Ireland and England, from a position at the beginning which was not unlike that existing on the arrival of the Anglo-Normans to the situation at the end in which the independent lordships had been extinguished and for the first time Ireland as a whole conquered. The change was due primarily to the expansionist policy embarked upon by the new Tudor rulers. With the end of the Wars of the Roses, and the victory of the House of Tudor over the Yorkists in 1485, the monarchy emerged as the effective centraliser of power, although early in the fifteenth century it was not at all apparent to the anxious Englishman that dynastic changes could result in the conquest of the whole country.

The collapse of Henry II's plan to organise Ireland became apparent during the reign of his eighth successor, Henry IV (1399–1413), who was unable to afford adequate resources for his Irish representatives. Viceroys found it impossible to secure the necessary subsidies from England, and consequently they abandoned the enterprise of directly ruling Ireland on the king's behalf, if, indeed, they had ever attempted it. With the accession of Henry V (1413–22) England turned once more to a glorious war in France, and victories like that at Agincourt gave the English in Ireland a desire to be ruled by a successful commander. About 1420 they appealed to the king and the pope to organise a crusade against the savage, barbarous, godless and awesome Irish.

After the accession of Henry VI (1422–61) and the unexpected collapse of England in France, the hopes of the loyal English failed.

Slowly there emerged a practical compromise by which the diminished royal authority in Ireland was entrusted to one or other of the warlike Anglo-Irish lords. It is in this light that we must see the viceroyalty of Sir John Talbot, subsequently Earl of Waterford. Although Talbot became involved in a struggle with the Earls of Ormond while he was viceroy, Ormond was eventually appointed to the same position, and the similarities between their periods in office cannot be overlooked. Both appointments reveal the virtual delegation by the Lancastrians of an active policy in Ireland to potential rivals. Alternating with Talbot and Butler was Richard, Duke of York, sent to Ireland in 1449 ostensibly to operate an expansion policy for Henry VI, but in reality simply to effect his removal from intrigues at court, where he was a potential menace to the dynasty. But the plan miscarried. York was able to exploit contacts and organise his forces for the Wars of the Roses into which England was plunged after its defeat in France.

For those in the English Pale who had desired a crusader, York was a disaster. He took a substantial army out of the country to fight his opponents, thereby accelerating the population drain to England, instead of proceeding against the new Irish ruling families which had recently won military power. These included the O'Mores, O'Connors, O'Dempseys and O'Dunnes in the central plain, and the O'Byrnes and O'Tooles, who reinforced the already feared MacMurroughs to the south of Dublin. It was by these active elements that the English in the Pale were being eroded. York was also responsible for encouraging the independent remnants of the colony to assert the autonomy of the kings' courts and parliament in Ireland, largely to protect himself against any attempt made in England to deprive him of his authority.

The Butlers of Ormond identified themselves with the Lancastrians in the Wars of the Roses, and ultimately the Earl of Ormond transferred to other estates in England. His interests in Ireland, in Tipperary and Kilkenny, collapsed. Some passed to minor Butlers, the rest passed into the control of new Gaelic families, such as the O'Ryans, O'Glissanes and O'Dwyers. At the same time, other Anglo-Irish families like the Fitzgeralds of Kildare and Desmond, expanded. A major encounter between Butler and the Fitzgeralds took place at Piltown in Kilkenny in 1463, and appears finally to have reduced the Butler strength to a few castles in the possession of collateral branches of the family in Ireland, after the Earl of Ormond's branch migrated to England. At this point the Yorkists, who had first suffered defeat and, indeed, the death of their Duke, spectacularly overwhelmed their opponents, so that the younger Duke of York deposed Henry vi and became Edward iv (1461–83).

Though Ireland at the accession of Edward iv might have appeared to be in the hands of the Fitzgeralds, friends of the Yorkists, the new king, who was virtually unchallenged for ten years, provoked a more positive royal policy in Ireland, particularly because of continued complaints that disorders created by a growing body of lawless landed gangsters were not being repressed. Edward IV made two unsuccessful experiments in direct government under Lords Worcester and Grey, before attempting to exercise a limited control over an Anglo-Irish viceroy.

In 1462 he also appointed the Earl of Desmond as viceroy at a time when Desmond was the most outstanding of the Anglo-Irish lords. In his short term of office Desmond appears to have organised an effective combination of supporters throughout the country and to have enjoyed the confidence of virtually every great lord, Gaelic and Anglo-Irish. It seems as if, for the first time in three centuries, Ireland was at peace and unified, and likely to remain so. Desmond in 1463 might have been described as all but king in Ireland. Then the king suddenly appointed in his place the Earl of Worcester, a noted butcher in the Wars of the Roses, who promptly had Desmond executed for infringing the Statutes of Kilkenny. Edward IV's object may well have been to demonstrate to independent Anglo-Irish lords that he would tolerate no rival in Ireland.

Still the experiment in direct government under Worcester was not immediately repeated, since England could not provide the funds necessary for a war against the Fitzgeralds and their friends. But the Desmond Fitzgeralds did withdraw and they kept themselves completely apart from the Dublin administration for the next sixty years, so that south-west Munster became alienated as south Connacht had become under the MacWilliams. However, by relying on the Kildare Fitzgeralds, Edward IV purchased peace at the price of abandoning Worcester's ruthless policy. The king simply attempted to control Kildare by appointing Sherwood, an active and aggressive Englishman, Bishop of Meath, occasionally replacing Kildare in the viceroyalty by him, or giving him a key office. Thus from 1470 until 1534, with a few minor exceptions, the Earls of Kildare controlled the interests of the King of England in Ireland, and, much as had been done by Desmond, they organised an effective

balance of allies to maintain peace throughout the country.
Of necessity this involved a selection between different rivals
and sometimes a switching of allies. At one stage, O'Donnell
was a friend of the viceroy, at another, O'Neill. Correspond-
ingly, alliance with a MacWilliam might involve Kildare
in an alliance with O'Donnell or against him. Similarly in
the midlands O'Connor could be supported against O'More
or, a little further to the west, O'Kelly against MacWilliam
of Clanrickard. Inevitably such a policy strengthened the
Kildares, so that they may well have been occasionally
tempted to set up an independent kingship, as their rivals
and the more positive administrators in London believed.

In 1478 Thomas, the seventh Earl of Kildare, died, and
rather than appoint his youthful son Gerald eighth Earl of
Kildare, Edward iv preferred to send over another English
viceroy, Henry Lord Grey. But the Geraldines, as the
Fitzgeralds had become popularly known, were too well
entrenched to be easily displaced. Ultimately the king was
obliged to give way and to recognise Kildare, while attempting to control him and avoid the risk of the viceroyalty
becoming hereditary. With this in mind, restrictive statutes
were enacted in an Irish parliament held by Grey. But
Kildare ruled not merely to the death of Edward iv, but
through the reigns of Edward v (1483), Richard iii (1483–5),
Henry vii (1485–1509), and the first four years of the reign
of Henry viii (1509–47). A hard-witted Irish soldier of
fortune, Kildare successfully maintained himself in his
sovereign's good graces by assuming in London the role of
court jester against more sophisticated, if duller, rivals and
critics. The Tudor rulers had to keep him in office, even
when he was believed to be involved in conspiracies to oust
Henry vii. He was accessory to the unsuccessful plot to
displace the king in favour of the Yorkist pretender Lambert
Simnel, for whose invasion of England Dublin was to be
the launching pad. In fact, Kildare, with his allies, was
able to maintain his position in Ireland by being given
virtually a free hand in domestic matters, on the under-

standing that nothing further would be done against the Tudors by intervening in foreign affairs.

At the same time it is important to stress the policy of the Earl of Desmond, and of his successors until after 1530, of negotiating with England's enemies abroad. They were taking up the position of such earlier independent Gaelic lords as the O'Neills, who had brought in the Bruces. The success of Henry VII in defeating conspiracies of pretenders like Lambert Simnel and Perkin Warbeck, should not blind us as to their potential danger to his throne. His own title had been very questionable before his victory at Bosworth in 1485 terminated the rule of the house of York. Henry VII hardly underestimated this when, two years later, Kildare crowned Simnel in Dublin as Edward VI. Simnel was defeated in England, but the decision taken not to displace Kildare as viceroy, even if he refused to agree to forfeiture of his lands should he again become implicated with the pretender, was another ignominious set-back for the Tudors. Henry was obliged to keep Kildare in office in order to control more dangerous men like Desmond. Perhaps it was only because Kildare was unable to curb Desmond that Sir Edward Poynings was appointed viceroy after the pretender Warbeck had returned to Ireland for the second time in 1493. Poynings has been long remembered for having held a parliament which passed what has come to be known as Poynings' Law. This made it illegal to summon future parliaments without previously securing the king's consent, together with the approval of his council in England for the draft legislation to be considered. But even Poynings' primary duty as viceroy was a military one, though whether this involved more than the immediate destruction of the forces hostile to the king is in some doubt. Like Worcester, Poynings imprisoned his predecessor, but only when he was convinced that Kildare was intriguing with the Irish in the north against whom he had opened a campaign.

Whether in fact Kildare was guilty was not left to

Poynings to decide. The king, no doubt recollecting that
Worcester's proceedings against Desmond had alienated the
south-west, probably for a generation, directed that Kildare
be sent over to England. The contemporary chronicler,
narrating proceedings against Kildare at London, told how
Kildare won royal support by provoking his critics. He
returned to Ireland, once more as the king's representative,
after Henry VII had answered those who commented
irritably that all Ireland could not rule Kildare by the
response, 'then shall this Earl rule all Ireland'. In addition,
modern historians have pointed out that, despite his legislative successes, Poynings had revealed military inadequacies
and substantially increased the costs of administration
without obvious revenue to meet them. The king decided
it would be cheaper to run Ireland by continuing the
Kildares in office and obliging the viceroy to provide for
his own expenses.

Perhaps also a careful review of the evidence not only
exonerated Kildare but adduced disturbing testimony as to
the ramifications of his power. Had he decided to replace
him, the king would have been involved in a far greater
outlay than he was prepared to envisage. He would also
have had to build up against Kildare a rival group of
alliances throughout the country, and he lacked the determination to do so. The fact that his successor, in reversing this
policy, was to inaugurate seventy years of warfare, might
suggest wisdom in the decision of Henry VII.

The restoration of Kildare served to bring out the manner
in which he was prepared to deal with potential enemies,
far and near, in the remaining seventeen years of his life.
In 1504 he defeated MacWilliam Burke, his son-in-law, at
the battle of Knockdoe, after a conflict involving many
autonomous Irish states and English lordships. There is
evidence that, during the preceding half-century, the power
of MacWilliam Burke had been expanding in the west,
possibly on account of the growth of Galway as a commercial
centre, newly linked by trade routes with Scandinavia and

Spain. Kildare's action may have prevented a successful revolt by a western ruler who could have weakened his influence at Dublin as well as in the north-west of Ulster. Thereafter the hegemony of the Fitzgeralds was unchallenged. Through another marriage alliance they became sufficiently powerful to build up a relatively obscure branch of the Butlers, which succeeded in the next generation to the earldom of Ormond after the direct Butler line had moved to England. The original Butlers ceased to have much significance in Ireland, at least until Henry VIII developed his strong interest in the emigré seventh earl's grand-daughter Ann Boleyn.

The Great Earl, as Gerald, the eighth Earl of Kildare, was known to the chroniclers, passed the rest of his life unchallenged by any comparable rival. He had successfully transcended by intermarriage the old racial divisions between Gaelic and Anglo-Irish. In his war against MacWilliam Burke he had led northern Irish lords as well as the gentry of the English enclave around Dublin known as the Pale. But Kildare was to fall a victim in one of his own minor campaigns against a midland chief. During his lifetime guns were first introduced into Ireland, and in 1513 he was shot while attempting to capture a castle of O'More. Once again his adversary is not without importance, as he serves to remind us that Kildare, like any north Leinster ruler, could not afford to permit the rise too close to Dublin of a persistent opponent, no matter how negligible.

The accession of Henry VIII in 1509 had brought no alteration in policy as far as Ireland was concerned, and Gerald, the ninth Earl of Kildare, succeeded his father as viceroy. Although Wolsey, the king's chief minister, came to regard the Kildares with a jaundiced eye, some time elapsed before any attempt was made to replace Gerald, who for some twenty years ruled Ireland almost without interruption. But Henry VIII, with a greater degree of self-confidence about his position, was better able than his father to restrain outstanding Irish lords. Both Gerald, the ninth earl, and

Thomas, his son, the tenth earl, spent some time at court and were provided with English wives. Ireland in this way became involved in the intricate matrimonial alliances favoured over western Europe by the Hapsburgs, the Valois and the Tudors alike. It was partly because of such alliances that Kildare became subordinated to intrigues at the English court. This led to his supercession in 1519 when Henry had him replaced by an English viceroy, the Earl of Surrey. But at the same time the king urged conciliation in Ireland 'by sober ways, politic drifts and amiable persuasions', rather than aggressive military action.

Over much of western Europe, the late fifteenth and early sixteenth centuries saw the emergence of new royal families which built their power around an incipient national feeling. This shifted the political centre of gravity from the papacy in Rome to Vienna, Paris, Madrid, London and other dynastic capitals. Thus the Hapsburgs of the Holy Roman Empire strengthened themselves by alliance with the victorious sovereigns of Castile and Aragon who built up Spain by expelling the Moors and conquering Mexico and Peru in the New World. The Valois kings of France consolidated their rule after successfully shaking off the Burgundians and the English. The Tudors were less important internationally, and having successfully supplanted the Yorkist kings by their victory in 1485, were glad to secure a Spanish alliance to balance the friendship of the Yorkists with the Burgundians and the alliance of the Stuarts, the Scottish royal house, with the Valois. Kildare's replacement by Surrey in Ireland, where O'Brien of Thomond and Fitzgerald of Desmond sought support from the Tudor king's continental rivals, was dictated partly by Henry VIII's concern over the international situation. Continental alliances and counter-alliances had reached a critical point. In 1519 the kings of England and France were the rivals of Charles I of Spain for the succession to the Holy Roman Empire. The predictable election of the Spanish monarch, who thereby became Charles V, accentuated the nervousness of England in being involved and perhaps overwhelmed in an international war, as indeed happened so disastrously to France some years later.

In Ireland Surrey was replaced after a short term by an Irish-born viceroy. By the 1520s, there seemed a reasonable chance of an alternative to Kildare, in the person of Piers Butler, recently ennobled Earl of Ossory, the collateral Butler whom the older Kildare had built up against the emigré Ormond. But Kildare was still all-powerful in Ireland in the 1520s, and, while an alternative deputy could be appointed, his supporters were neither sufficiently numerous nor reliable to make of him an effective ruler. In fact there is evidence that Kildare was able to work upon the fears of former friends. The dependability of smaller allies sometimes proved decisive when the leader in power seemed to be removable. As long as London could be employed to strengthen one potential leader against another, diplomacy could become quite intricate, centering on speculations as to the likelihood of continued English support. So it was not easy to find in Ireland an effective alternative to Kildare as viceroy.

After 1530 Kildare's replacement was attempted once again in an effort to prevent a backdoor invasion of England from Ireland. This was after the fall of the king's chief minister, Cardinal Wolsey, over Henry's projected divorce from Catherine of Aragon, the aunt of Charles v. International complications were feared in Ireland and the king decided on a military viceroy, Sir William Skeffington. Skeffington was supported by energetic English officials, appointed to key posts in the Church as well as in the state. The first steps in this direction had already been taken by Wolsey when he appointed, with the acquiescence of the pope, the English official John Allen as Archbishop of Dublin. The new experiment to replace Kildare was not persisted in, however, in the uneasy months in which Thomas Cromwell was climbing to power after Wolsey's death. It was Cromwell who had advised the king to appoint

Skeffington and who had already drafted the plans to make England independent of the papacy. But Kildare himself unexpectedly revealed his inadequacy when he was severely wounded in an encounter with a minor midland chief, one of the Irish lords in Wicklow whom he could not prevent from raiding Dublin city. Nor was Kildare strong enough to resist pressure from Henry VIII to sign the petition to the pope asking for the nullification of the king's marriage with Catherine of Aragon. Being still very powerful, however, the viceroy's final removal required preliminary enquiry and his attendance at London.

Kildare's deputy was his heir, Silken Thomas Fitzgerald, who soon became aware of a plan to supplant his family which Archbishop Allen and his namesake, the master of the rolls, were organising for Skeffington and the Butlers of Ossory. Thomas went into rebellion on the rumour that his father had been executed by the king in the summer of 1534, and so launched the Kildare crusade against the heretical and lecherous Henry VIII. This was how Silken Thomas described the king in his appeal to Charles V and to the pope, which, however, was ineffective. Because of the king's anti-papal legislation as well as the divorce, the pope had been prepared to declare him deposed, and excommunicated together with his supporters. But such enterprises, so successful in an earlier age, were the exception in the sixteenth century. Charles V advised the pope, in the interests of Catherine's daughter, Princess Mary Tudor, to abandon any attempt to replace Henry as King of England.

Thomas won control of all Ireland, apart from the cities of Dublin and Waterford and the Butler territory around Kilkenny. However, the rapid capture of Thomas, who had become Earl of Kildare when his father died in London, of natural causes, was sufficient to end the first pressing episode of the war. Skeffington, now restored as viceroy, was to plan a meeting of parliament in Ireland to support the English policy of subordinating the Church to the crown and liquidating some of the monasteries. This led to a war which dragged on fitfully for some five or six years, but early in 1535, when the dramatic capture of Kildare's stronghold at Maynooth, the first time in Ireland that gunpowder destroyed a hitherto impregnable fortress, ended all opposition in the Pale.

Thus the Kildare rebellion resulted in the reconquest by English armies of this area. It also precipitated the radical change in administration which re-established the English viceroyalty, financed from the capital of dissolved monasteries and of lands confiscated from absentees and rebels.

Already in England a conflict of wars was making it difficult for ecclesiastics to give a complete obedience to both the law of Church and the law of state. Canon law ruled against the interference of any layman, no matter how exalted, with the affairs of a priest: but to the judges of the common law, which they administered in the king's courts, the trafficking which went on within the church courts ultimately controlled from Rome, smacked of treason. Frequent clashes took place between Church and state over ecclesiastical appointments, and the state insisted on treating such offices as material property held under royal donation or feudal lease. Ecclesiastics, from the pope to the lowest official of a church court, sometimes resorted to ecclesiastical sanctions of which the most formidable were interdict and excommunication. But these were always dangerous weapons and were avoided if at all possible. Ecclesiastics, however, became indifferent to civil and common law where they were not actually obliged to observe it.

The appointments of the Holy See in Ireland were regarded with a respect and approval which is not easy to explain, in contrast to England, where papal power had long been exercised through monarchical channels. The papacy often acted as umpire in the strife between Gaelic lords and Anglo-Irish administrators. It also condoned the Gaelic takeover of decayed and depopulated English areas in the fifteenth century, where Irishmen were appointed to spiritual benefices from which their ancestors had for so

long been debarred. From time to time the English government tried to enforce regulations securing for the state a
monopoly of papal appointments just as contemporary
rulers in France, Spain and elsewhere were doing. But by
the fifteenth century the jurisdictional area of the English
courts in Ireland had diminished and the area in which
appeals to the court of Rome were normally made had
extended. By the time of Henry VIII's break with Rome,
the tradition of looking to the Holy See was too strong to
be easily eradicated.

Yet once Henry had defeated the Kildare rebellion,
overwhelmed the Irish Catholic crusade and re-established
his power in Dublin, he was able to enforce a theoretical
recognition of his claim to be head of the Church. The
confiscation of the monasteries was effected by the surrenders
of their superiors which were nominally voluntary. But as
far as English influence in Ireland was concerned, this was
a disaster. While the diocesan clergy, in the now somewhat
enlarged English sphere, acquiesced, many of the regular
clergy, particularly the friars, who received next to no
compensation from the state, withdrew to the independent
Gaelic areas, where they maintained a fitful contact with
Rome. This tradition was so widely and continuously
adhered to as to make it impossible to secure in Ireland a
state dominance over the Church comparable to that which
was achieved in contemporary England.

In the last ten years of Henry's reign the power of the
English in Ireland substantially increased. The achievement,
however, was largely superficial. An acquiescent parliament
in 1536 decreed that the pope was without power and that
it was treason to support him. It asserted the claim of
Henry VIII, as the ruler of an 'empire', to be head of the
Church as well as the state, with the right to regulate and
confiscate monasteries. It secured recognition of the extinction of the Kildare order and imposed acquiescing bishops
in successive vacancies, beginning with that created in
Dublin, where the followers of Silken Thomas had murdered

Archbishop Allen. A substantial body of legislation and extensive submissions by chiefs, comparable to those achieved by Richard II, undoubtedly seemed to have secured the new power, but the cost was considerable. Although a new viceroy, Lord Leonard Gray, effectively terminated the open warfare by a decisive victory at Bellahoe in 1539, which drove O'Neill and other Irish supporters out of the war, from the king down there was dissatisfaction and unease. Gray failed to secure the next heir of the Kildares, spirited out of the country by a secret combination to protect the defeated Anglo-Irish family from complete extinction. In the event, Gray's policy of endeavouring to win to his side a strategic element in every Anglo-Irish and Irish lordship beyond the English sphere of influence proved to be the viceroy's downfall.

The position by 1540 was that sullen resentment existed extensively in the one area within the country where the tradition of loyalty to England had always been strongest. The reasons are not far to seek: a conservative people resented the rejection of the pope and the preaching that it was treason to believe in his spiritual authority. Traditionally the Anglo-Irish had maintained a strong devotion to Rome and the popes had generally supported the English interest against rebellious Irish lords. The liquidation of monasteries added to the dissatisfaction of the loyal Anglo-Irish, since it deprived them of other time-honoured allies against the undisciplined Irish. The decision in favour of monastic dissolutions had been taken in London under Cromwell's influence, in order to provide funds for the increased costs of administration. As in England, the alliance against the Church was to be built up by rewarding deserving laymen with bargain leases of church property. In Ireland, however, it was the new administrators from England who were the chief gainers, and they also started to be the main benefactors in office by monopolising appointments to the exclusion of the Anglo-Irish.

The sense of limited achievement among the reformers,

however, was not fully appreciated at first. Gray was sacrificed to a group of hostile critics who secured his disgrace and execution, on the fantastic charge that he was seeking to restore the Geraldine interest. But Gray's removal in 1540 and his subsequent execution did not alter the way in which politics took precedence over spiritual matters. His successor, Sir Anthony St Leger, though pressing forward the dissolution of the monasteries within the Pale, renewed the conciliatory policy of twenty years earlier, restrained the more fanatical anti-papal activities of Henry's new ecclesiastics, like Archbishop George Brown of Dublin, and even induced another parliament to declare Henry King of Ireland, possibly in the hope that the abandonment of the papally conferred title of Lord would end popular attachment to the pope.

It seems to have taken the spectacular visit to London of leading independent Gaelic lords to have brought about an apparent victory for the English crown. They submitted to the king, who converted their traditional elective lordships into hereditary estates, granted them English titles and ennobled them with peerages. Conn O'Neill became Earl of Tyrone and Donal O'Brien Earl of Thomond. Even MacWilliam, who had usurped royal lands in Connacht, accepted the earldom of Clanrickard in place of chieftainship. Nominally these Gaelic lords admitted Henry's ecclesiastical claims and undertook to extend Anglicanism in their spheres of influence. Bishops too had been encouraged to surrender their papal briefs of appointment and accept a regrant of their offices from the king.

'The policy of surrender and regrant', under which these changes took place, was a compromise arrangement to meet the political difficulties created by a situation in which Irish lords held their lands in defiance of English law and nominal English proprietors, notably the crown. The intention was to extend Henry VIII's anglicisation policy for the Fitzgeralds and Butlers to all great chieftains throughout the country. The idea was good but not thought out sufficiently, for basically it involved bribing the chiefs to abandon Irish law. It operated on the assumption that the old hostility of the English in Ireland towards Irish civilisation must be fully adopted, and the community of Ireland transformed so that it became part of the community of England. But insufficient attention was paid to the landed rights of the freeholders as against the former chiefs in Gaelic areas. The people in those autonomous states were to refuse to consider themselves bound by the agreements made with the king, but the king's ministers assumed that loyalty demanded absolute compliance and assent in the establishment of a uniform system with England. That there was some immediate success is clear from the failure of international intrigues at the beginning of the 1540s. The first Jesuit agents of the papacy, like most of the first post-Reformation papal nominees to bishoprics, were unable to hold their positions. The Jesuits abandoned their mission when it became clear that the Earl of Tyrone, and other chiefs who had recently submitted, were afraid to receive them. But although the independent lordships had been destroyed by the end of the sixteenth century, the tradition of resistance in church matters was maintained and the forces of the Counter-Reformation secured a sufficient foothold to build up an effective independent Catholic Church in Ireland in the succeeding centuries. Thus the community of Ireland did not merge with that of England.

The real failure of Henry VIII with the Anglo-Irish began to be apparent when London sensed the hostile attitude of public opinion towards the changes. Perhaps the trend had already gone against the government before the death of Henry VIII in 1547. Forcing the Irish to become English may perhaps have called the Anglo-Irish bluff; certainly in the religious sphere, under his successor Edward VI, evidence of their dissatisfaction is very compelling.

Ten years earlier, the new officials had been full of enthusiasm for the king's religious policy. As long as Henry lived there was a nominal acquiescence in his pretensions—

the more distant from Dublin the more nominal. But even within the English sphere, subordination of church policy to state necessity involved an acceptance of apathetic attitudes towards the preaching of royal supremacy. This was in marked contrast to England, where executions and martyrs among upholders of papal power were much more numerous. Among the administrators in Ireland there may have been a few crypto-Protestants, and certainly some were genuine supporters of royal supremacy. But this did not prevent St Leger, like Gray, from diminishing the powers of the loyal Butlers, since they were suspected of political ambitions on the highest level. By the end of the reign both Archbishop Brown and James Butler, Earl of Ormond, had been weakened in power as well as in enthusiasm for religious reform. The officials may have changed their views, perhaps after the execution of Thomas Cromwell in England, or else their apathy in Henry's last years was simply due to their increased uncertainty about the complexities of the Irish situation.

Not everyone will agree that the Reformation is the key to the failure of Henry VIII's policy in Ireland. Certainly, in the independent parts of the country the attempted anglicisation could not be carried out, since the policy of surrender and regrant failed to take adequate note of timeless Irish traditions safeguarding the property rights in land of every freeman. Apparently the Gaelic and Anglo-Irish lords who secured English grants assumed that, as much of their power came from land won in battle, which they treated as their own for military purposes, they could depend on English arms and administration to operate surrender and regrant. They particularly wanted to apply it to the landed families over which they traditionally ruled, both allied kinsmen and subordinate tributaries. But they overlooked the strength available to these minor gentry, and appear to have underestimated the opposition which the English rule of succession by primogeniture would provoke. Rivals to their heirs under English law could recruit support from the military class threatened by an English landed system and by a monarchy whose policy was to get rid of military followers and retainers.

Perhaps it is going beyond the evidence to see an early failure in the Pale in the absence of sufficient minor officials to popularise the changes, if this was possible. But there is no doubt that whenever the question of religion was involved, the new régime was exposed to criticism, privately at least, by those dissatisfied with change, as well as by those dispossessed by monastic confiscations and not adequately provided for in subsequent church vacancies. Thus the Anglo-Irish began to desert the Reformation.

We have seen that at the end of the fourteenth century the community of Ireland was still very clearly the Gaelic-speaking element. But after the accession of the House of Lancaster in 1399 and the virtual abandonment of the English in Ireland, this was no longer quite so clear. Within about a century, so far as contemporary historians were concerned, the English in some areas in Ireland had become recognised as part of the Irish community. The effect of the Gaelicisation which had begun before the Statutes of Kilkenny was that many of the Anglo-Irish were accepted, at least in part. Thus a body of genealogical material relating to the Burkes of Connacht was put on record, and described in Irish documents as *Seanchas Burcach*. Similarly, in the great lordships of the Fitzgeralds of Desmond and Kildare, and also among the Butlers of Ormond and Ossory, the Gaelic acceptance is on record. Nor were the minor families of early medieval Ireland excluded; such material tells us that the Gaelic MacQuillans had formerly been Mandevilles of Norman origin.

The obsession of the Tudors with the Church thus accentuated the differences between England and Ireland, and blurred the distinctions between Gaelic and Old English within Ireland. The argument, however, must not be taken too far: a sense of difference still existed. But the fusion of literary interests and the growth of some compatability between Gael and Anglo-Irish did lead to acceptance of the Old English outside the English Pale as belonging to the community of Ireland. This was in contrast to the mentality represented by those who had framed the Statutes of Kilkenny, out of hostility towards the Irish community, who glorified its great wars of the past, rejoicing in the recollection of former victories over the Irish barbarians, and lived for the return of such heroic days.

Could the Gaelic Irish have been persuaded to abandon their laws and customs? In Ireland the rights of a subject under common law tended to be eroded, particularly in times of war. The quasi-military mentality embodied in the Statutes of Kilkenny encouraged the royal administration in ignoring the legal niceties which could not be overlooked in England. Anglo-Irish lords, such as the Burkes, who had abandoned the king's law were also stigmatised as lawless, if not as outlaws, by those adhering to the Statutes. The crime alleged against Desmond as late as 1468, that he had defied English custom by enforcing a system of quarterage and provision for his troops, was declared so abominable as to justify execution in accordance with the Statutes. A fusing of English and Irish traditions, then, would undoubtedly have meant reverting to more primitive conditions. Also, the constant levying of quarterage and provision for the upkeep of troops by the population would have hampered the transformation of the country's self-sufficient economy into a capitalistic one. Whether there might have evolved any other fusing of the two systems, like the laws of Kilcash, as the military exactions were called, in the Butler area, we cannot say, but the possibility of Gaelic participation in parliament is worth investigating.

It is important to remember that early parliaments had essentially a judicial function. Even though parliament in Ireland became increasingly concerned with financial matters and with the subsidy for the administration, its judicial functions were maintained.

In fact, for certain purposes in the fifteenth century, they would appear to have increased substantially when the king's courts weakened. The existence in medieval parliaments of a third house representing the clergy suggests that this could have provided one way of extending the parliamentary system to the whole country. The summoning of the newly ennobled Gaelic Earls of Thomond, Clanrickard and Tyrone to the House of Lords indicates that the community could certainly have been accustomed to participating in parliament at this upper level. Unfortunately, the government was primarily concerned to pressurise the existing parliament for its own purposes, and no one seriously entertained the idea of trying to assimilate the Irish at two levels, as lords and also as commoners who would represent the freeholders. The community of Ireland, therefore, remained to a large extent outside the formal activity of what should have been the most representative institution in the country. In such circumstances it is difficult to see how anything but war could have broken the closed circuit.

In Ireland under Edward VI (1547–53) a more Protestant policy than that of Henry VIII was pursued by the government administered by the Duke of Somerset. This was also true of England, and the religious changes brought about in England were extended to Ireland. English was substituted for Latin in public church services, and the Communion Service and the Book of Common Prayer took the place of the Mass and the Roman Missal. This only accentuated popular resentment and reforming bishops, such as John Bale in Ossory, faced considerable opposition. Many of the clergy resisted the government's policy. Archbishop Brown of Dublin tardily accepted the new liturgy, but George Dowdall, a Palesman whom Henry VIII had made Archbishop of Armagh and who had accepted the royal supremacy, left his diocese and went into exile rather than agree to the liturgical changes.

The problem of the pope was in one way not so obvious as the problem of Protestantism, since the omission from the liturgy of prayers for the Bishop of Rome did not automatically impinge on the ordinary people. Admittedly, it was another matter when anti-popery sermons were preached and ecclesiastics prosecuted for resorting to Rome. The destruction of the monasteries and of venerated images, long the object of pilgrimages, created more dramatic revulsion. The crisis came in the reign of Edward vi, and primarily, it would seem, in the English Pale, where the hitherto loyal Anglo-Irish turned against Protestantism. The hostile reaction to reformers who preached against transubstantiation made it clear that the government would have to move much more slowly in matters of worship than it was doing in England if it was to achieve a nominal acquiescence, even among the loyalists of the Pale. Protestantism in Ireland was confronted with an entrenched opposition, in contrast to England, where it met with some sympathy and had been welcomed in high places. Determined reformers in Ireland, such as John Bale, Bishop of Ossory, were to find that political considerations came first, and that none of the administrative officials were prepared to reinforce their efforts.

In other matters the government was more popular with its traditional supporters in Ireland. The festering sore represented by Offaly and Leix, the area ruled by O'Connor, O'More and other midland chiefs who had brought to their deaths the eighth and ninth Earls of Kildare, became the object of a settlement by colonists. Ultimately the scheme eradicated a great menace to the Pale by extending royal authority and intimidating Irish chiefs by force of arms. The proposal to turn these areas into King's and Queen's counties respectively in the next reign was attractive to the Palesmen, since it supported a state-sponsored military system. They could invest their wealth in it and perhaps raise their social positions by participating in it. In the long run the scheme was successful, though the period of war with the Gaelic chiefs lasted to the end of the sixteenth century. In this area at least the hostility between Anglo-Irish and Irish remained permanent, and traces of it were still to be found in the parliaments of the seventeenth century and in the confederacy of Kilkenny.

The revival of foreign intrigues indicated that the government of Edward VI had little reason to fear outside intervention, even on religious grounds. O'Neill and other Ulster lords, who had not even made a nominal submission, demonstrated their loyalty and passed on essential information to the authorities. The good offices of Archbishop Dowdall of Armagh had done much to make this possible, and even better relations might have been established with the northern lords had the introduction of Protestantism not been too much for the archbishop. Robert Wauchop, the pope's nominee in Armagh in opposition to Dowdall, was unable to remain within the country through lack of support, and fear of the military power of Dublin. England's international position also improved slightly under Edward VI. The Earl of Kildare, exiled under Henry VIII, was permitted to return, and he understandably dissociated himself privately from his papal friends and relations.

The unexpected death of Edward VI in 1553 and the accession of his half-sister Mary I (1553–58), Catholic daughter of Henry and Catherine of Aragon, terminated the first Protestant experiment and displayed how shallow the impact of the Reformation had been in Ireland. When Mary went back to Catholicism and restored the Mass and the old rites, the rapid Catholic reaction in the Pale indicated that even within the English sphere of influence, Protestantism had gained no foothold. England and Ireland were reconciled with the Holy See by papal bull, and an act of parliament re-established papal jurisdiction, though guaranteeing absolution and protection from prosecution to those who had been accessory to the secularisation of church lands. While in England the parliamentary measures to restore Catholicism, particularly those affecting former monasteries, were not passed without difficulty, in Ireland the objections appear to have been minimal, being confined merely to some of the new official class which had been built up since the Geraldine rebellion.

Under Edward VI it had been apparent that the Reformation could not advance beyond the area controlled by English arms. Once the state would again turn to Protestantism under Elizabeth I (1558–1603), any future general conformity would depend upon new English officials and colonists. But even in the case of those among them who held ecclesiastical offices, religion on the whole was subordinated to the exigencies of politics. In consequence, there were few martyrs; persecution, except on a sporadic basis, could be dangerous to the state if it alienated the traditionally loyal Old English. Indeed, even Mary's short reign revealed the divergence between the ruling classes in England and the Old English in Ireland.

Apart from religion, the reign of Mary was a yard-stick on Tudor policy in Ireland, for it brought out the essential similarity between the methods of all the Tudor rulers dealing with it. Like her father, Mary intimidated parliament into passing the government's programme of legislation, and the beginning of a new policy of colonisation was given statutory approval. Two new counties were established, and were called King's County and Queen's County, in honour of Mary's husband, Philip II of Spain, and herself. The names of Offaly, Leix and other Irish midland territories were abrogated, and their Irish inhabitants, such as the O'Connors, O'Mores, O'Dempseys and O'Dunnes, were exterminated or transplanted, as a prelude to a plantation which took shape under Elizabeth I.

The restored Dowdall of Armagh sought permission to use his ecclesiastical powers to curse the recalcitrant and excommunicate the rebellious Irish, whom, he urged, should be given the full treatment of the policy envisaged in the Statutes of Kilkenny, in an effort to save the English community in Ireland. Even if Dowdall was only trying to assert his loyalty to the government, it should not be forgotten that his mentality represented that of many of the Old English of the Pale.

The Tudor pattern of subordinating church interests to those of the English state was maintained even under Mary, since she had to seek the allegiance of new English planters and officials of the courtier class. The queen followed a policy of toleration at the highest level in Ireland, in contrast to England where her reign has always been associated with the burning of Protestants at the stake. She restored to their titles and estates Archbishop Dowdall of Armagh and Gerald Fitzgerald, eleventh Earl of Kildare, who avoided taking any action which might suggest he was anxious to regain the prominence of his ancestors. Even the Earl of Desmond temporarily enjoyed royal favour, perhaps because he had made a timely submission to Edward vi.

The London government privately protected certain persons in Ireland, giving them permission to hold Protestant services in their own homes, though such services had been declared illegal and heretical by Mary's parliament. The list of these persons, though short, is instructive: it included the treasurer, Sir Henry Sidney, the master of the rolls and the secretary of the privy council—all important officials of the kingdom. Yet some of these, such as Sidney, introduced the measures in Mary's parliament restoring Catholicism and were later to be the chief pilots of their repeal in the first parliament of Elizabeth. An indifference to religion on their part must not be inferred: they simply accepted it that religion should be controlled by the monarch. Mary's toleration of Protestantism anticipated the policy towards Catholicism which Elizabeth had necessarily to follow in Ireland, since there she could not afford to be as hostile to the pope as she was in England. Just as Mary had been prepared to tolerate, and the pope to absolve, the state-appointed bishops of Henry viii and Edward vi, or at least those who had not violated canon law by getting married, so Elizabeth i carefully avoided persecution of those against whom treason for political purposes could not also be alleged. Under both Elizabeth and Mary state interest led to a different policy being adopted in Ireland, where the law in practice varied from England. This policy of the government is clearly on record from the middle of the sixteenth century.

The death of Mary had been a tragedy for Catholicism in England. A reaction set in, caused by the shortness of her reign, resentment towards her intense persecution of Protestantism, and the bankruptcy of a foreign policy through which England had lost Calais, her best continental foothold, in a disastrous war against France in which Mary had been involved by her Spanish husband. With such inauspicious beginnings, Elizabeth moved carefully and diplomatically, under Spanish patronage, to the peace of Chateau Cambresis with France and the international recognition of her own position as ruler of England, despite her doubtful legitimacy and the pretensions to her throne of her cousin, Mary Queen of Scots, who was married to Francis II of France. As the daughter of Henry VIII and Anne Boleyn, however, Elizabeth was not prepared to let the fact of her succession be questioned by the pope, and so England moved back to the position in law which had existed under Edward VI. Parliament revoked Mary's pro-papal legislation, and the Book of Common Prayer, with minor modifications, was again made the sole public liturgical manual. But the queen wisely altered her own spiritual title and chose to be called, not supreme head of the Church of England, but merely supreme governor in all things ecclesiastical as well as temporal. It was a settlement which subordinated the Church to the state and it was almost as little pleasing to the Protestant clergy she appointed as to the Catholics she dismissed.

As in England, but more slowly, Protestantism was officially re-established in Ireland. Sussex and Sidney dealt effectively and quickly with the Irish parliament; but there was no attempt, nor could there have been, to enforce the new laws throughout the country as a whole. Elizabeth was concerned to avoid any extreme action which might enable a conspiracy group to appeal successfully for intervention from a Catholic power. The wisdom of this policy was such that no general rebellion broke out in Ireland until the last decade of her reign.

But the danger of foreign intrigue did revive with Elizabeth's accession. The very success of her policy in England, where she quickly secured parliament's endorsement for a renewal of the Anglican settlement of her brother Edward VI, seems to have provoked in Ireland a revival of Catholic designs, even within the Pale. Both French and Spanish ambassadors in London appear to have been lobbied by persons offering evidence of Irish support for an anti-English invasion. However, the papacy was to regret that it had David Wolfe as an agent of undefined diplomatic status operating among the clergy in Ireland; his presence and alleged political scheming were used by Elizabeth as an excuse to refuse entry to England to a papal representative commissioned to invite her to the Council of Trent.

The enactments of Elizabeth's first parliament in Ireland in 1560 included the law, recently passed in England, abolishing papal supremacy and re-asserting royal authority over the Church. Furthermore, for failing to attend Sunday service in their local churches, parishioners rendered themselves liable to a fine of one shilling, while attendance at any other form of public prayer was decreed, with penalties, to be illegal. Those holding ecclesiastical and official positions were obliged to subscribe to an oath accepting the royal supremacy and denying that of the pope. The problem for the historian is how far such provisions were enforced or enforceable throughout the country as a whole.

Several bishops whom Mary had got the pope to appoint as replacements for Protestant clergy refused to conform, but others acquiesced. There the matter stands. The absence of evidence would suggest that the government decided not to press matters, particularly in those parts of the country where isolation from Dublin would have made it impossible to enforce the law, particularly in the event of the growth of a pro-papal movement, centered around the memory of persons regarded as martyrs at the hands of the government. The foreign situation, if properly handled, was not in danger of getting out of control. The pope, however hostile to Elizabeth as the daughter of Henry VIII and Anne Bolcyn, was unlikely to take action without some secular support. But in the reign of Henry VIII the emperor had advised him against such a plan, and in the reign of Elizabeth his successor did the same. So did Philip II of Spain, who was quite ready to marry Elizabeth after the death of her half-sister, his previous wife. Moreover, Elizabeth's presumptive heir was the Catholic Mary Stuart, Queen of Scotland and queen-consort of France. With Spain and the empire wary, the pope was slow to act against Elizabeth. His emissaries in Ireland were not committed to conspiracy, as other clerics evidently were. David Wolfe was subsequently at pains to explain that he had taken care to observe the law and not preach rebellion until after the pope decided to excommunicate Elizabeth in 1570. In fact, Ireland might have remained relatively quiet if there had not been trouble from an unexpected quarter, in the person of Sean (Shane) O'Neill, the younger son of the Earl of Tyrone, who gathered the forces of the O'Neills and threatened the very life of the English colony.

Sean O'Neill came of a family which had been inter-married with the Kildares, and was thus partly of Anglo-Irish origin. He had been excluded from succeeding his father as earl, however, in favour of an elder son Matthew who, he alleged, was not legitimate. Although no bar existed in Irish law to preclude the election of any member of a family as successor to a previous chief, according to the English law of primogeniture Matthew's illegitimacy should have debarred him from succeeding to the earldom of Tyrone. Sean's grievance against the government, therefore, was that in supporting Matthew it had violated common law. In a series of confrontations between the brothers Sean secured popular support in the O'Neill country, and ultimately defeated both his brother and his father in battle. Sean was proclaimed O'Neill in accordance with Irish usage and shortly afterwards his followers killed Matthew in an ambush. By the middle of 1559 the old earl himself had also died, but the government decided to support Matthew's heir against Sean, with disastrous consequences for the peace of the country. Sean raided the Pale with impunity and so intimidated English commanders that none was prepared to take the field against him. For nine years he defied the Dublin administration and brought it into ridicule. Besides defeating the queen's forces, he overcame the expanding MacDonnells of Antrim and the powerful O'Donnells of Tyrconnell. Protestant and Catholic primates alike were kept out of Armagh if they attempted to support the queen, or oppose Sean.

Once he had become the most powerful lord in Ulster and the only one capable of defying the government, Sean agreed to negotiations with a view to obtaining recognition as head of the O'Neill lordship. In 1562 he visited court where he and his followers were a nine-days' wonder. He used the occasion to intrigue with the Spanish and French ambassadors, and ostentatiously attended Mass in a Catholic embassy. In spite of this, the queen and he seem to have got on extremely well, and negotiations appeared likely to be fruitful.

But the queen's ministers seemed incapable of appreciating the consequences of their own dishonesty or intransigence. The difficulties might not appear to have been great: it is hard to conjecture what O'Neill would have demanded in the religious sphere when the choice was simply between the queen and the pope. O'Neill, while maintaining his right to attend Catholic services, was in no way committed to a papal crusade. The Anglo-Irish Primate of Armagh appointed by the pope thought that O'Neill was no more to be trusted than a gangster without reverence for religious proceedings. Certainly it would appear that O'Neill, in so far as he had any policy beyond ensuring his own ascendancy

in Ulster, would have been content with the solution of
Richard II, for he continually insisted that only the earls of
Ireland could be regarded as his equals. But he came back
to Ireland to find no readiness on the part of the Dublin
Castle authorities to meet the claims which he apparently
thought had been acquiesced in by the queen. He returned
to the north where he defeated his outstanding rivals
individually, only to succumb unexpectedly and be killed
after battle in consequence of combined quarrels with
O'Donnell and the MacDonnells.

The head of the murdered O'Neill was bought from the
MacDonnells, and the viceroy, Sir Henry Sidney, did not
hesitate to credit O'Neill's destruction to his own military
prowess, secure in the taciturnity of the head which he had
spiked on the gates of Dublin Castle. At a parliament in
Dublin two years later, in 1569, virtually the whole of
Ulster was declared confiscated and resumed by the crown.
But the royal government was in no position to enforce its
title, a weakness revealing the limitations of the English
forces, which during the preceding thirty years had been
regarded as invincible. Thus an uneasy situation was created
in the crises that rapidly followed in other parts of the
country.

At about the time of O'Neill's final defeat, a crisis arose
among the Old English settlers since the government was
encouraging the land claims of Sir Peter Carew, who was
allegedly the legal successor to grantees preceding Richard
II. Antiquarian investigations, which in this and other
instances were highly questionable, were upheld in the
queen's council, and fighting broke out in Munster in 1568
between Carew and such threatened Anglo-Irish gentry as
some of the Butlers of Ormond and the Fitzgeralds of
Desmond. The new claimants got the worst of the quarrels,
but the government treated the matter as one of rebellion.
The parliament which had attainted O'Neill and declared
his lands confiscated, made similar declarations against the
rebellious Butlers and Fitzgeralds. But the queen, who was

extremely friendly with the Earl of Ormond, was induced to interfere to prevent her representatives from going to extremes. All the same, a state of unrest and distrust was perpetuated throughout the English spheres of influence in the east and south, giving rise to rebellions and conspiracies in the next twenty years.

The meeting of parliament at which these measures were passed was the first on record where an opposition organised itself successfully against the government. Resentment ran deeply among members of the opposition, particularly towards John Hooker, the English antiquarian who had established Carew's title, and who missed no opportunity of directing the Irish parliament to the proper English procedures to be adopted.

But cautious diplomacy and careful avoidance of the religious issue enabled Sidney to regain control of a situation which had reached open warfare. In his closing speech to parliament the viceroy discreetly made no reference to the queen's excommunication by the pope, thanked the members for their loyalty and expressed regret at being unable to provide funds for an Irish university. A precious twenty years were let slip before the government decided to set up the University of Dublin as a college which could educate some native clergy and attempt the almost hopeless task of winning the people for the Reformation. At the same time, papal efforts to maintain an archbishop at Armagh and a national nuncio were thwarted by the arrest and incarceration of Richard Creagh and David Wolfe, appointed respectively to those offices by the pope.

Formally the government in Ireland appeared to avoid any attack on the pope, since it realised that what in England was a cause of strength was the reverse in Ireland. The unexpected excommunication of the queen by Pius v in February 1570 led to several defiant government speeches in the English parliament and the enactment of anti-papist measures. But while nothing was openly admitted, there existed seemingly a readiness to follow a more pacific policy

7

in Ireland, at least for as long as Irish and Anglo-Irish lords were likely to gain support from those who resented what was being said in England.

The establishment of provincial presidencies in Ireland during Elizabeth's reign suggests some awareness of the wisdom of delegating decisions and allowing divergencies within reason in the different areas. The presidencies also represented an effort to extend royal power and weaken the independent Irish and Anglo-Irish, though this policy was obstructed by official speculation and serious restrictions on administrative resources. In the event, the resort to war or rebellion in one area after another gave a military emphasis to the new officials in Munster and in Connacht, and thereafter, till the end of the century, any devolution of powers to the provinces seems to have been only on routine levels.

Among those who rebelled on the land issue in the late 1560s, an outstanding personality was James Fitzmaurice Fitzgerald. At first, after the parliament of 1569–71, Fitzmaurice was agreeable to peace, but different forces soon appeared to play upon him which led him to take up the leadership of a papal crusade against the queen in Ireland. A first outbreak took place before 1570, when Fitzmaurice held authority from his cousin, the Earl of Desmond, who was under restraint from the government over land disputes with the Earl of Ormond. Fitzmaurice's own territories too in Cork had been the subject of claims by enterprising English adventurers. In the quarrel between Desmond and Ormond the partiality of government for the latter must have been plain, and indeed the queen herself had secretly ordered Sidney, her deputy, to secure a verdict in Ormond's favour.

When Desmond weakly surrendered his claims Fitzmaurice left the country for France, Spain and Rome, trying to organise an Irish expedition against Elizabeth 1. The land question had occupied most of his attention in his first rebellion, but on the continent he identified religion with the issue. His ultimatum to some of the new adventurers denounced them as Huguenots, which he took as his main justification for forcing them out of the country. An exile with a sense of mission, Fitzmaurice emphasised this religious issue in his negotiations with Catholic powers.

The proposals of Fitzmaurice for a Catholic crusade in Ireland coincided with a new papal policy towards Elizabeth. The pope had excommunicated the queen in 1570, partly because he was aware of a conspiracy of English Catholics to replace Elizabeth by her Catholic cousin, Mary Queen of Scots. Mary had fallen on misfortune after the premature death of her husband, the king of France. She had returned to Scotland and married a Scottish noble, by whom she had a son who was to become James I of England. But she had also become involved in deadly intrigues to which her husband was a party, and which led to his murder and her own deposition. She fled to Elizabeth, only to be imprisoned. Conspiracies to replace Elizabeth by her cousin might well justify, in the English queen's mind, the execution of Mary. From the pope's standpoint, the excommunication of Elizabeth could be warranted if it brought about her deposition and replacement by a Catholic. In the atmosphere of the Reformation and the passionate wars of religion, the pope's decision was disastrous for many English Catholics, torn between loyalty to Elizabeth and to their Church. The situation seemed different to Catholics in Ireland, however, where government officials were continually irritating the Anglo-Irish and causing them more and more urgently to consider opposition to the régime before the country was handed over to Protestant adventurers.

On the continent Fitzmaurice received polite speeches but little real aid from Catholic princes. The pope was more generous, but the insufficiency of his resources left Fitzmaurice's mission without adequate support. Although he optimistically expected that a papal crusade would secure general support in Ireland, Fitzmaurice was mortified to find that virtually no one was prepared to come forward.

English influence in Ireland was still sufficiently strong to intimidate sympathisers from joining him, and he was attacked and killed by one of the Old English of Munster in 1579. Although Desmond tardily took his place, English forces defeated the enterprise, and a scorched-earth policy brought famine and fever to Munster, from which it scarcely recovered in ten years. The death of Fitzmaurice and the delay in securing Desmond for the rebellion did nothing to alter the administrator's belief that terrorism and extreme measures would most effectively terminate the outbreak. Furthermore, once the movement collapsed, Elizabeth commenced a new plantation scheme on the extensive lands confiscated in Munster.

But the policy of ruthlessness carried out in Munster so antagonised the people that Elizabeth herself came to realise that Lord Grey de Wilton, her viceroy, who had tortured and executed all the foreigners captured from Fitzmaurice's forces, would have to be replaced. Even the Pale was hardening into an attitude of obstructive neutrality. Viscount Baltinglass, who renounced allegiance to a female head of the Church, rebelled and fled the realm in 1580. A conspiracy involving Chief Justice Nicholas Nugent was detected and executions followed in 1582. Soon afterwards a papal archbishop of Cashel, Dermot O'Hurley, who had recently landed from Rome, was arrested and tried at Dublin under military law for treason committed beyond the seas, which strictly speaking was not indictable by English law in Ireland. O'Hurley was tortured and hanged, but the Government subsequently saw that a policy of persecution, however successful in England, would clearly be disastrous in Ireland, even in the Pale.

Not surprisingly Elizabeth's third Irish parliament, in 1585, rejected the Government's proposals to extend the laws against Catholics, and Sir John Perrott, though extremely resentful of Catholic opposition, was the first top official to direct Protestant bishops to exercise discretion. Plantation in Munster was, however, pushed ahead, and a substantial part of the upper structure of society came under the power of new English landowners. But these landowners failed to bring over with them a sufficient number of tenant farmers to alter the complexion of the southern population as a whole.

Whatever the reasons, the country was quiet in 1588 when the Spanish Armada reached its coasts. The great enterprise of Philip II was wrecked by storm and few of the survivors in Ireland were permitted to escape. The power of Elizabeth had been so substantially extended that the inhumanity of the Government's local officials against the shipwrecked provoked no considerable protest. For the moment it appeared as if Ireland had been pacified, and as if the opposition in parliament might well grow into a constitutionally accepted political group.

Yet almost from the day after the last survivors of the Armada had disappeared, English local officials created such exasperation as to lead to the greatest rebellious outbreak of the sixteenth century. The war of O'Neill and O'Donnell against the queen, variously described as the fifteen years' war and the nine years' war, secured substantial support in every province of Ireland. It began with isolated protests again venal officials and persecuting sheriffs, and it finally witnessed the involvement of people traditionally connected with the queen's government, notably O'Donnell and O'Neill themselves. The former was the son of a loyal friend of Dublin Castle, illegally imprisoned for years as a hostage for his father. O'Neill's loyal association was even more positive, as the second son of Matthew O'Neill, murdered in the succession war with his brother Sean. Protected for many years by the government against Sean's long-lived successor, Turlough Luineach, Hugh O'Neill was ultimately created earl of Tyrone like his ancestor Conn. He had experience in the field on the queen's side in the Munster rebellion, and was a witness to the extortion of English officials in the north. He was responsible for bribing Lord Deputy Fitzwilliam to release Red Hugh O'Donnell, and subsequently entered into an alliance with this descendant of his hereditary enemies.

In the years after the defeat of the Spanish Armada a group of Catholic bishops, mainly in the north, successfully urged O'Neill and O'Donnell to organise a nation-wide war against the government. It was perhaps the execution of O'Hurley which led so many outstanding clergy to involve themselves openly for the first time in the struggle against Elizabeth in Ireland, and at the same time to take the first steps to proclaim the decrees of the Council of Trent. But while O'Neill and O'Donnell put demands for religious toleration in the forefront of their programme, it should not be forgotten that their armed protest was largely directed against the expanding English administration and the methods of its officials. In this they had the connivance and sympathy of many in the Pale, and in the old English walled towns of the east and south, though even among the Catholic ecclesiastics in these areas there were some who favoured neutrality and even loyalty to the queen. Although the Catholic bishops must have had little readiness to make terms with Elizabeth in an age when Rome was still far from prepared to countenance Protestant rulers, O'Neill's careful diplomacy won him increasing support among the Anglo-Irish, since he represented himself as a moderate, reluctant to be involved in rebellion and ever prepared to renew his loyalty to his queen.

In the military sphere, perhaps because of the queen's parsimony, English forces were disastrously defeated in three provinces, and after O'Neill's victory at the Yellow Ford in 1598 the Dublin administration sent a whining letter to conciliate him. In the following year Elisabeth's favourite, the renowned Earl of Essex, appointed as Irish Lord Lieutenant, was completely out-manoeuvred in diplomacy by O'Neill, who appears to have convinced him that the victory of Catholicism in the wars of religion in continental Europe was only a short time away.

At this stage it was apparent that O'Neill was prepared

to stand on terms similar to those conceded by Henry IV to the Huguenots in France, which virtually ensured them self-government and their own religious establishment without interference from the rest of the realm. A new era was dawning in Europe. A new pope, Clement VIII, modified his predecessor's policy sufficiently to let Catholics determine the allegiance question locally, both in France and in Ireland. While he was quite prepared to bless and give crusaders' indulgences to the rebel Irish and their Spanish supporters, and even to appoint a Spanish Franciscan, Matthew of Oviedo, to the archbishopric of Dublin, Clement was not prepared to condemn those who fought for Elizabeth or to make a Spaniard his Irish nuncio. But the queen was too old and too involved to countenance any new policy, and Essex too rash to bide his time; on his return to London he made an armed protest against Elizabeth's ministers, a rebellious gesture that cost him his head.

Elizabeth, however, was obliged to agree to the suggestion of her new viceroy and Essex's successor in Ireland, Viscount Mountjoy, to terminate the persecution of Catholics. In 1600, Mountjoy and Sir George Carew, the able president of Munster, were most careful to subordinate religious to political issues. Philip II was now dead and his less dilatory successor, Philip III, planned an Irish expedition which arrived under Don John de Aguila at Kinsale towards the end of the following year. Mountjoy and Carew, however, were able to reduce O'Neill and his allies, contain the forces of the small Spanish expedition, and ultimately defeat O'Neill at the battle of Kinsale. Aguila withdrew to Spain and O'Donnell followed. Although O'Neill held on, hopeful of further foreign aid, credulous about promises of goodwill from Elizabeth's potential successor, James VI of Scotland, he was ultimately driven into submission in the last days of the queen's reign, and at Mellifont signed his surrender to Mountjoy, unaware that the latter's authority had expired, as the queen had just died.

The treaty of Mellifont, as patriotic historians have

described the proceedings which, according to Mountjoy, involved O'Neill in abasing himself before the Lord Deputy, was, perhaps inevitably, an unreal one. Submission on the understanding that James I, as James VI of Scotland had become when he succeeded Elizabeth in England, would pardon and restore the leading rebels and give them permission to practise their own religion, provided they abandoned their Spanish connections, depended too much upon good will all round. Although the new sovereign from Scotland had been in communication with O'Neill before his succession, he had yet to reveal the kind of policy he intended to pursue.

The death of the last of the Tudors raises difficult questions as to the extent of involvement with O'Neill in the wars. To the forces in the field it was a matter for exasperation that so many elements in society, and notably the towns, observed neutrality. There is no doubt that the strength of the loyal tradition influenced many who resented the government's policy against taking the ultimate step of defiance. Among the lords, great and small, there was a steady shift, according as the forces of the rebels or the government were in the ascendant. In all these decisions the question of religion was made to appear of first importance, but in fact it frequently took a secondary place. To Mountjoy, however, the question of religion was crucial. So fearful was he of the support O'Neill might get if he insisted on a Catholic viceroy and the restriction of offices to Irishmen, that the Protestant Church authorities were roughly handled when they made use of their legal rights to persecute Catholics. The wisdom of this was apparent, since convincing evidence showed, firstly, that the overwhelming mass of the urban population of the south boycotted Protestant services and, secondly, that some Munster gentry who refused to associate with O'Neill insisted that since the queen's government had never persecuted their religion she could be relied upon to continue giving them immunity. That there should be a new government line on religion, conceding some toleration, would not have appeared unreasonable to the younger people who had grown up since the ardour of earlier religious conflicts had cooled. Neutrality in the war, however, was considered by the government to be a more serious matter, and the towns which had prided themselves on their independence in earlier ages were to find that a tougher policy would be employed against them once peace had been restored.

4

A Stuart kingdom, 1603–1691

AT this stage we can consider the community of Ireland in relation to the various groups which identified themselves, usually exclusively, with this concept. These groups were made up of the exiled Catholics, the depressed Irish, the old or pre-Tudor English, the Palesmen, the new English and the resident Catholic clergy.

The exiles were at all times a significant element in the history of Ireland, particularly when they sought to intervene in its internal affairs, as they did from Europe in the seventeenth century and from Britain and America in the nineteenth and twentieth. On the eve of the accession of the first Stuart ruler of England the exiles of the Gaelic and Anglo-Irish traditions on the continent became quite critical, an outlook which accentuated, in a foreign context, differences at home. Their Catholicism, the common element which had taken them out of the country influenced them both towards an utter rejection of Protestantism and the Protestant Irish as having any claim to be regarded of the community. But as time went on, the exiles became more and more dominated by their new surroundings, and their attitudes to Irish affairs were increasingly coloured by loyalty to the policies of their patrons. The pope as a temporal sovereign in Italy, the authority in the Catholic Netherlands, in Lorraine and in other lesser states, influenced those he had received towards his point of view. The exiles in Spain too tended to become more remote from England, though the years of peace after 1604 must have restrained them somewhat. In France the Irish were inclined to accept England as an automatic, or at least as a potential ally while Henry IV lived, and as long as his successor maintained his policy, so that more moderation against England prevailed amongst the exiles there. It would appear that the Anglo-Irish gravitated more towards France, and the Irish towards Spain. Of course both these groups of exiles had a sense of Irishness, or an interest in Ireland. The record, vis-à-vis Ireland, of isolated soldiers abroad fighting in Protestant armies, has not survived however, apart from their writings, which are of a very specialist and partisan kind and not in the Irish literary tradition. Finally, there were the Irish ecclesiastics among the exiles in Europe, noted for their devotion to the universal Church, to their own order and houses of residence, and above all for the high degree of sophistication in their writings.

In Gaelic areas the accession of James I (1603–25), who quickly made peace with Spain, seems to have favoured the restoration of O'Neill and his allies to their former independent authority. The king made Rory O'Donnell Earl of Tyrconnell, and one can assume that other lords felt equally convinced of their autonomy, at least in regard to religion. But apart from outstanding individuals like O'Neill, there were still some Irishmen who held on to the tradition of rejecting the Old English as not being part of the community.

At first the Government of James I appeared capable of maintaining a position in which Irish and Old English participated in the affairs of Ireland. James I kept Mountjoy as his viceroy and Mountjoy regarded it as a matter of honour to observe the understanding which he had reached with O'Neill at the end of the war. However, two years later Mountjoy left Ireland and his successors took up a more self-centred attitude. To the Old Irish, viceroys thus became remote, and many of the Old English persisted in the mentality formerly represented by the Statutes of Kilkenny. This was the view of the Irish with which the viceroys became linked.

The Pale and the towns were still largely detached from the atmosphere left over from the strife. They remained self-centred and jealous of their independence. Their reluctance to proclaim James 1, their readiness to open churches to Catholics and to provide publicly for the saying of Mass, so forcing the new government to recognise a *fait accompli*, demonstrated the strength of Catholicism from Drogheda to Cork, and the resentment of Elizabethan policy. This was to play a decisive part in the future of these centres of Old English interest; ultimately under Cromwell they were extruded from strategic centres and reduced in government eyes to the despised category of Irish papists.

The New English hardly conceded that the community of Ireland was of any consequence except on very formal occasions, and then always in close association, if not subordination, with England. In 1603 they might be divided into three categories, military, adventurer and planter, though these categories should not be construed too rigidly. But all of them were almost as hostile to the Old English as they were to the Irish, particularly since the great majority of these were either Catholics or crypto-Catholics. The military element among the New English was extremely resentful of Mountjoy's settlement at Mellifont, which precluded them from winning a monopoly of the lands they had hoped to see confiscated. The adventurers aspiring to civil office were hardly to be distinguished from the soldiers, though they produced at least one remarkable character in Richard Boyle, who arrived in Ireland with five pounds in his pocket and died Earl of Cork, the richest man in the realm. The planters, a sorry element of survivors of the relatively unsuccessful plantations in Leix and Offaly, and in Munster after the Desmond rebellion, had been particularly exposed in the war against O'Neill and his allies, and regarded themselves as deserving more encouragement than the government was prepared to give them. But this attitude naturally changed after the Flight of the Earls from Ulster, when the government reverted to a policy of plantation. The New English were prepared to fight in their own interests, and by the end of the century had won control of Ireland. But they quickly began to see Irish affairs from a different viewpoint to England's, if only because of commercial discrimination against Ireland and the English tendency to regard all colonists as inferior, whether in Ireland or the New World.

Finally the Catholic Church as an international organisation, with a supra-national attitude, must be included in a survey of the elements concerned with the community of Ireland. From the time of the Reformation, Rome was inclined to regard Irish affairs in close association with those of England, and after 1603, with those of Scotland. In fact the papacy still tended to classify peoples in relation to their princes and to regard kings as more important than their subjects. The realisation by more receptive Catholic reformers that this was hardly adequate resulted in greater attention being paid to the affairs of peoples, or at least to those connected with the upper classes. Rome's new thinking on this question was also influenced by that of Irish exiles, whose distinction of Gaelic and Old English frequently affected papal policy. As for the clergy in Ireland, the Franciscans enjoyed the widespread confidence of the people in Gaelic areas, and the Jesuits had perhaps a similar position among the Old English. Fear of the Jesuit order so dominated the English administrators at home and in Ireland that the Jesuits were frequently credited with responsibility for the more nefarious enterprises against the state. English officials often used the term 'Jesuit' to describe any outstanding Catholic priest.

Having considered the community, it is also necessary to look at those forces or factors which were calculated to bring about change. Of these I have noted four, the Roman Church, the Scots, the monarchy and the English parliament.

As far as the Church was concerned, the accession of James I created a problem. Although a Protestant, the king had allowed some of his Catholic subjects to represent him

at Rome as being drawn to the religion of his mother, Mary
Queen of Scots, whom many Catholics regarded as a martyr.
Even if within a short time the king emerged as hostile to
the papacy, the historian must beware of assuming that
what happened was inevitable. James I, 'the wisest fool in
Christendom' as he was called by Henry IV of France,
probably tried to impress the papacy with his learning,
which was prodigious if undisciplined, and deeply resented
the lack of appreciation of his literary efforts. Entertaining
an exalted notion of his own station, believing in the
absolutism of monarchy, he wanted to avoid the bloody
persecution of his predecessors, but rapidly lost his self-
control with foreign monarchs who were unprepared to
receive him at his own estimate. The papacy was accordingly rejected. About the same time, efforts were being
made by Anglo-Irish scholars like Peter Lombard, created
Archbishop of Armagh by the pope, to find a formula
whereby the community of Ireland could relate itself
rationally to the new dynasty. This became papal policy,
and it found particular favour during the more resilient
pontificate of Clement VIII. But the very anxiety of
Lombard, and of Jesuit theologians like Bellarmine, gave
rise to suspicions among leading English Protestants, who
were not convinced that the Church was ready to abandon
its claims to depose monarchs.

Scots migrants to Ireland increased substantially in the
middle of the sixteenth century. Corresponding to the new
Gaelic families which had flooded into abandoned English
areas in the south, were the MacDonalds and other highland
families entering the Glens of Antrim, from which the Old
English had virtually disappeared. They successfully resisted
viceregal efforts to dislodge them. Ultimately however,
their leaders condescended to make peace, to become
naturalised subjects of the kingdom of Ireland, and even,
in the last years of Elizabeth, to take titles of nobility. These
Scots, largely Catholics, who were already in the country
at the death of Elizabeth, must be distinguished from the

newer elements who appeared increasingly after the accession of James, and who came mainly from the lowlands and the Scottish border. Thereafter a lowland and Presbyterian Scottish community developed in Ireland, which constantly looked back to its motherland, rejected rival claimants to speak for the Scots and co-operated only reluctantly with English Protestants. Since the Scots wars of religion they were dominated by a fear of catholicism, and the Catholic community in Ireland became virtually anathema to them.

The monarchy of necessity created an element of change, as the king of three kingdoms had no anxiety to be dominated by Scotland and Ireland, though he resented English reluctance to receive the Scots as full citizens. By the end of the century James II was to advise his son against any integration of the parliaments of the three kingdoms. James I, who had been King of Scotland since his infancy, began his reign as King of England with considerable favour for closer relations between his old realm and the new. It became usual to employ the term British and to refer to England and Scotland as Great Britain. But the English parliament did not favour legislative union as long as this would appear to give greater privileges to the Scots and so strengthen the monarchy. By the time the power of parliament had become predominant, the monarchy had become less enthusiastic for union. Charles I (1625-49) was prepared in a limited way to give some countenance to the idea of a distinct community of Ireland, but there are few positive signs of such an attitude on the part of his father, James I.

The English parliament, from the 1640s on, was trying to assert itself over the king, and also to control the affairs of Ireland and of the colonies in America. There were two spheres in which parliament was particularly interested in Ireland—religion and land. Its Puritan members had no time for Catholicism, resented the rivalry of Catholic towns, favoured the acquisition of land by the English, and smarted under the exploitation of the country for the king. But their policy was eventually a selfish one, with few imperial ideas and little regard for the community of Ireland, whether in respect of the colonists or the country as a whole.

Having considered the community and the forces likely to bring about change within it, it remains to deal with the most significant events in its history during the seventeenth century, taking as a half-way point the destruction of the Irish armies by Cromwell.

The hostile reaction in England to the arrival there of O'Neill and O'Donnell after their pardon by James I gives some indication of the resentment towards Irish rebels which Elizabethan propaganda had created. O'Donnell, who had been recently ennobled Tyrconnell, and O'Neill recently restored in Tyrone, were both stoned in the streets of London, and their unpopularity in England did not go unnoticed by the king. However, the question of religious toleration did not arise clearly in James's mind until the outbreak of Catholic conspiracies, such as that of Guy Fawkes on 5 November 1605. If modern scholars are in doubt as to how far this conspiracy facilitated former Elizabethan ministers in bringing the king more smartly into line with their own views, the fact remains that, with the Guy Fawkes plot, English Catholics sustained a major rejection from the dominant Protestant community.

Two years later, after proclamations were issued in Ireland banishing the Catholic clergy, Tyrone and Tyrconnell were induced to leave the country. The Ulster chiefs, resenting indignities against them and fearing allegations that they were conspiring against Dublin, fled to the mainland of Europe in what has come to be known as the Flight of the Earls. Their disappointing reception on the continent, with maimed rights, was a grim indication to them that they had ceased to play a decisive role, such as they had played in the wars of Elizabeth's reign. British diplomatic influence was sufficiently powerful to make their presence an embarrassment to all Catholic powers until they took refuge with the pope. In Ireland, their passing was lamented by their poets, but not without the implication that they had deserted and abandoned the country to the exploiter and adventurer.

In Dublin, the king's administrators convinced him that the Flight of the Earls was due to their involvement in a rebel conspiracy, and James was converted to a policy of plantation, particularly on the lands of those who had fled from Ulster. James I was easily impressed by his English ministers, and through them Elizabethan army officers were promoted and sustained in Ireland. In this way, successive viceroys in Ireland maintained the Protestant and colonial policies of Elizabeth I. While the rights of individual Irish freeholders were ignored or scandalously taken from them, the policy of plantation was based primarily on military exigencies, and this itself necessitated measures for the continued concentration of the Irish in the least dangerous areas.

Ultimately, however, economic forces prevailed, and the planters adjusted conditions to their own advantage, some-times embroiling themselves in serious quarrels with the government. Considerable property changed hands as a predominanely pastoral system of agriculture gave way to the more intensively cultivated system of the planters. Estates of landowners like Conn O'Neill in Down, confronted with the expensive demands of a more sophisticated society, were broken up. Their poets mourned the passing of the great plains and the cutting up of the green fields in the enclosure movement. These northern plantations were generally successful. They were built up by migrants from Scotland and the English side of the Scottish border, where the warring families of the past were no longer required and were easily transplanted on to corresponding borders in Ireland. Although later their greed nearly led to their destruction, during the rebellion of 1641, they had, by the end of the century, transformed the greater part of the northern province into Presbyterian and Anglican comm-unities. During this period power passed finally from the Old Irish and English upper classes to the new landowners

8

and colonists including those who later came into the country in further confiscations under Cromwell and William III.

Once the Gaelic lords of Ulster had fled the realm, the early Stuarts were disembarrassed of a potential military threat. This perhaps made them over-complacent with their success and ever ready to take the advice of those interested in exploiting the king's less fortunate subjects. Only in religious matters were there some doubts about their success. Gaelic culture and traditional English medieval usages in Ireland were subordinated to the new cosmopolitan Protestant society. The mass of the people, however, continued to give their allegiance to the Holy See; but the mass of the people were despised by the ex-army officials and the Protestant clergy who believed that they could easily be dragooned and intimidated into conformity.

Aware as he was of the newer spirit among Catholic churchmen such as Peter Lombard, who was prepared to make no distinction between a Catholic and a Protestant sovereign, Mountjoy had been slow to go with these ecclesiastics along the lines of coercion.

But the Guy Fawkes conspiracy in England led the government to panic and it gave its approval to coercion against catholicism. Proclamations were issued banishing the clergy, and ordering all officials, including town mayors, to take the Oath of Supremacy and attend parish services on Sundays. A long-drawn-out struggle followed, however, in which the government was not successful. Parliament, summoned in 1613, was fully prepared to ratify the attainder of the exiled earls and endorse the Ulster plantation, but not to enact additional penal laws against Catholics. By the end of his reign, James's government, partly under the influence of the Catholic rulers of France and Spain, agreed reluctantly to informal toleration. But the policy of plantation and expansion of Protestant power in local administration was only partly modified.

The parliament of 1613 in Ireland was remarkable, since

it was the first occasion on which the whole country was represented in the commons. The government tried to make parliament representative of the community as a whole, and abandon the legislative tradition of the Statutes of Kilkenny. Serfdom was abolished. The principle of equality before the law was proclaimed, and this must be regarded, at least in part, as due to the influence of James. On the other hand, however, an attempt was made to give statutory sanction for the anti-Catholic measures taken by the viceroy in a continuation of the Elizabethan policy of maintaining religious uniformity with England. Although no additional anti-Catholic legislation was enacted in James's reign, the result was to exclude from full citizenship the Catholics, who outnumbered the other denominations by more than two to one. In creating additional parliamentary boroughs, James 1 provided so amply for the representation of recently planted areas in Ulster as to give them a wholly disproportionate number of seats. Indeed he virtually established parliamentary constituencies for towns which were still under construction. The object was to secure for the government a reliable majority, otherwise, as substantial Catholic opposition in the commons in the last parliament of Elizabeth had shown, the administration's legislative programme might be imperilled. In this way, the evil principle of the Tudors was maintained, whereby undue influence was used to muzzle parliament. The idea of integrating the various population groups into one community was seriously endangered.

The proceedings of this parliament resulted in the emergence of two parties, one supporting the government, which was largely the party of the New English, and the other the opposition, which was composed of the Old English and the Gaelic Irish. As far as the opposition was concerned, the parliament performed the useful function of bringing the two elements close together. Their unity was accentuated by a common allegiance to Catholicism. Indeed, many modern historians have represented religion as being the real division in the Irish parliament under the Stuarts. But it might be more correct to see as the vital distinction the difference between the newer and the older elements; this, rather than religion, it appears to me, was the real division in seventeenth-century Ireland. Admittedly, when passions were aroused the religious issue came much more into prominence, but more was involved than questions of landed power and religion. All the upholders of older traditions found themselves coming together in the face of a growing threat from the new interests, which were ultimately to overwhelm them.

The plantations did incalculable damage to Anglo-Irish relations. Since the reign of Henry VIII the government had encouraged people to regard feudal traditions as preferable to the older Irish system of landownership. But from the time of Elizabeth I it began to emerge that forfeiture of landed property to the crown, with immediate loss of social and political status, was a major liability. Government policy began to favour corrupt officials, who, under the Stuarts, became dominated by the need to amplify revenue even by the most questionable means.

The increase in crown revenues derived from the new grants of land in Ulster stimulated questioning of land-owner's rights elsewhere. In the predominantly Irish areas of Connacht, Leinster and Munster, in the counties of Leitrim, Longford, Westmeath, Offaly (King's County), Wexford, Wicklow and Tipperary, further colonial experiments were pushed through. Then the titles of Old English proprietors were queried. Now, the parliament of 1613 had taught the government that Catholics could be loyal, even if it might still be necessary to condemn as criminals, attaint or execute the discontented Irish on planted lands in Ulster. But extreme government pressure, even at the highest level, against prominent Old English parliamentarians had aroused such a degree of passive resistance that the government was obliged to climb down on the issue of Old English proprietary rights. By 1617 it became necessary to issue commissions to remedy such titles as were theoretically defective in law.

Perhaps it should be added that for the first time the Gaelic Irish within the country, as distinct from the Gaelic exiles who fled abroad and might yet hope to return, accepted the constitutional order of society in the Old English tradition. Circumstances were to strengthen this position to some extent when the next parliament was held twenty years later under Wentworth, but the outbreak of civil war in the 1640s and the setting up at Kilkenny of a quasi-parliament by the Catholic confederates was to reveal how seriously both elements continued to diverge. Not until the Cromwellian conquest were Old English and Gaelic Irish to be forced to abandon their basic differences.

In 1613, however, as far as the government was concerned difficulties with the opposition seemed in danger of making it impossible to continue the parliament in existence. After a conflict over the election of the Speaker of the House of Commons, the king sent for leaders of the two parties and lectured them on their duties. The government for its part, while it upheld the majority, agreed to moderate its programme, and in the long run the co-operation of the opposition was a notable consequence of this concession. Indeed, it could be said that both the king and his ministers had learned the valuable lesson that the old interests in Ireland, despite their attachment to a proscribed religion, were prepared to play their part in the public organisation of the community. Unfortunately, the exigencies of civil war, coupled with the rising of 1641 and its subsequent involvement of the Old English, dispelled for England any belief in Irish trustworthiness.

The Thirty Years' War (1618–48) created a good deal of nervousness in the kingdom of James 1 for some time. The war had little real importance for Ireland until the king became involved in a proposed alliance, first with Spain and then with France. General English hostility towards the Hapsburgs created an attitude favourable to a war in defence of Protestantism. This was accentuated by the expulsion of the king's son-in-law, Frederick the Elector Palatine, from Bohemia whose crown he had accepted in 1620. The government's failure to support him damaged the prestige of the king in England, and the projected alliance with Spain was highly unpopular there, both for this reason and because of the traditional enmity between the two countries. But for Ireland, the Spanish alliance was important, as it meant the king would have to adopt a more tolerant attitude towards Catholicism.

On the whole, the reign of James I demonstrated the strength of Catholicism in Ireland, especially when the government tried to enforce laws regarding uniformity of religious service, the taking of the oaths by muncipal office holders, and the banishment of the clergy. Public opinion reacted unexpectedly, particularly when the state resorted to extreme measures, such as the execution in 1612 of the Bishop of Down and Connor as an alleged party to conspiracies of the exiled Tyrone. After 1620 it could be said that the government came to the conclusion that these laws could not be enforced, largely because of the attitude of its local officials, who were overwhelmingly Catholic. A promise of toleration, as part of the negotiations for the Spanish alliance and the projected marriage of James's heir to a Catholic Spanish princess provided a suitable excuse for abandoning a policy which was unpopular and unsuccessful.

These Spanish negotiations broke down in 1623, but they were replaced by successful proposals for an alliance with Catholic France, culminating in the marriage of the future Charles I (1625–49) with the princess, Henrietta Maria. The same provisions as in the abortive Spanish negotiations were agreed to regarding Catholics. The policy of persecution came practically to an end. After this it was employed only spasmodically until the whole situation was transformed in the 1640s by civil war.

The viceroyalty of Thomas Wentworth, Earl of Stafford,

during the 1630s is important for the clearer emergence of the New English interest, which became readily distinguishable from that of the government. In dealing with parliament, Wentworth balanced the old interests against the new. He successfully strengthened the position of the government and built up a steady revenue for England. His achievement, however, was made at a cost which was to prove disastrous. His policy of toughness on Old English petitions for redress reversing the main propositions known as The Graces—concessions which the king had already indicated to be acceptable and sponsored in principle— provoked hostility to the monarchy and above all to himself.

Titles of landowners were again called into question. Over the greater part of Connacht grand juries were intimidated and even imprisoned in order to find titles for the crown against Old English as well as Old Irish proprietors. In the process of building up the resources of the Anglican Church, adventurers such as the Earl of Cork were compelled to disgorge some of their ill-gotten wealth. Even the city of London was judged to have forfeited its Irish grants, including the county and city of Londonderry, on technical breaches of its charter. In addition, the radical Protestants of the north, sympathetic with the anti-episcopal Scots, were harried and coerced, and excluded from Anglican Church benefices. Catholic ecclesiastics who attempted to discipline their clergy, including members of religious orders ready to challenge episcopal authority, were threatened with prosecution for exercising illegal jurisdiction. Under the influence of Archbishop Laud of Canterbury, the viceroy's authority was used to compel the episcopal Protestant Church in Ireland to assimilate its public articles to those of England and abandon more Calvinist articles approved in 1615.

Wentworth's rule in Ireland coincided with a period in which Charles 1 sought to strengthen the monarchy in Scotland, and attempted to replaces Presbyterianism by the Anglican liturgy and church organisation. This, in 1638, provoked the Scots' Solemn League and Covenant against popery and episcopacy, which culminated in the Bishops' War. It was in this way that the period of warfare began in the Stuart kingdoms which was to end in the disestablishment of episcopacy in England and the execution of the king. In Ireland, Wentworth's policy was attacked, since the English parliament was determined to prevent the king using against the Scots a virtually Catholic army which had been organised by Wentworth at Carrickfergus. Wentworth, now Earl of Strafford, was recalled to face legal proceedings which ended in his own execution. Both parties in the Irish parliament had combined to pull him down. But this temporary alliance, entailing a commitment to the leaders of the parliamentary majority in England against the monarchy, was not to last. Once the issue between king and parliament emerged in England, and gave rise to the issue of religion, the parliamentarians were determined to have nothing to do with the Irish Catholics in the opposition. These, in any case, had turned again to the king, fearing the intolerance of the English parliament. The failure of Charles i's government to crush the Scots rising created a pro-Presbyterian party in Ireland among the settlers of Scottish origin. The Dublin administration which succeeded Strafford became more puritan in outlook and more favourable to the English parliament. Strafford's Carrickfergus army was demobilised, but the king privately empowered a few prominent persons, such as the Earl of Antrim, to maintain forces for his use, nominally against the Scots, but perhaps also to overawe the Dublin governors.

In October 1641 plans were discovered in Dublin for a rising which aimed to seize that centre of English power. Though failing in this, its immediate object, rebellion broke out in Ulster, and this for a period led to the occupation of most of planted Ulster by Old Irish forces, who drove the settlers into their fortified towns. The war between Catholic and Protestant which then began in Ireland lasted until the Cromwellian conquest. In this war the king's representatives in Dublin publicly denounced Catholicism as if all Catholics were traitors, and this moved the gentry of the English Pale to combine with the Ulster rebels, and, under the influence of the Catholic hierarchy, to set up their assembly at Kilkenny. They avoided the term 'parliament', but organised themselves virtually as the parliamentary forces had done in England. Their assembly was to represent all Catholic interests, including the hierarchy, and took as its motto 'for God, king and country'. The confederates communicated with the pope, and asked the governments of France and Spain for support and supplies. Outside of Dublin, and some fortified cities of the south, east and north coasts, the greater part of the country soon fell to their hands.

The influence of the English parliament did more than lead to the setting up of the Kilkenny confederation. On the news of the outbreak of rebellion in Ireland, Westminster enacted a provision to confiscate all lands of those captured in rebellion against England. This measure was intended to guarantee repayment to those prepared to invest money in the re-conquest of Ireland. Thus, even before the outbreak of hostilities with Charles I in England, the parliamentary leaders were determined not to permit the king to utilise the Irish crisis as an excuse for establishing an army which might overawe them. They had collected war propaganda regarding Irish excesses against Protestants in order to force the king to give them control of war policy against the rebels. Having given way on this issue, Charles I found himself subjected to allegations that the Irish had his royal warrant to massacre Protestant settlers, and the Irish lords justices in Ireland ordered all Catholics to disarm, whether or not they claimed to be loyal.

The English parliament, for its part, began to negotiate with the Scots rebels. The king, alarmed by increasing denunciations of Catholics, which he believed were aimed at his queen, Henrietta Maria of France, attempted to arrest the leading parliamentarians, but was unsuccessful. He then decided to raise his standard at Oxford against the parliamentarians who had allied with the Scots and had undertaken to accept the Covenant, and agreed to replace episcopacy by Presbyterianism.

The action of the English parliament in legislating for Ireland coincided with a growing resentment in the Irish parliament at the undue influence exercised on the king's behalf by Wentworth and his successors. During the 1640s the activities at Kilkenny of men such as Patrick Darcy were significant, since they were attempting to work out a relationship between the king and his Catholic subjects in Ireland, largely in continuation of their parliamentary outlook under James I and under Wentworth. Darcy, an Old English Catholic lawyer, had issued an anonymous pamphlet in 1641 challenging both the powers exercised by viceroys under Poynings' Law and the powers claimed by the English parliament in Ireland.

Thus, once the king and English parliament went to war, many of the Old English Catholics in Ireland tried to bring about a reconciliation with their monarch. But the confederates' insistence on the rights of the Irish parliament, as they saw them, was not upheld by the Irish Protestants, or the party of the New English, who emphatically rejected the independent attitude which they themselves had supported earlier, and which many of them, in a different context, would support after the restoration of the monarchy. The outbreak of war had brought about this difference and, so far as Ireland was concerned, the savagery of the fighting created a further divergence between Protestant and Catholic that the centuries did not bridge.

At the beginning of the rising in Ulster it was alleged that the Irish who attacked the planters were guilty of excesses against non-combatants, a report which led to the belief in a general massacre of Protestants. This, linked in popular imagination with the masscre of the Hugenots in Paris on Saint Bartholomew's Day, 1572, created among seventeenth-century English Protestants such fear, distrust and horror of papists, particularly of Irish papists, that it became impossible to discuss rationally any matter involving the conflicting religions.

In Ireland, Catholic success in the field was notable in Ulster and Leinster. In the north the planters were restricted to a few strongholds, and in Leinster the power of the king, or rather of the official authorities who were increasingly drawn towards the parliamentarians, was confined to an area of not twenty miles radius from Dublin. Within this area English rule was maintained in the king's interest at least nominally until 1648, when it was handed over to the forces of parliament.

The state of war between the Catholic assembly at Kilkenny and the Dublin government had not persisted for long when proposals were made for an agreement between Kilkenny and the king, which might have concluded successfully had the safeguards which the Catholics considered essential been accepted. Such an agreement could have transferred to the king a force of more than ten thousand men. The negotiations themselves quickly resulted in a cessation, as contemporaries called the armistice, which enabled a small royal army to be sent for service to Chester. Concurrently the Dublin administration was forced to recognise Lord Clanrickard, despite his Catholicism, as the king's commander in Connacht. But so far as the larger army of the Kilkenny government was concerned, much longer negotiations with the government were necessary. The result of these was the abortive treaty of 1646, known as the first Ormond peace, which was followed by a second Ormond treaty on the eve of the king's execution.

The Old English had successfully prevailed at Kilkenny, to the extent that the confederation had not adopted a papal policy of denying English monarchial rule. But in little else were they successful. The difficulty in an assembly representative of every Catholic element in Ireland was that the consequences of persecution and confiscation were diverse and that peace terms might result in the frustration of those whose interests were not provided for. James Butler, Earl of

Ormond, who had become the leading representative of the king first in military and later in civil matters, was theoretically in an admirable position to negotiate, since most of the members of his family at this juncture were Catholics. But he himself had been brought up a Protestant, and his own intransigence slowed up the discussions and ultimately made progress impossible, except in moments of the greatest crisis. So great was his influence among the Old English that these came to be nicknamed 'the Ormondists' by their opponents who eventually secured endorsement for their own views.

The first Ormond peace, although it was officially proclaimed by the supreme council of the Kilkenny confederates, was abrogated under the influence of the Papal Nuncio, John Baptist Rinuccini. The unexpected arrival of the papal legate at Kilkenny had strengthened the claims of the Catholic clergy who wanted to maintain thier control over churches in the areas dominated by Catholic forces. That Ormond had not been prepared to support any such plan permitting the retention of church land by Catholics was not surprising, because the very idea of negotiations with Catholics was anathema to all Protestant interests. Rinuccini's arrival was hardly popular with some of the Old English Catholics either, since they had come into possession of former monastic property, and feared that a victory for the Counter-Reformation in Ireland might deprive them of these lands should they be reclaimed for the Church. Rinuccini, though empowered to negotiate for the recognition of the transfer of monastic lands to secular owners, was in fact extremely slow to admit his powers in this area. In the negotiations generally he took up an attitude of hostility towards Ormond, which only the Old Irish appreciated.

This term, the Old Irish, was used by contemporaries usually to refer to the Ulster forces of the O'Neills, who over-ran the greater part of the plantations and defeated a Scots Presbyterian army under Robert Monro which had been sent to protect the northern Presbyterians by allies of the English parliament in Scotland. In retrospect, it should be mentioned that Wentworth's policy of religious uniformity, though successful at first, had provoked radical Protestant resistance when he had attempted to enforce an oath, nicknamed the Black Oath, against the Solemn League and Covenant. Hitherto Presbyterians in Ireland had been content to remain organised within the established Protestant Episcopalian Church, but, in 1643, after the outbreak of war, the first presbytery from which the modern Irish Presbyterian Church is dated was established in Belfast. Other communities were organised at about the same time and probably outnumbered the Anglicans, so that in Ulster, after the first stages of the rising, the forces opposing the Catholics were predominantly Presbyterian. But the war in Ulster, ultimately represented as one of religion, was basically for or against the plantation.

The Catholic successes were in large part due to the coming from the theatres of war in Europe, particularly the Low Countries, of experienced officers such as Owen Roe O'Neill. O'Neill's victory over Monro at Benburb in 1646 led him to be regarded as the outstanding military tactician of the day. But O'Neill's forces suspected the Kilkenny negotiators of being prepared to permit the continuation of the plantations of James I. They therefore supported Rinuccini in condemning the Ormond peace of 1646, a condemnation endorsed by most of the Catholic community, particularly as ecclesiastical sanctions involving interdict and excommunication were invoked. Even though two years later the majority of Catholics probably came out against Rinuccini, there is little doubt that his intervention against the treaty of 1646 was closely in accord with contemporary Catholic opinion. Moreover, Rinuccini, though accentuating divisions by attempting to secure the king's agreement to the public restoration of Catholicism, had good reason to believe from Charles's agents in France that such a development was feasible, even though this was at the very stage when the king was seeking to convince his

British subjects that he was totally committed to a Protestant policy. The execution by the parliamentarians of the powerful Anglican Archbishop Laud in 1645 was one indication of how much Charles had to contend with.

The renewal of negotiations, in an effort to find generally acceptable terms, was facilitated by the arrival in Ireland of the Earl of Glamorgan. He had been secretly empowered to make the concessions on religious issues which Ormond had earlier refused. Glamorgan's negotiations seem to have paralleled those between Charles 1's Catholic queen and papal representatives in Paris and Rome. Such an agreement would have virtually established over most of Ireland a position comparable to that approved in 1598 by Henry IV for the Huguenots of France. The Catholic hierarchy would have been re-established in Ireland and civil positions opened to Catholics. Proposals on these terms were agreed to by Glamorgan and accepted secretly at Kilkenny. A few months later, however, they were published by the parliamentarians in London after the Glamorgan treaty had been discovered in the baggage of a Catholic bishop killed in battle in Ireland. It was, perhaps, inevitable that Charles 1 should disavow the agreement, but it did nothing to strengthen his position or his credibility. Nevertheless, Charles was still hopeful of Irish reinforcements and privately permitted negotiations to continue, even after he had surrended to the Scots in 1646 and publicly denounced the negotiators.

In the province of Munster, under Lord Inchiquin, a Protestant army concentrated on the towns had tended to align itself first with the parliamentarians, but later reverted to the confederate royalists. Once again, however, armistice negotiations with Kilkenny created difficulties with the nuncio. But on this occasion his condemnation of the agreement with Inchiquin precipitated a division among the clergy, as most of those who were Old English disobeyed him. His supporters at Kilkenny being defeated, the nuncio withdrew to Galway and finally left the country, concurrent with the endorsement of a second Ormond peace.

In this instrument Ormond agreed to concessions involving his own replacement as viceroy by the Catholic Clanrickard. Thus, within three weeks of Charles I's execution the anti-parliamentary forces in Ireland had been concentrated under the royalist flag. Nevertheless, such a situation was essentially a temporary one, prompted by the military crisis. For a moment it looked as if the forces of Owen Roe O'Neill might ally against the royalists in agreement with a parliamentarian general, like George Monck. In the event such a division between the Catholics did not take place, but the dissolution of the Kilkenny confederation, on the eve of the Cromwellian re-conquest of Ireland, revealed how politically diverse were the elements claiming to represent the community as a whole. Division among the generals nominally attached to Kilkenny created a stalemate which made it impossible to concert any successful attempt against Dublin, where Ormond decided to make way for the parliamentarian, Michael Jones, in 1647.

The defeat of Charles I and his execution in 1649 led all the opponents of the English parliament in Ireland and Scotland to combine in support of his son Charles. Almost inevitably this committed the latter to incompatible Calvinist conditions in Scotland and Catholic conditions in Ireland. It was then that the parliamentarian general, Oliver Cromwell, afterwards Protector of the Commonwealth of England, Scotland and Ireland, entered Ireland to defeat the royalist armies. Cromwell commenced his victorious military career in Ireland by replying to the decrees of a Catholic synod at Jamestown, which had urged the people to crusade for their religion, with an appeal to 'the poor deluded people of Ireland' against the self-interested Catholic hierarchy. Cromwell's victories and his ruthlessness with opponents, massacring garrisons, including clergy, in the Anglo-Irish towns of Drogheda and Wexford, shortened the war but perpetuated the recollection of the victorious general in Ireland as the most odious of Englishmen.

Cromwell's campaign was followed by a decree of the Commonwealth classifying the people of Ireland according to their degree of disloyalty to the English state. In the first category, a number of specified persons, including Ormond, Inchiquin and Clanrickard, were pronounced guilty of treason and declared to have forfeited their lives and property. Secondly, all Catholics were to lose their lands, but those who could prove constant good affection to the parliament of England would be permitted to enjoy lands in Connacht valued at two-thirds of what they previously held. Thus in three provinces, the royalists and rebels were expropriated, and the Commonwealth of England imposed a decree transferring to Connacht the few innocent Catholics among the landowners, but retaining some of the labouring class in the remaining provinces. In these areas there was superimposed a new landed class, made up of soldiers and adventurers to whom money was due after the war and who were thus recompensed in land. All Catholic clergy were deemed to be enemies of the Protestant state, but by a special indulgence if they could prove their innocence of complicity in the killing of Protestants, might transport themselves abroad. The significance of the Cromwellian landed settlement was that even after the restoration of the monarchy in 1660 it was virtually maintained, except for a few privileged royalists who were restored for a brief period until final resettlement was made after the revolution of 1689.

The Cromwellian settlement followed the civil and the Down surveys of Ireland, by means of which the government of the Commonwealth had systematically mapped out and analysed the landed situation in the country, thereby providing the earliest mapped survey in western Europe. The surveys noted who were the proprietors at the beginning of the war in 1641 and divided the whole community simply into English Protestants and Irish papists. In a few instances Scottish Protestants were also noted as British. For most purposes those designated as papists were deprived of political rights. These were restricted to Protestants, among whose rival sects Cromwell imposed a toleration which he denied to Catholics.

The Commonwealth of England was virtually a military dictatorship. There were occasional meetings of parliament to which representatives of Scotland and Ireland were summoned, but this procedure did not in any way modify Cromwell's absolute rule. Formally, the British in the three countries of England, Scotland and Ireland became simply one community. However, it soon emerged that trading interests demanded discrimination against Ireland, a trend which was accentuated when the restoration of the monarchy took place in 1660. It was in this situation that the Old Irish and Old English traditions tended to be fused.

About 1670 Sir William Petty, who had been mainly responsible for the surveys of the Cromwellian plantation, made a computation of the number of inhabitants in Ireland in 1659. His estimate put the total population at 1,100,000 at that date. In terms of religious denominations he allocated 100,000 to the English Protestant Episcopalians, 100,000 to the English nonconformists, 100,000 to the Scots Presbyterians and 800,000 to the Catholics. Petty's figures would suggest that the Protestant community of Ireland, formally recognised as such by the Cromwellian régime, amounted at the most to three-elevenths of the population. Of the 800,000 Catholics probably not more than 100,000 were Old English.

The more rigorous enforcement of laws against Catholics by the parliamentarians, who extended to Ireland the more extreme anti-Catholic measures which had been enacted since 1559 for England only, might have reduced the Catholic clergy to a very small number. To say Mass became a treasonable offence and the organisation of the Church was seriously obstructed. Though a number of Catholics, including even some priests, had conformed, very few higher clergy, and hardly any members of religious orders, dared remain within the country. In practice, however, once the war was at an end, few of the clergy suffered death, but many endured long terms of imprisonment, or were transported to the West Indies or exiled to the mainland of Europe.

As far as the Catholic laity were concerned, the Eliza-

9

bethan penalties against those who had failed to attend Protestant services on Sundays were no longer enforced. Within five years the régime was aware that Catholicism still persisted, and by 1658 reports indicated an increase in the number of cases where Catholics met for devotional purposes. In 1658, the year of Cromwell's death, there is evidence that Catholics were becoming more active, and that they remained as determined as ever to resist persecution. It cannot therefore be assumed that the Puritan Commonwealth community would have successfully integrated the proscribed Catholic majority, had the Cromwellian régime been maintained.

The government of the Commonwealth in Ireland concerned itself primarily with working out the great transfer of land and securing its position by keeping an effective army in the country, under Cromwell's son, Henry. In this period the Presbyterians of the north continued to cause concern, particularly while war persisted in Scotland. The fact that they had become associated with the heir to the executed Charles 1, who claimed to be Charles 11 and had agreed to subscribe to the Solemn League and Covenant, made the Cromwellians more concerned with the Presbyterians than with the defeated and disowned Catholics, the remnant of whose forces were agreeable to transportation abroad. For a moment the possibility that the Scots in Ulster might be sent to Connacht was seriously considered. Presbyterian protests at the execution of Charles 1 as an unjustifiable infringement of the scriptural direction to 'touch not the lord's anointed' had provoked the hostility of the English parliament. But the danger from Scotland, and with it the proposed transplantation of the Ulster Presbyterian colonists to Connacht, was terminated when Cromwell reduced the Scots to impotence at the battles of Dunbar (1650) and Worcester (1651).

Perhaps one other element might be noted in Cromwellian Ireland, the emergence of the first Quaker community. This group originated among some of the soldiers of the Commonwealth, among whom William Edmundson was the best known, though not as prominent as his contemporary, George Fox, in England. The Quakers, like the Fifth Monarchy men in England, deprecated the way in which Cromwell's government abandoned the independent principles which had looked to the rule of the saints upon earth. Yet, since they were only an infinitesimal proportion of the population, the Quakers were prepared to abandon their earlier attacks on ungodliness of church functions and simply to devote themselves to seeking government protection against tithe proctors and test oaths.

The Cromwellian régime destroyed the theocratic claims of the militant Calvinists who had deposed Mary Queen of Scots and who would have put the kirk before parliament as well as before the monarch. After the Scots deviated to the king after 1646, it was easier for the English parliament to drop its commitment to Presbyterianism. After the battles of Dunbar and Worcester, tolerance, which was already denied to Catholics and Episcopalians, was only accorded to those Presbyterians who were prepared to accept that the state should determine the public position of religion. In fact Cromwell went further. He persuaded the Commonwealth to abandon the co-existing Church and state. He gave public support to individual Protestant congregations, but not to the concept of a national Church. He denied recognition to the Anabaptists who, like some Presbyterians, might still interfere in politics, but he tolerated Quakers and Jews who, in his experience, had no ambitions to dictate to the state. And even after the restoration of the monarchy in 1660 little was heard of theocratic position. Henceforth Catholic diplomats were to be prepared in practice to accord Charles II a substantial degree of influence in papal appointments. Presbyterians and Quakers became compliant in a way they had not been a decade earlier, although the Restoration led to a new situation in which the monarchy's interests came first.

The restoration of the monarchy in 1660 seems to have been partly the outcome of a combination between Presbyterians and former Anglican Episcopalians, in order to prevent the army re-establishing its rule after the failure of the protectorate of Richard Cromwell after his father's death. In Ireland, however, Presbyterians were clearly disillusioned when Charles II permitted the restoration of Anglicanism and the burning of the Solemn League and Covenant. The same dissatisfaction existed among Presbyterians in Scotland, who, however, after the revolution of 1688 successfully supplanted the Episcopalian establishment there. Presbyterians in Ireland shared largely the same attitude. Ordinary Presbyterians were particularly irked by the fact that the landed element among them conformed to the Episcopalian establishment, and at the same time maintained contact with their old co-religionists, advising them towards moderation in times of crisis. In this, however, they were not influential with all. In 1663 a small minority of Presbyterians and Independents became involved in an unsuccessful conspiracy against the Dublin Castle administration; they were convinced that the defeated papists were about to be restored to their confiscated lands by the new régime of Charles II.

The Catholics in Ireland included some who expected the Restoration to lead to the re-establishment of their Church. Those of the exiles on the continent who understood the political scene can hardly have believed that this would come about. But the fact that so many of those who had been involved in the Kilkenny confederation had fought for the king certainly roused the hopes of the more military minds among the exiles for the recovery of their lands in Ireland. Charles II, however, was reluctant even to permit them to return home; such concessions as he made to Catholicism were due to his private toleration.

The restored Episcopalian Church, both in England and in Ireland, made full use of the monarchy to establish special religious commemorations of outstanding events in the struggle of the preceding decades. The anniversary of the execution of King Charles the Martyr was decreed to be observed by a fast, and the anniversary of the Restoration of Charles II by a feast. The date of the discovery of the Irish rebellion in October 1641 was honoured annually with sermons reminding the faithful of the horrid massacres perpetrated by the papists, which were seen as fully justifying their exclusion from power. In addition, the régime of the Commonwealth was treated as illegal and Cromwell in particular held up for public reprobation as a usurper; the enactments of his Commonwealth were treated as legal, except that certain measures concerning land were amended to suit the more privileged royalists. But in general, Charles II was obliged to acquiesce in the Cromwellian land settlement. It is in this context that we must see the continued employment of the story of the massacre of Protestants, which was carried over from the propaganda of the Commonwealth, justifying the maintenance of the decrees against royalists and Catholics and, therefore, still to be maintained against Catholics.

The Restoration saw a meeting of parliament in Ireland in 1661 from which all Catholics and nonconformists were in practice excluded, though no specific law was imposed to ensure this. For the government, the main problem was the resettlement of land, and, ultimately, the control of the Cromwellian majority in the Irish parliament. It was decided that an Irish Act of Settlement must first be drafted in England.

The necessary negotiations which this measure involved became linked with an attempt by Peter Walsh, a scholarly Franciscan friar of Old English origin, who had previously supported Ormond against Rinuccini, to work out a formula of allegiance which would enable Catholics to testify their devotion to the monarchy. After the Restoration such formulae interested some supporters of the government as a method of dealing with political rivals. It was easy for them to dispose of the feared Cromwellians, since they could decree the trial of regicides who had personally signed the death warrant of Charles I and use an opportunity, such as Venner's Plot to proclaim Jesus Christ as king, for breaking up the religious meetings of the Fifth Monarchy Men, Quakers,

Baptists and other groups. The Presbyterians were a more serious problem because they had originally been associated with the Restoration, but ultimately an oath was devised to compel benefice holders either to conform or face exclusion. This oath obliged Presbyterians to declare that they did not believe in the right to take arms against the king, even in the king's name, which of itself was most objectionable to Calvinists.

Peter Walsh, in his proposals for Catholics, known as the Remonstrance or Loyal Formulary, would have conceded a similar recognition to the king's position; to him, only royal grace and dispensation made any deviation from the establishment permissible. To the Irish, however, the mere fact that Walsh had adapted a formula devised by an English priest in the 1640s did nothing to advance the popularity of his proposals. Walsh unintentionally provoked trouble from two quarters. Gaelic tradition had never recognised absolute monarchy, and the papacy considered that the idea was a contradiction of the principles asserted by Gregory VII and Innocent III in the eleventh and twelfth centuries, which gave the pope the right, in the case of an unworthy king's sin or heresy, to release his subjects from obedience to him. On these two divergencies the Remonstrance perished, and the surviving clerical supporters of Rinuccini, whom Ormond had never forgiven, became linked with the anti-Remonstrance majority among Catholics. But the Remonstrance did at first create a great deal of hope among lay claimants to expropriated estates, though they quickly lost interest when it emerged that Walsh was primarily concerned with a mere theoretical statement of loyalty. Further difficulties arose because the papal representative at Brussels, who also dealt with affairs in the Stuart kingdoms, condemned successive formulae that appeared to encroach on the pope's authority or might bring his dignity into contempt.

It was also possible that opponents of the Catholics might represent their refusal of the Remonstrance as a demonstration of their essential disloyalty. But after the recall of Ormond from the viceroyalty in 1669, Catholics were permitted to express their loyalty in a less controversial way by his successors. Under Charles II Catholics were rarely persecuted for practising their religion, although some of those higher clergy who had sided with Rinuccini against the second Ormond peace were not permitted to return from exile. In general, Catholics considered conditions under Charles II to be sufficiently satisfactory to lead the Catholic negotiators in the preliminary conversations to the Treaty of Limerick in 1691 to accept the immunities of his reign as adequate basis for their future protection.

As far as political power and landed property were concerned, however, the Catholics failed to recover their position. On any occasion under Charles II when they attempted to reverse the situation, they found the Protestants of Ireland, much as they were divided among themselves, united against the common danger from the overwhelming Catholic mass of the people. Whereas the Restoration Act of Settlement had extended the definition of Catholic 'innocents' to include various royalists, the Act of Explanation, hurriedly brought in after the 1663 plot of old Cromwellians, put a further legislative bar to the hopes of Catholics recovering their estates. Catholics had few political privileges, in an age when these were accorded chiefly to major landowners. They did not extend to membership of the Irish House of Commons, whose only Catholic member returned at the 1661 elections was declared improperly elected. Charles II, as the restored monarch, was very much in the hands of his Protestant supporters, in Ireland as well as in England. He realised they could well decide to send him away once more 'on his travels' as indeed they were to do to his less perceptive brother, James II, in 1688.

Although Charles II appointed the Earl of Clarendon, a constitutional royalist, as his chief adviser in England, it had not at first been clear that Ormond, the outstanding royalist in Ireland during the 1640s, would be restored as viceroy there. As in Scotland, certain preliminaries were necessary before power was given back to royalist adherents. Nominal power was entrusted to such men as William Bury, Lord Broghill and the Earl of Mountrath. Orrery, as Broghill became, was probably more able than Ormond. He had helped to link the Munster Protestants to Cromwell, but, more importantly, had emerged as a key man when it became clear that the power of the Cromwellians was at an end. He was not trusted, but he could not be disgraced either. Ultimately he was provided with the presidency of Munster, a position of honour without power, though until his death, some ten years later, he remained the real leader of the Irish Protestants, who were dissatisfied with any readjustment of the land settlement which might lead to the restoration of a substantial number of Catholics.

For six years after 1662, and again for a period towards the end of Charles ii's reign, Ormond ruled Ireland for the king. Ultimately he secured general approval, but failed to react resiliently to the crisis of the Dutch war. His intransigence in negotiations, perhaps his strongest weapon in time of peace as likely to preserve an impression of stability, could be a liability in a crisis, as past events had shown. He protected the Remonstrants after their formula had been condemned in papal circles, fearing they might be persecuted by their Catholic opponents. As a result, he earned among some Catholics the name of being a persecutor of their religion. Nor was the viceregal position made any easier by the fact that local influence in Ireland had completely changed. Ex-Cromwellian magistrates scattered throughout the country enforced penal laws, except when directed not to do so by the viceroy. Ormond, therefore, was put in the awkward situation of having to order the non-execution of the law. The fact that Charles ii, like his father and grandfather, was basically tolerant did not ease the situation for the viceroy who was less clement than the king.

Moreover, the whole question of loyalty was complicated both by the land settlement, which had provoked the

Presbyterian conspiracy of 1663, and by a move in the English parliament to put an embargo on Irish cattle exports. During the seventeenth century economic rivalry arose between Ireland and England, and already under Strafford there had been some anxiety about the way Irish and English interests were diverging. In the second half of the century, English jealousy of Irish cattle exports led to discriminatory legislation against Irish trade being passed on several occasions, despite the integration proclaimed for the whole British Isles. In these two great matters of land and cattle the royalist Ormond was dealing with a landed interest which was still basically Cromwellian. In addition, in England he was exposed to parliamentary intrigues of those who were using the unpopularity of Irish cattle against him, in an effort to terminate his power, as that of his friend Clarendon had been terminated for being too old-fashioned in politics to deal with a situation of international war.

Thus Ormond interpreted royal directions to observe leniency very narrowly. After his replacement in 1669 Catholics enjoyed a greater degree of immunity. For a brief time, while the king was negotiating the Treaty of Dover with his cousin, Louis xiv of France, the leading archbishops Oliver Plunkett of Armagh and Peter Talbot of Dublin, actually enjoyed a gift of £100 each from the king, though both were to suffer persecution at a later date.

Charles ii's secret negotiations with Louis xiv in the 1670s provided him with adequate, if temporary, financial resources to maintain his rule without recourse to parliament, either in England or in Ireland. The Treaty of Dover, however, boomeranged on the royalists closest to the king when it began to emerge that Charles had taken money from France and promised to advance Catholic interests, even to the extent of announcing his own conversion. A new Declaration of Indulgence for Protestant nonconformists and for Catholics alike resulted in an outcry among Anglicans in England and was withdrawn. Plans to permit Catholics to hold office had to be abandoned. Even Prince

James, the heir to the throne and a convert to Catholicism, was obliged to retire from public life. The Titus Oates plot of 1678 created a further crisis, and a number of outstanding Catholics were executed on perjured testimony, having been charged with conspiracy to bring in a French army, Even the Archbishop of Armagh, Oliver Plunkett, was hanged in 1681. His fellow archbishop, Peter Talbot of Dublin, had already died in prison. Plunkett had hitherto been almost an excessively loyal subject and had induced many Catholic ex-soldiers to go into exile.

But on a long-term basis, the king was able to use the Oates conspiracy to defeat his most dangerous critics. He allowed Protestant mass hysteria to go to such extremes that a reaction set in, bringing about the discrediting of parliamentary critics and, consequently, the unqualified royal absolutism of his later years. On the eve of his death in 1685, Charles 11 was more powerful than he had been at any time previously. although during the Oates crisis such was the fear of popery that neither king nor viceroy could save innocent men from legal murder.

In Ireland in the 1680s, although Ormond had been once again restored, Catholics were given more latitude, still, of course, within limits, while the nonconformists, of whom Ormond continued to have great fears, were given less. Considerable uncertainty was aroused among the nonconformists of Ireland when Charles 11 permitted Richard Talbot, brother of the archbishop who had died in jail during the Oates conspiracy, to initiate enquiries into the Act of Settlement, and to revive legal hearings which had been stopped after the passing of the Act of Explanation in 1665. Talbot's power grew because he was a favourite of the Duke of York, the king's brother, who in 1685 succeeded as James 11.

The accession of James 11, then in his middle fifties, resulted in a quick change in Ireland, where the Cromwellian ascendancy was replaced by the descendants of those expropriated since 1641. Talbot was the architect of this new and brief Catholic ascendancy, so warmly applauded by the Gaelic poets. The army was thrown open to Catholics and offices were made available to them by suspending the penal laws and dispensing with the statutory Oath of Supremacy.

It was, perhaps, against his better judgement that James permitted Talbot, whom he had created Earl of Tyrconnell, to exercise wide powers. He was made commander of the Irish army and then replaced Protestant viceroys as head of the government in Ireland. Tyrconnell acted so quickly that he caused panic among Protestants and a hysterical migration to England. So dominating and recurrent was the atmosphere of conspiracy in the seventeenth century that the records of the Oates conspiracy indicate how on that occasion English Protestants lived in fear of their throats being cut by an Irish papist army. In these circumstances the withdrawal from Protestants in Ireland of the right to bear arms in self-protection, besides the reopening of the land question, led a number of nervous people to abandon their estates, lest they be massacred in their beds. Later those who fled were to exploit their withdrawal by implying that those Protestants who had remained in the country were traitors.

Under James II, the established Episcopalian Church, accustomed to preach the doctrine that the king could do no wrong, found itself seriously embarrassed when its head the Catholic monarch used his position to keep benefices vacant in order to endow the Catholic hierarchy. Some prominent Anglican prelates chose to ignore their oaths to the head of their Church and became involved in negotiations with James's son-in-law, the Dutch ruler, William of Orange. William King, then Chancellor of St Patrick's, Dublin, and a future Bishop of Derry and Archbishop of Dublin, even acted as an intelligence agent for the Dutch stadtholder.

The crisis in England became so serious that James was forced to withdraw to France when he saw that he was about to be abandoned by his non-Catholic subjects, who feared that the king was determined to deprive them of their offices and destroy the Protestant structure of the state. The unexpected birth of a son to his second wife, who was a Catholic, in July 1688, deprived his Protestant daughters, Mary and Anne, of their rights of succession and seemed to ensure a line of Catholic rulers in England. The birth of James's son, coupled with the mistaken idea that the king would automatically align himself with Louis xiv, precipitated a conspiracy which brought his Protestant son-in-law to England in November 1688 to defeat the Catholic alliance.

From France, James was invited to Ireland by Tyrconnell. However ill-advised Tyrconnell's action turned out on a long term basis, in that it provided justification subsequently for fresh penal laws against Irish Catholics, it ensured in the immediate crisis that the greater part of the country would flock to the standard of James ii.

James held a parliament in Dublin, whose proceedings were later declared null and void. In the nineteenth century the nationalist writer Thomas Davis described it as 'the patriot parliament', since for the first time it had established the principle of toleration, thereby anticipating the egalitarian ideas of a century later. But perhaps the most noteworthy action of the 1689 parliament was to reassert its independence of the parliament of England and attempt to build up once again, as the confederation at Kilkenny had done, a unified community based upon the law of the land, with, however, a recognition of Protestantism which the Catholic bishops at Kilkenny would not have permitted. But although this was the first occasion when an Irish parliament was held in Dublin with the king himself as a participant, no interference was permitted with his right under Poynings' Law to approve draft legislation in advance. James, however, did condone the virtual expropriation of the Protestants who had fled from Ireland, and who by this time must have included the greater number of Protestant landowners. Charles II's Act of Settlement was repealed and provision was made for the restoration of the desendants of former owners. An Act of Attainder was passed, expropriating those who had left for England and who failed to appear in public by a specified day. These attainders amounted virtually to indictments for treason, and they included some migrants who were not, in fact, landowners, and who may, perhaps, have been listed at the instance of their personal enemies.

The proceedings of the Irish parliament of 1689 converted the war between William and James into a war between Catholics and Protestants. The threatened Protestant landowners were reinforced by the Presbyterians, who feared James's reputation for being even more hostile to Presbyterianism than he was to Anglicanism. William was, however, rather unexpectedly supported by a Catholic Donegal group including Neachtan Ballderg O'Donnell, whom Tyrconnell had alienated, and who perhaps rather credulously believed that William might secure some form of Catholic restoration, in spite of a century of confiscation. But the sober citizens of fortified towns in the north were glad to leave dicisive action to the Williamite partisans among the townsfolk. In Derry it was the teenage apprentices who shut the gates against the Catholic king's army. For a hundred days the city resolutely held out against the besiegers, until it was relieved by sea from England.

On the arrival of William and his army in Ireland most of the Protestant population rushed to his support. William had just been proclaimed by the English parliament joint sovereign with his wife, James's daughter, Mary. James, who had been given some military support by Louis XIV of France, as part of the latter's expansion policy against the Hapsburg powers and William of Orange, now William III of England, was unable to hold the line of the river Boyne. He retreated hastily to Dublin and thence sailed for France. William's victory at the Boyne subsequently justified intense Irish Protestant celebration. But it was also a cause for celebration to Catholic opponents of Louis xiv, including the Emperor Leopold and Pope Innocent xi, who had refused aid to James as an ally of the aggressive and insulting Gallican king. James's lack of courage in Ireland was not forgotten by the Gaelic poets, despite their increasing attachment to the royal Stuarts. Even without him, a Franco-Irish army stubbornly but unsuccessfully fought a series of pitched battles. After a campaign lasting over two years, they were ultimately advised to surrender. Unlike Cromwell, however, William iii was prepared to make some concessions to Catholics to end the war in Ireland, since this would enable him to concentrate on his main objective, the frustration of the French attempt to dominate Europe.

In the articles agreed upon at Galway and Limerick in 1691, Jacobites who were prepared to accept William's rule were guaranteed their lands against further confiscation. The civil articles would have ensured for Catholics the immunity from persecution which they supposedly enjoyed under Charles ii, a questionable guarantee, considering that it was at that period that Oliver Plunkett had been sent to his death.

It was subsequently alleged that the Treaty of Limerick was deliberately broken. In fact this treaty was complied with in many particulars, and those in which it was breached were limited. Its primary purpose was to safeguard the garrison which had defended Limerick on behalf of James ii. It was understood that many of them would follow the Stuart king into exile and provision was made for this to be carried out peacefully. For those who were prepared to live under William iii the treaty provided safeguards, and entitled them to be regarded as of the gentry class, a position which to some extent was carefully observed.

Further provision was made that, when possible, William iii and his co-sovereign, Mary ii, would try to procure an amelioration of the status of Catholics in parliament. This, however, was never attempted. The English parliament had already excluded Catholics from parliament in Ireland, and had also declared void the proceedings of the Dublin parliament of James ii. The Irish parliament refused to ratify the treaty's clauses of tolerance for Catholics. Like Charles ii, the joint sovereigns were slow to test the limits of their constitutional powers. The government of the oligarchy which ruled England after the revolution of 1688 was not prepared to share power with the Irish Protestant ascendancy but could not very well compel it to improve the position of Catholics in Ireland when they still aspired to succeed to the lands they had attempted to recover under James ii.

Ratification or non-ratification of the royal provisions for Catholics became a public controversy in Ireland. For urging 'no peace with treacherous papists' the Anglican Bishop Dopping of Meath was removed by William from the Privy Council. Bishop William Sheridan refused to take the oath to William as being contrary to his oath to James ii as ruler of the established Church. However, only a tiny minority of Irish Anglicans became non-jurors like Sheridan. But the vagaries of politics later led to the displacement as chancellor of one of William's early supporters, Sir Richard Cox, for being too lenient to the papists.

For the Catholic clergy after 1691, allegiance to William iii often could not be reconciled with their loyalty to the Restoration monarchy. The pope had given James ii the right to nominate higher prelates. As James still claimed to be king, and set up his court at St Germain in France, he continued to exercise his claims and the papacy still recognised them. Probably many of the Irish Catholic clergy, in the event of a second Stuart restoration, hoped to revert to the position visualised by Rinuccini. They sympathised with, if in fact they did not teach, the Anglican doctrine of the hereditary divine right of kings, and applied it to James ii. The vast majority of the priests refused to take the oath of abjuration, forswearing the succession rights of the exiled Stuarts, although the clergy were tolerated by statute. Their continuing allegiance to James provided Protestant justification for the later penal laws against them. Laws against the laity were prompted by fear that they would become strong enough to secure restoration to their forfeited estates.

But it was at this point that a gifted writer, William Molyneux, presented in his pamphlet, *The Case of Ireland*, the first attempt to convince by full legal argument some of the English in Ireland that they belonged to the community of Ireland and were, in fact, that community.

Politically, however, the community of Ireland was a minority at the end of the seventeenth century. Presbyterians continued to look to Scotland, and Catholics in exile looked to their patrons. The leaderless Catholics at home seemed less articulate: some of them accepted the exiled Stuarts and few in their hearts adhered to the House of Orange. Hardly anyone alive in 1700 was to survive to 1782 and see the reassertion of the belief in an Irish self-governing community, enunciated by Protestant descendants of seventeenth-century planters.

5

Colonial Ireland, 1691–1800

THE history of the eighteenth-century community of Ireland began in an atmosphere of civil war. After the efficient army of William III (1689–1702) had routed the Jacobites, the exiled Gaelic and Old English political traditions merged with those of the Catholic and Stuart royalists. Rome accepted fully the monarchical claims of James II, including the privilege of nominating bishops, and it did the same in the case of his son, who ruled in exile as James III and had the longest reign of any English monarch. Until his death in 1766 Irish Catholics were taught to pray for James III as their king.

The revolution of 1689 had made the new monarchy constitutional in England. The Bill of Rights made it impossible ever again for the ruler to dispense with regular meetings of the English parliament. In Ireland, however, the monarchy was not obliged to enact the Bill of Rights and continued to control much of the affairs of the Irish parliament through the English council's powers over the initial stages of legislation under Poynings' Law. The English parliament increasingly vied with the king and council to exercise supervisory powers over Ireland, both by direct legislation and by supporting the English House of Lords in its claim to be a superior court of appeal from the decision of the Irish judges. It was against this trend that Molyneux was to write *The Case of Ireland* in 1698, even if his concern was with a limited concept of the community of Ireland. Molyneux's pamphlet, however, was too much for the English House of Commons, which ordered it to be burnt by the hangman.

10

From the beginning of the eighteenth century the political community in Ireland was confined by law to the Protestant Episcopalians, who saw to it that neither Presbyterians nor Catholics were permitted to share power or have equality before the law. In this way, when the struggle arose for denominational equality it became involved with the question of reforming the constitution. So this continued to be linked with the relief of Dissenters, as Presbyterians and subscribers to non-episcopalian Protestant denominations were called, and with the emancipation of Catholics, until after the beginning of the second quarter of the nineteenth century. By that date their exclusion from power had left both Dissenters and Catholics with few parliamentary traditions.

In Scotland, as in England, the powers of parliament were enlarged. Presbyterians in Ireland maintained their Scottish connection. The bargain with William and Mary that replaced Episcopalianism by Presbyterianism in Scotland continued to preoccupy Irish Presbyterians, who were doubly resentful of their inferior position under an episcopal establishment in Ireland.

But the political and landed interest settled by William in Ireland accepted the confirmation of the position of the Protestant Episcopalian Church. Thus the Episcopalian Church of Ireland, as after the Restoration, became again the church of the upper level of society. Even some landed Catholics conformed to it in an effort to save their social positions. However, this Anglican Church in Ireland, while theoretically linked to that of England and uniform with it, was more influenced by Calvinism, because of the infusion in it of conformist Puritans and Presbyterians of the landed class.

Their dependence upon England, vividly emphasised during the struggle against James II and against Catholic claimants to their lands, accentuated the desire of the Irish Protestant upper class for uniformity with England. At the same time, however, that class began to resent the government's refusal to accord the colony the liberties of British subjects or to grant its parliament equal legislative powers with those of the English parliament. The Irish parliament was subjected to restrictions similar to those imposed on colonial legislatures in the New World; and, indeed, Irish politicians complained that their ancient kingdom was treated as casually as a new English colony in America. The aggressiveness to which this discontent gave rise in the Irish parliament made English statesmen apprehensive. Successive viceroys after 1691 sensed that among Irish Protestants there were some reservations about the monarchy's exercise of its powers. Out of the English refusal to grant either equality or union there slowly developed the concept of the Protestant nation, popularly associated today with Henry Grattan and his patriotic movement two generations later.

Early in the reign of William and Mary, Irish rivalry with England over cattle exports extended to the export trade in wool manufacture. Ultimately, the Irish parliament was obliged to discourage the export of manufactured goods, and its members had to accept the power of the English parliament to legislate for Ireland. In return they were permitted to pass penal, discriminatory legislation against Catholics and, to a lesser degree, against Protestant nonconformists. Beginning with the war between William III and Louis XIV, and making use of every political excuse and convenient opportunity until the end of the reign of George I (1714–27), the first ruler of the House of Hanover, the Irish parliament passed a series of acts which brought Ireland closely into line with anti-Catholic legislation in England and which were similar to restrictions on the Huguenots in France at that period. Concurrently, the clergy of the Established Church, apprehensive of any attempt to emulate the recognition of Presbyterianism in Scotland, took every opportunity to weaken nonconformity in Ireland, politically and socially.

Acts against the Catholic clergy decreed the banishment of prelates and of all monks and friars. The parochial clergy were supposed to be restricted, one to each parish. These were to be registered and their good behaviour guaranteed by reputable persons. They were to swear allegiance to the Protestant sovereign, but when, under Queen Anne (1702–14), the oath of abjuration was imposed in 1709 against the claims of the Stuart Pretender, James III, the system broke down, as not forty out of a thousand priests complied. The extreme penalties could no longer be applied, as the English monarchs were constantly under pressure from their Catholic allies, such as the Holy Roman Emperors. The parochial priests on the whole were ignored. Banished clergy might be imprisoned if they were discovered in the country, but executions except over some additional involvement in a criminal offence were abandoned.

To exclude the laity from political power, a declaration against transubstantiation was imposed on all public office-holders, and proved to be an effective bar. Similar restrictions were introduced by municipal corporations and by professional, craft and trade guilds. An obligation to receive Communion annually in the Anglican parish church was directed as much against nonconformists as against Catholics. There was discrimination in the law of succession to Catholic estates, since these had to be divided equally among all male children of the deceased Catholic landowner. Social discrimination, justified by alleged fears of a Stuart invasion, deprived Catholics of the right of carrying swords, a privilege customarily conceded to all gentlemen. In local areas, levies could be imposed on Catholics to pay for damages inflicted by invading Catholic forces in time of war. In contrast with the non-enforcement of extreme penalties against the clergy, the discriminating measures against the laity could and did operate. By the end of the eighteenth century, Catholic land holdings, which had dropped to fifteen per cent of the total by 1704, had fallen to about eight per cent. While few conversions took place among landless people, some 4,000 upper-class Catholics conformed to the Established Church during the eighteenth century. The bulk of these would appear to

have made the transition in the later part of the century,
after the more severe laws against Catholics had been
repealed. Social pressures thus proved more effective than
legal threats.

Throughout this period the Catholic Church was severely
handicapped in its organisation. By the mid-century, however, imprisonment of priests was a thing of the past. The
mass-rock and the vigilant sentries on the lookout for the
priest hunters had long ceased to be realities. The mass-house
in a humble back street or the modest cabin similar to any
small farmhouse in the countryside, became the normal
centre of the Catholic parish and its religious practice until
emancipation.

The question of allegiance did not present the same
difficulties for the laity as it did for the clergy. Representative
lay addresses were submitted privately as expressions of
loyalty to the king, and were accepted, at the beginning and
at the end of the reign of George II (1727–60). After the
accession of George III (1760–1820) the Dublin Catholic
clergy offered prayers for the Hanoverian royal family,
without previous resort to Rome, as far as we know.

The Irish abroad also played a significant part in their
country's history during the eighteenth century. Most exiles
are notoriously attached to their country of origin, and the
Irish exiles were particularly rich in a sense of history and in
vivid recollections of former glories. With these characteristics must be included their deep dense of gratitude, which
made them loyal and reliable elements in the lands which
gave them refuge—even if it happened to be England. As
soldiers and as missionaries they served half the countries of
Europe in this period. In the seventeenth century the Irish
and British colleges at Rome, and in the dominions of the
Catholic sovereigns of Europe, had directed the Counter-
Reformation towards Ireland, and so played a decisive part
in building up the post-Tridentine Church at home. We
know little, however, about the exiles who became significant
in international commerce, trading and smuggling between

the ports of Spain, France, the Low Countries and Irish ports south of Dublin and Sligo. But it is being increasingly realised that trade, even through Britain, was of decisive importance in maintaining Irish contact with Europe.

Coercion in Ireland failed in the spheres of politics and nationalist feeling; and the Gaelic Irish survived, at least in part, because of the exiles of the eighteenth century. The Old English constitutional clergy of the seventeenth century had often deplored the indiscretions of irresponsible clergy, many of them friars, who used to tell their flocks in Ulster or else-where in unassimilated Gaelic Ireland that 'Spanish ale' or 'wine from the royal pope' was 'on the ocean green.' True these intractable friars, redolent of and dependent on the lowest levels of the people, were displaying political inepti-tude, and to the more subtle minds concerned with the position in the Pale they were a liability and a menace. But outside the Pale Catholicism might well have perished had it not been reinforced in this way from abroad.

Among the Ascendancy the idea of a legislative union between England and Ireland came under discussion, particularly in Molyneux's remarkable pamphlet. Molyneux followed Darcy and the English political thinker Locke in arguing that government was based on a contract between ruler and ruled. For this reason he urged a parliamentary union, or alternatively, legislative independence for the Irish parliament. But Molyneux's view, while of interest to many people, was an embarrassment to others, even to Protestant patriots, who were affected by a sense of dependence on English good-will. They feared that a statement of claims on behalf of the parliament of Ireland would cause an upsurge of anti-Irish feeling among English politicians. Molyneux, however, was an example of how the New English planter class of the seventeenth century were linking themselves to the medieval parliamentary tradition in Ireland, which had been upheld before the 1640s by Catholic lords of the English Pale.

Molyneux's thesis for fusing the communities of England

and Ireland was taken up in the Irish parliament during Queen's Anne's reign. Twice it proposed such resolutions unsuccessfully. Anne's reign, however, did witness the amalgamation of the parliaments of Scotland and England, and thereafter those combined kingdoms were known as the United Kingdom of Great Britain. But the Scots had been able to overcome British reluctance to accord them full rights of citizenship, refused since James 1's time, by threatening to exclude the next English sovereign from the succession in Scotland. The Irish parliament was not in a position to make a comparable bargain, since under Poynings' Law it could not initiate legislation without the prior consent of the English king and council, which at this stage was dominated by the English parliament. Thus the proposal to unite the communities was postponed until the French revolutionary menace forced it through at the end of the century. By then, however, it was too late to effect and maintain a real integration of the communities.

Under George 1 the British parliament asserted itself absolutely and by a Declaratory Act in 1720 affirmed its legislative power over Ireland as well as the authority of the British House of Lords to hear appeals from Irish courts to the exclusion of the House of Irish peers. Government distrust of the indigenous upper class in Ireland led increasingly to the appointment of Englishmen, frequently ill-equipped, to the highest administrative, ecclesiastical and legal positions in the country. Archbishop King of Dublin, a patriot who was interested in building up a native administration, was denied translation to the primacy of Armagh on the excuse of age in 1724; he remained seated when greeting the English nominee, Hugh Boulter, with the sarcastic apology that he must be considered too old to rise. Resentment in Ireland had become so general in this time that Jonathan Swift, Dean of St Patrick's Cathedral in Dublin, disappointed at being denied a bishopric, satirically declared that English nominees were invariably good men, but that they were murdered on their way to Ireland, and that it was their killers who, having stolen their robes, were masquerading in their offices.

Rejected by England, and with the added humiliation that Scotland had been accepted, the Irish Protestant landed class gradually developed during the next two generations a vague sense of being the community of Ireland. This assumption, however, would have been rejected not merely by the exiled Irish Catholic Jacobites and their secret supporters at home, but also by resentful Presbyterians. But this limited, self-centred community of the eighteenth century was of importance, as it helped to strengthen in Ireland a parliamentary tradition, something which was largely foreign to contemporary Irish Presbyterians and Catholics.

The tradition of community consciousness developed in a pragmatic way. The Irish parliament, despite its limited powers, gradually became identified with an extra-parliamentary popular group which helped to reinforce its position. The popular element, both inside and outside parliament, changed from time to time, even in its religious allegiance. What these popular groups shared was a common obsession with local interests, particularly in Dublin. This extra-parliamentary influence, unknown to the Constitution, proved decisive in several crises of the eighteenth century and anticipated similar manifestations in England, both in town and country.

The affair of Wood's Ha'pence and the intervention of Dublin opinion in the crisis in 1724, under the influence of Jonathan Swift, is a case in point. Swift became known in the political sphere at this juncture as the author of *The Drapier's Letters*, which, like Molyneux's pamphlet, were burnt by the common hangman, since they alleged scandalous jobbery and the use of inferior metal in Wood's Ha'pence, a copper coinage manufactured for Ireland under an English patent. Swift insisted that Wood's coins were worthless and would drive good coin out of Ireland, impoverish the Irish community and bankrupt its tradesmen. In the fourth *Drapier's Letter* he appealed to the whole people of Ireland to regard the issue as being whether England should be permitted to rule the country in this illegal and destructive manner. The result was that public opinion compelled the government to withdraw the coins; insignificant as the squabble might appear, and unreliable as were the allegations against the coins and the inferences as to their effect, it provided a convenient pretext for exposing the arbitrary nature of government and for expressing resentment against interference from England. The worst of the affair, commented the Primate Archbishop Boulter of Armagh, was that papist, Protestant, and all conflicting interests in Ireland, had combined against England.

The failure of Lord Carteret, the viceroy, to stem the popular tide against Wood's Ha'pence led to the adoption of a system of government by undertakers. The system was maintained for over a generation, until after the accession of George iii. During these forty years key officials guaranteed the government a compliant parliamentary majority, provided they were allowed dispense royal patronage and were themselves appointed lords justices in the absence of the lord lieutenant, who normally visited the country only for the six months in every two years when the eighteenth-century parliament was in session; in this way Ireland was administered usually by the Primate, the Lord Chancellor and the Speaker of the House of Commons. In the long reign of George ii (1727–60) these key men included Primates Boulter and Stone and Speakers Connolly and Boyle. Membership of the Irish House of Commons consisted of two representatives from each of the thirty-two counties and one or more members for a number of parliamentary boroughs, the whole amounting to some three hundred MPs. In the parliamentary boroughs the number of electors was often severely restricted, and in some instances even confined to the borough corporations. By gaining ascendancy in one or more boroughs, local landowners, frequently members of the House of Lords, could virtually ensure the return to parliament of their own nominees.

Borough owners sold their interest to persons aspiring to be
MPs. just as officers bought commissions in the army. The
system was similar to that which existed in contemporary
England under Ministers like Walpole and Newcastle, and
it was accepted that borough members would not vote
against their patron's wishes. Until a change of policy took
place under George III the system was maintained in Ireland,
though it could rarely resist extra-parliamentary pressure
in crises comparable to that over Wood's Ha'pence.

Arid as politics was under the early Hanoverian kings, it
was not entirely without its dramatic moments. Ocasionally
the undertakers were startled out of their lethargy by
outraged public opinion. When in the early 1750s Dublin
Castle, the seat of administration, proposed to appropriate
a revenue surplus for reducing the national debt, an extra-
parliamentary element became active, partly because of
recent agitation in Dublin municipal politics by a reforming
crank and anti-Catholic bigot, Charles Lucas. The undertakers as a result were faced with a mutiny. Primate Stone
sought to intimidate the ringleaders by dismissing them
from office, but ultimately the government was obliged to
hand out an unusual number of appointments and promot-
ions in order to break the recently formed opposition and
re-establish its own majority.

The answer of the Dublin mobs was to burn in effigy the
so-called patriots, notably Anthony Malone and the Earl of
Kildare. However, parliamentary affairs remained quieter
for more than a decade. Although sensitivity had been
aroused by a flagrant demonstration of the subordinate
role of the Irish House of Commons regarding public finance,
by contrast with the control exercised by the English Commons in the same field, in general only lip service was paid to
the political principles of Molyneux and Swift.

The accession of George III was followed by a more
vigorous display of royal interest in politics, both in England
and in Ireland. The policy was not without some vestiges of
enlightenment. At an early date in his reign it was decided

to replace the undertakers by a viceroy who would remain permanently in Ireland for the duration of his office, control patronage himself and, with the assistance of his chief secretary, manage the House of Commons. Lord Lieutenant Townshend, sent over in 1767 to inagurate the new system, brought with him some concessions to local feelings. It had been a grievance that in Ireland the duration of parliament was limited only by the length of the king's reign, unlike England, where under a Septennial Act general elections took place regularly. It was decided to restrict the duration of parliament in Ireland, much to the mortification of the former undertakers who saw their power limited by this measure, just when they hoped to pose as patriots in opposition to the new policy of the crown. The party names of Tory and Whig were revived in Ireland, the former to denote a supporter of the king's policy, the latter to denote an opponent and, by implication, an Irish patriot.

The leading claimants to the name of 'patriot' were now William Ponsonby and Henry Flood. Unable to oppose the Bill for the restriction of parliament's duration, they were determined to pick a quarrel on the initiation of a Money Bill. Since under Poynings' Law parliamentary measures had to be approved previously in England, the council had got into the habit of using a draft Money Bill as the reason for summoning parliament in Ireland. The patriots, who had not challenged this practice on the accession of George III in 1760, elected to make it an issue in 1769 when they succeeded in defeating the government. They gave as their reason the fact that the measure had not originated in the House of Commons. By his oratory alone Flood had linked constitutionalism and Protestant patriotism. After an adjournment of more than a year, during which Townshend and his chief secretary systematically built up a new majority without the aid of the undertakers, the measure was reintroduced and passed, but at a price. The government had to face it that an extra-parliamentary interest, patriotism, was now represented in the House of Commons, and that to secure a majority was only too easily represented as corruption.

In an endeavour to meet this situation the brusque and unpopular Townshend was removed. His successor, the more diplomatic Earl Harcourt, attempted a smoother managerial system, and pacified parliament, if not the patriots, by seducing Henry Flood into taking office. Thanks to the American War, however, Harcourt's system did not last.

No sooner had Harcourt re-established the aura of somnolent inertia in politics than the outbreak of the War of Independence in America in 1775 reawakened colonial aspirations and impelled the Protestant colony in Ireland in two opposite directions. Harcourt had little difficulty in securing loyal addresses to the king, and parliament dutifully denounced the Americans as ungrateful and disloyal. A representative Catholic address to George III, reprobating the conduct of America, was even more servile. But the Irish parliament was anxious to secure more freedom, and, like the American colony, resented its subordinate position. A ban on the export of provisions which could have benefitted the Americans provoked a vigorous protest from the Cork members and raised the whole issue of free trade.

Since the government had used the occasion of the loyal addresses to transfer the substantial British army in Ireland for service in America, the question of a militia became topical. Danger of a French invasion gave rise to Protestant alarm. Local gentry, led by a rather moderate patriot, Lord Charlemont, organised and equipped local defence forces which were described as 'Volunteers'. They sought from the Lord Lieutenant and from Dublin Castle the weapons to arm themselves. Harcourt's successor, Lord Buckinghamshire, was acutely embarrassed, but ultimately advised Lord North's government in England to recognise the Volunteers in an effort to keep them under control.

The government, however, decided to test the Protestant patriots, and it was perhaps with a certain sardonic pleasure that it confronted parliament with relief measures for Catholics and Dissenters in 1778. These exempted from the penalties of the law any Catholics taking a newly-drafted declaration of loyalty, which involved a repudiation of the doctrine that a foreign potentate could release them from allegiance to their sovereign. In the general atmosphere of liberty the measures secured ratification, and were accepted by the Catholic archbishop of Dublin without formal consultation with Rome. The declaration touched upon the delicate question of the pope's secular authority and the claims, generally ignored, of the Stuarts, as represented by Bonnie Prince Charlie, who had nominally succeeded his father as Charles III in 1766. Catholics in Ireland, however, had become more reconciled to the Hanoverians since George III's accession and the Catholic question was, therefore, one in which the government appeared to have a trump card in dealing with the patriots, whose tolerance was open to question. They had condoned the judicial murder of Nicholas Sheehy, a rash priest involved in agrarian agitation in the 1760s and allegedly an accessory to the murder of a landowner's agent. The Protestant Ascendancy had insisted that the agitation was a front for Austrian intrigue on behalf of the Stuart pretender.

The Catholic Relief Bill, together with a measure giving nonconformists the right to become members of corporations and of parliament, was passed in 1778, the patriots making the best of the situation by praising the concessions faintly. In the following year, however, a government embargo on the export of meat as cheap victualling for the army in America was used by the patriots to demand free trade. The Volunteers at a Convention were committed to the same cause. In 1780, after a great demonstration in Dublin concentrating around the statute of William III, the great Protestant hero of liberty, an appeal for free trade was moved by a new patriot MP, Henry Grattan, and was coupled with a threat that parliament would restrict the administration's financial supplies. The government gave way, since it would have been too dangerous to hold out against public opinion in Ireland while England faced possible invasion from France and Spain.

Having won on free trade, Grattan publicly proclaimed the birth of the Irish nation, after a successful Commons' resolution to demand the removal of restrictions on the legislative powers of the Irish parliament. As this had been privately favoured by the English Whigs who succeeded Lord North in office in 1782, the government agreed. The British parliament repealed the Declaratory Act of George 1 and the Irish House of Lords recovered its appelate jurisdiction. Poynings' Law was substantially amended so as to give the Irish Houses of Parliament the right to initiate legislation directly. The news of these concessions was received by the Irish parliament with tremendous excitement. It had won control of its own legislative programme, subject, however, to the continued right of the government to monopolise the greater part of its time and the greater part of the proposed programme of legislation. Such was the Constitution of 1782.

Concurrently, a further Catholic Relief Act empowered those subscribing to the declaration of loyalty to exercise the full rights of British subjects regarding property. They were, however, still excluded from the franchise, municipal corporations, and from membership of parliament.

Moreover, parliamentary reform, to which the Whigs in England had been favourable while out of office, was now frowned upon. In Ireland the tide of revolution was stemmed. Conservative men of ability were added to the Dublin Castle administration, such as John Fitzgibbon, later Earl of Clare, and John Beresford. But beneath the sunburstry and brilliance of 'Grattan's Parliament' there was still much misery and economic stagnation.

'The Constitution of 1782', as the new position after the legislative changes was grandiloquently described, created a sense of participation for the landed gentry, but did not alter the existing situation as regards the holding of office.

The Dublin Castle administration was still established and appointed by the British government of the day, and while in England a minister not enjoying the confidence of parliament was theoretically unable to remain in office, no similar provision existed in Ireland. In these circumstances, the fact that the great offices in Ireland should be held by men conforming to the views of the British Cabinet was not seen as such a glaring abuse of public opinion, although difficulties could arise in moments of crisis and did, in fact, create the same anxiety for the government as in the days of Molyneux and Swift.

A grave problem developed towards the end of the 1780s, almost coinciding with the outbreak of the French Revolution, when George III became insane. Differences between the two countries as to the powers to be exercised by the new regent, the Prince of Wales, appeared likely to cause the government serious embarrassment. Since the prince had been connected with the Whig opposition, the government in England favoured a strict delimitation of his powers. In Ireland the Whig opposition was prepared to support his being offered the regency without qualification, and thus a disparity between the power of the executives in both countries might have arisen if the king had not recovered and made the issue irrelevant.

During these years the question of parliamentary reform, and in particular the concession of the francise to Catholics, had become an issue in a small way. While the Whigs had generally on such matters become identified with what was regarded as the patriotic position, the Catholic question gave rise to further complications, since ambitious middle-class Catholics in Dublin were anxious to participate in political affairs. The well-known Dublin brewer, John Keogh, for instance, who was rich, ambitious and vulgar, was pathetically anxious for acceptance as a respectable citizen deserving of admission to polite society. But from the time of Charles Lucas the popular patriots had been hostile to popery, and were inclined to regard any concession to Catholics as likely to increase the influence of the crown.

The revival in 1791 of a Catholic committee to secure emancipation, as the right to sit in parliament came to be called, precipitated a difference within the Catholic body largely on a social basis. In the propertied and aristocratic Europe of the years prior to the French Revolution, it was unthinkable that the leaders of society would permit themselves to be led by middle-class tradesmen. In Ireland, the few Catholic peers had in the past regarded it as their privilege to address the government, without reference to the wider body of Catholic opinion. They might in special circumstances consult outstanding Catholic bishops, a full complement of whom operated in the country since the penal laws had dropped into disuse after the abortive Stuart rising on Scotland in 1745. In the late 1770s, however, the securing of Catholic relief meant lobbying influential persons and, since the Catholic peers were penniless, it was the Cork butter merchants who in 1779 contributed £5,000 to win the support of persons supposedly close to the king. When, therefore, the question of further Catholic concessions arose about 1790, the financial aspect of organising a relief committee necessarily put the Catholic peers at a disadvantage. Social pressures were so great that. although few Catholics conformed to Protestantism early in the century, when the penal laws had first been imposed to satisfy the Protestant ascendancy, the proportion of religious conformists increased after the enactment of the relief measures of George III. There seems little doubt that, rather than be overwhelmed by the rising middle class, individual Catholic gentry increasingly gave way to the temptation to conform to epscopalianism and break down the last barrier between themselves and the Protestant upper class.

The outbreak of the French Revolution in 1789 was greeted with some complacent approval by admirers of the English revolution of 1688–9. The revived interest in parliamentary reform soon made it clear, however, that the unity of the Irish nation against English legislative interference had disappeared. Only a small minority were now concerned with the question. Most of these were Catholics or Dissenters (a term usually meaning the Presbyterians by this time), the two religious denominations not of the governing class. The younger advocates of reform became critical of the dilatory attitude of Grattan and his generation, as well as of the more conservative elements among the Catholics and Dissenters, who felt adequately satisfied with the relief acts passed between 1778 and 1782. These divisions enable us to distinguish between the influence in Ireland of the American and French Revolutions respectively. The first was justified as an indigenous British event, legalistic and traditional, moulded by the historic concepts of British liberties and privileges, founded on the rights of property, which were elevated to an altar of respectability beyond which there was no notion of the people. In the development of the French philosophy of revolution, however, the necessity for social upheaval became paramount. In any such movement in Ireland, success could only result in the redistribution of the economic assets of society, with confiscation of the wealth and power of the privileged Anglican minority. Thus reform imperceptibly passed into revolution, and was eventually outlawed by the government on the excuse of the new French war.

The French Revolution, therefore, provoked reactions which differed according to class. The aristocracy was hostile and fearful, the middle class excited and attracted. In these circumstances renewed applications for parliamentary reform and Catholic relief split the Catholic committee, which came under the influence of its middle-class element. This group became so strong as to be able to organise for the whole of Ireland a representative convention to discuss its proposed emancipation.

However, by 1793, the British governing class, with few exceptions, had reacted against the French Revolution. The Prime Minister, William Pitt, having decided on war with France, brought a group of Whigs into the Cabinet in 1794.

They included Earl Fitzwilliam, who was sent to Ireland as viceroy in 1795. On the advice of Grattan and the influential Whig reformer, Edmund Burke, who had close Irish and Catholic connections, Fitzwilliam proceeded to support Catholic emancipation and to liberalise Dublin Castle. But his dismissal of John Beresford from the office of First Commissioner of Revenue provoked a crisis and he was recalled. Catholic emancipation was dropped. The forces of counter-revolution were now fully in the saddle, and were determined to prevent in Ireland the development of any popular movement which might create nation-wide unrest. Under the influence of Lord Clare a convention act was passed, prohibiting the summoning of any representative body which might allegedly overawe parliament or lead to its being regarded with contempt in the public eye.

Edmund Burke, through his son Richard, secretary of the Catholic committee, had advised the Catholics to moderate their demands, But in 1792 the more radical element on the committee secured the services of a new secretary, a brilliant young Protestant barrister, Theobald Wolfe Tone. Under Tone's influence the case of the committee was carried over the heads of the Dublin administration to the king in person and to the government in London. Concessions, including the grant of the franchise to Catholics, were dictated to a reluctant Irish parliament. From the standpoint of the Irish parliament and its connection with the development of the community of Ireland this was an unfortunate lesson, since Catholics had been taught to rely on the English government as more likely to be liberal. Thus was created a moral climate which eventually facilitated the union of the kingdoms.

The lesson on a short-term basis was perhaps different, and even suggestive of undue pressure, since after the outbreak of war against the new French Republic further concessions were postponed. Ultimately the government turned its back on reform. Meanwhile, however, since it was concerned with the spread of French revolutionary ideas of liberty, equality and fraternity, or death to tradition, as it appeared to conservatives, it took the unprecedented step of setting up in Ireland in 1795 a Roman Catholic seminary at Maynooth. This measure was aimed at providing an adequate education for the Catholic clergy to prevent their continuing to resort to the continent, where the influence of revolutionary ideas on them might be subversive. Concurrently with the setting up of Maynooth the Catholic bishops in Ireland became converts to constitutionalism of the English variety, and exercised their influence against revolution fairly consistently. They condemned the ideas of the revolution and denounced potential supporters of any French invasion during the war. At the end of the century they agreed to closer association with the government as part of the great constitutional readjustment proposed by Pitt.

But while the Catholic clergy and gentry were drawing nearer to the government, the middle-class members of the Catholic committee were coming closer to another organisation, the Society of United Irishmen, first founded in Belfast in 1791 and followed by a second society in Dublin. Under the impact of this and other bodies the patriots divided, most of the younger element going revolutionary, while Grattan and the Whigs went with Burke against France. Under the influence of Tone many middle-class members of the Catholic committee joined the United Irishmen. These societies devoted much time to the question of parliamentary reform, and they finally came, somewhat diffidently, to the conclusion that no property qualification should be imposed on voters. But the decision of the government to turn from reform led to the repression of organisations like the United Irishmen. They went underground and established connections with France, with a view to altering the Irish situation by revolutionary means.

In writing his memoirs of these events in France, where he subsequently went to secure a naval expedition to Ireland, Tone insisted that his policy was to substitute for Protestant, Catholic and Dissenter the common name of Irishman. To later generations the autobiography of Wolfe Tone became the gospel of nationalism and this phrase in particular, referring to the divided communities, or to the division of the community, was remembered when the more immediate consequences of Tone's policy was forgotten. For paralleling his substitution of the name of Irishman for those of religious denominations was Tone's support for a social policy in favour of the men of no property. Tone realised that the property owners and other vested interests were opposed to revolution, and, at this juncture, to change. His interest in social questions was not, however, predominant.

In the event revolution proved abortive in Ireland. Several attempted invasions in 1796 and 1797 were turned back by storms at sea, while the French expedition of 1798, which succeeded in landing, did not gain sufficient support. This rebellion of the United Irishmen in 1798 was unsuccessful both because it was an amateur urban affair, inadequately organised by comparison with the counter-organisation, however inefficient, of the government. In the north of Ireland the movement was confined to a radical element among the Presbyterians. The respectable Protestants in the Volunteers had been regrouped as yeomanry against the forces of invasion. Protestant agrarian secret societies were wound up and replaced by a new quasi-secret body with aristocratic patronage, the Orange Society. In the south, apart from a few Protestant revolutionaries, the majority of rebels in the field were drawn from traditional Catholic areas.

Under Henry Joy McCracken in Antrim and Henry Monro in Down, disappointingly small forces went into action. They were defeated and their commanders tried and executed. In Dublin the government anticipated any rebellion by arresting the ringleaders. In Wicklow and Wexford, following preliminary successes under Beauchamp Bagenal Harvey, a Protestant gentleman, and John Murphy, Catholic curate at Boolavogue, the rebels were defeated at Vinegar Hill and the surviving commanders hanged.

The failure of the rising was attributed by subsequent

patriots to the unexpected arrest of leaders given away by spies, and to the unco-ordinated outbreaks of peasantry, goaded by government forces into rebellion. But the whole circumstances of the rising require careful reassessment of the evidence. It seems clear that Ireland was economically more prosperous during the reign of George III than it had been at any time earlier in the century. In these circumstances movements of political liberty arose more easily, but the impact of war in the last decade of the century affected the prosperity of agricultural workers and textile manufacturers in the towns. The resultant discontent, often associated with unemployment, and the prevailing ideas of revolution and war, created popular unrest. Unexpectedly, this brought about in some areas a revival of the old religious animosities. The fear of papist risings could still provoke a Protestant community. Old stories of massacres were again bandied about and led, almost inevitably, to sectarian clashes once the risings began. This was particularly notable in the county of Wexford. Although the leaders were Protestant gentlemen, rumours led the government forces to turn to Catholic centres and burn several chapels. In the event the rebellion of 1798 became associated with the revival of religious denominational distrust, and the whole ideal of the United Irishmen was adversely represented.

The success of the French Revolution in throwing up outstanding military leaders brought about the unification, under Napoleon Bonaparte, of great areas of Europe which had hitherto been divided among different monarchical dynasties. It was in this situation that the idea of political union between Ireland and Great Britain was proposed once again. This time, it was adopted by William Pitt, the British Premier. But despite the substantial activities of Lords Clare and Castlereagh the amalgamation of the two parliaments was not easily accepted in Ireland, the counter-revolutionaries in parliament being divided on its merits. But after a first reverse in the Irish parliament in 1799, Castlereagh carried through a systematic extra-parliamentary canvass to secure support from various interests, including the Catholic bishops.

Castlereagh's plan, and, indeed, that of Pitt, proposed to substitute for Englishman and Irishman the common name of Britisher. However, the planned integration would have involved Catholic emancipation and this, as it turned out, ran into insuperable difficulties in England. But before these became evident the Catholic bishops individually agreed to support the plan, and also to accept a relatively generous government scheme to endow the clergy throughout the country. Part of the scheme meant accepting the right of the government to veto papal appointments to Catholic bishoprics and other benefices if the persons proposed were suspected of sympathies with revolution. In the aftermath of the attempted French invasions and of the abortive rebellion, the proposals were accepted by the principal bishops, who at that time were associated with the government as trustees of Maynooth.

On its line of approach to the Presbyterians, the government was also successful in securing a degree of support. It undertook to increase substantially the *regium donum*, a small royal gift to the Presbyterian clergy dating from the time of Charles II. But, above all, the Protestant Episcopalian clergy were won over by a provision that, in the amalgamated parliament, the maintenance of the Episcopalian Church as the Established Church, would be a fundamental article.

The passing of the Act of Union in the second attempt resulted in the dissolution of the separate Irish parliament. From 1 January 1801 there came into existence the United Kingdom of Great Britain and Ireland, with a single legislature. Provision was made for safeguarding other interests and, particularly in the smaller country's case, it was understood that separate exchequers would continue to function until the national debts of the two countries had reached a more equitable proportion. While a number of parliamentary boroughs were extinguished, Irish peers, including a representative number of Protestant bishops, were to sit in the House of Lords.

The measure did not, however, include any provision for Catholic emancipation, nor for endowment of clergy, nor a royal veto on episcopal nominations by the pope. The Catholic bishops with perhaps one exception had supported the measure, having approved Castlereagh's plan to subsidise the clergy, concede emancipation and give the government a veto on appointments from Rome. The Union passed, but the Catholic plan miscarried. Royal scruples were aroused at admitting papists to a sovereign body in a Protestant constitution. George III felt that emancipation would be a breach of his coronation oath. Pitt was constrained to retire temporarily, though he did return in a few years, assuring George III that he would never again make the same proposal. Not until 1829 did the change take place.

Since the Union, and particularly since the rise of the movement to secure its repeal, the allegation that the measure was passed only by colossal bribery was put forward by patriotic politicians and by historians who took the view that in some way such an action invalidated the amalgamation. In the light of modern research the actual incidence of bribery and corruption appears to have been grossly exaggerated. The number of seats for Irish constituencies in the united parliament was approximately one third of the 300 seats in the former Irish parliament. For this reason compensation was paid to the recognised owners of disfranchised boroughs. But to provide a capital sum to buy out the interest of borough owners was not unreasonable to the eighteenth-century mind. Securing support for the termination of their political careers from individual members of the Commons, who considered that their demands on the government should be all the greater for that reason, can easily be represented to a more critical generation as bribery and corruption. In fact, these terms only became commonly accepted when higher political standards were expected. This did not take place until after the Battle of Waterloo (1815) and the emergence of a more liberal atmosphere in British political life.

It might be said that the Union was successful in extending within Ireland the idea of the political community, since it was accepted by the Presbyterians, who had previously been accustomed to regard themselves as connected only with Scotland. Thereafter they became attached to Great Britain as a whole, and were more drawn to it as the industrial revolution progressed and brought increasing wealth to the north-east of Ireland. However, the tradition of the United Irishmen still persisted among a few.

Three years after the Union an abortive rising took place in Dublin under Robert Emmet—a belated attempt to secure a base for a new French invasion by the victorious Napoleon. Emmet in his trial insisted that the French would have in no way interfered with his plans to establish the dream of a Republic of Ireland, in accordance with the principles of the United Irishmen. His execution after a remarkable speech from the dock was long remembered in ballad and song, and revived an interest in revolution nearly fifty years later when the third French Revolution broke out. But to many of those first stimulated by revolutionary ideas the principles of the United Irishmen had been weighed in the balance and found wanting because of their defeat, and because they had led to the extinction of the independent Irish parliament and to the Union.

Apart from the bishops and the gentry many Catholics appear to have had reservations about the Union. A resolution condemning it was passed by a meeting of Dublin lawyers in 1800 at which a notable speech was delivered by the young Daniel O'Connell, future leader of the emancipation movement. In attacking the Union, O'Connell declared he would prefer to see re-enacted the penal laws against his Catholic fellow countrymen rather than approve the extinction of the independent legislature. O'Connell's romantic demonstration of trust in the Protestant Irish parliament should properly be regarded as a vote of confidence in a moment of crisis, rather than as an objective statement based upon political judgment. The actions of the Protestant

Ascendancy in the past could hardly have led anyone to regard his assertion as based on mature reflection. The exclusion of Catholics from membership of parliament continued the irresponsible tradition of that Ascendancy which had developed in the course of the eighteenth century. It may also have contributed substantially to the inability of the Catholic community to adjust to integration with Britain and to Britain's failure to accept the Irish Catholics as an element in the amalgamated body politic, if this was really to work as a unity.

Thus at the close of the eighteenth century the idea of Irish nationalism seemed very inconsequential indeed, and the future of an Irish community uncertain and unlikely. During the debate on the Union in the Protestant Irish parliament Grattan had said that he had witnessed the birth of the nation and was now to be present at its obsequies. It was a prophetic declaration that the future of the community of Ireland would not be with the Protestants, and that the nation of the eighteenth century, representing only an upper class, would become merged with that of Britain. Irish nationalism, on the other hand, came to be mistakenly regarded as something which first originated with the United Irishmen. Another century was to elapse before it was recognised as having cultural antecedents going back for more than a thousand years.

6

Ireland in the Community of Britain, 1800—1870

WOLFE TONE in his autobiography stressed the need for separating Ireland from England on the grounds that throughout history England had been the source of all Ireland's ills. The United Irishmen seem to have accepted it as a fact that the political Union terminated the existence of the Irish nation: when Emmet came to the peroration of his speech from the dock, he urged that no one should write his epitaph until Ireland had regained her place among the nations of the earth. The purpose of this chapter is to consider the way in which the association with Britain operated in its first phase, and the way in which the case against the Union was advocated during the same period.

The case for amalgamating the two kingdoms and their parliaments, as put forward by Pitt, visualised an integration of the communities. Their united parliament would govern in their common interests, protecting the weaker as well as the stronger kingdom. As Pitt put it, the great wealth of the major partner to the amalgamation would undoubtedly enrich the lesser. But the industrial revolution belied him; in Ireland, to an even greater degree than in England, it drew the wealth from the rural parts and left them impoverished. After 1850, the catastrophe of the famine in Ireland could be laid at the door of the Union.

In one way it is perhaps more realistic to regard the integration as one of property, a combination of England with the Protestant Ascendancy of Ireland. This was challenged by the middle class, both Presbyterian and

Catholic, and until Catholic emancipation was conceded, in the year after the Protestant nonconformists of the United Kingdom had secured recognition as first-class subjects, the challenge to an integration of upper class Britain with the Irish Protestant Ascendancy was maintained.

Although it concerned an English minority as well as the Irish majority, the struggle for Catholic emancipation was almost inevitably carried on by the Irish, and as an Irish question. The failure to liberate Catholics fully in 1800 transformed what had been largely, though not exclusively, a parliamentary question into a popular one.

But the complexities of the Union did not begin to emerge until after the Battle of Waterloo in 1815. British cabinets during the Napoleonic wars had been predominantly Tory. After Napoleon's defeat they tended to remain conservative at home, but occasionally appeared liberal abroad. Ireland, as part of the United Kingdom, was excluded as long as possible from liberalising influences. Catholic emancipation was canvassed from time to time by Whigs like Grattan and some survivors of the former Irish parliament who had opposed the Union. The Whigs as a party traditionally connected with reform became more identified with the question. A few Tories, such as the well-known George Canning, were also favourable, but in order to obviate fears and objections such sympathetic Tories tended to favour legislation along the lines of Castlereagh's original proposals to the Irish Catholic bishops at the time of the Union.

It was in this atmosphere that the middle-class Catholics struggled to secure participation in politics. Owing to the impotence of the English Catholic minority the initiative in organising the campaign passed to successive Irish groups. Because of the vicissitudes of politics and the dangers of public prosecution, particularly under the Convention Act, these changed from the Catholic Committee to the Catholic Board, the Catholic Association, and organisations with similar titles. In these bodies the outstanding personality was Daniel O'Connell, who from about 1824 until his death in

1847 was the most notable Irish political leader. The reversal of Tory policy on the issue of Catholic emancipation can be ascribed to O'Connell's methods. Wellington, the victor of Waterloo, who became Prime Minister in 1828, was obliged to consider what would be the full consequences of a resort to force in Ireland over the Catholic question. The climax came when O'Connell was returned as member of parliament for Clare and at the bar of the House of Commons refused to take the declaration against transubstantiation and the anti-Catholic oath of allegiance. Tory feelings were aroused to an intense heat, but in their wisdom, Wellington and his home secretary and political heir, Sir Robert Peel, forced George iv to give way. In the United Kingdom as a whole, the feeling was that there should be no further delay in conceding emancipation. The Catholic Emancipation Act was passed in 1829 and ended the restriction of parliament to Protestant members. In view of middle-class Catholic hostility, particularly in Ireland, proposed safeguards like a government veto on bishops' appointments were dropped. The community as a whole had learned its own power when it emerged that England really feared the possibility of civil war in Ireland. It was in the course of this struggle, directed by O'Connell, that the non-propertied Irish Catholics came to regard themselves as being the real community of Ireland.

Concurrent with the revival of religious feeling in Europe and the Catholic come-back which followed the French Revolution there was a noticeable increase in sectarian animosity. This was particularly true of the years after 1825. Inter-denominational jealousy emerged more viciously in Ireland than it had since the aftermath of 1798. This jealousy affected relations between Protestants and Catholics, especially after the resolution of the question of parliamentary reform had terminated the political grievance which kept Anglicans and Presbyterians divided. After 1829 the question of additional parliamentary reform no longer centred on religious disabilities, and Protestants and Catholics in Ireland alike became preoccupied with their own interests.

O'Connell stressed it that he was prepared to abandon other struggles, such as that for more reform, if Irish Protestants would combine with him in a movement for repeal of the Union. But Protestant apathy led him to revert to parliamentary reform, and thus to link himself with the Whigs as the reforming party, until he felt strong enough to advocate Repeal once again. The discontent of Presbyterians was turned into a new channel under the influence of Henry Cooke, who argued that Protestantism was threatened by the rising force of Irish Catholicism. From Cooke's time the Union was accepted by Irish Presbyterians as a bastion against the dreaded forces of popery and their intimidating leader, O'Connell.

Since the beginning of the century, the government of the United Kingdom had moved only reluctantly from a position of defending the realm against Bonapartism to a general defence of property. This was particularly true of the conservative Lord Liverpool, who was Prime Minister from 1812 until 1827 and whose attitude was to avoid any action as far as possible. In 1832, however, agitation for parliamentary reform resulted in the passage of an Act drafted by the more conservative Whig politicians under the leadership of Lord Grey, who had replaced Wellington as Prime Minister in 1830. Grey's government saw that the Irish question was involved in the enactment of reform; and the problem was how far reform could be extended in Ireland without interfering with the existing balance of society. O'Connell, who had renewed his alliance with the Whigs in 1830, launched his own campaign in favour of reform under the influence of contemporary revolutions in Europe. But Grey was sufficiently conservative to refuse to sponsor any major readjustment in parliamentary representation. Although the Irish Parliamentary Reform Act of 1833 allotted a handful of extra seats to the counties, the closed boroughs monopolised by a few men remained. It was a deep disappointment to O'Connell who had contributed substantially to the success of Grey's corresponding English bill. Grey's reluctance to interfere in Ireland and give it equality with England emerged with this Irish Reform Bill which was introduced separately from the British and proposed no more than minimal changes. The unpopularity of the Irish in England was a major liability to the Whigs, and it made it difficult for reformers to do justice to Ireland.

After the Union, responsibility for the government of Ireland remained, as before, with one of the two cabinet ministers who were nominally subject to the secretary for Home Affairs. At Dublin Castle Irish officials continued to interpret their duties in terms of the protection of property. Inevitably this involved special protection for the upper class, predominantly Protestant and predominantly Tory. To English statesmen, whether Whig or Tory, their political rivals in Ireland were preferable to their Catholic Irish allies at Westminster. More extensive reform would certainly have strengthened O'Connell and his supporters in Ireland. The government did little more than to remind property owners in Ireland that they had their duties as well as their rights,and even this mild rebuke, which was denounced as outrageous by upper-class grand juries, was not made until after Grey's replacement in 1834 by the slightly less conservative Lord Melbourne.

In those years the career of O'Connell was very important as far as the political education of his co-religionists was concerned. With a vast knowledge of law, and a remarkable capacity for intimidating less talented opponents, O'Connell broke the tradition by which the law was used in favour of the upper classes, and against the middle-class and non-propertied Irish. In a certain sense O'Connell's assertion of the rule of law was all the more remarkable, as it destroyed the theocratic legal safeguards of the revolution of 1689 in Ireland, the Calvinistic anti-Catholic oaths. It became possible to show the inarticulate Irish that the law was not just an engine of repression, and that abstract principles of justice existed behind it. For O'Connell's generation, however, the lesson seemed closely, too closely, associated with the power and magnetism of one man, and it was to be necessary to relearn the lesson when the hero had passed to his reward.

Great as was O'Connell's influence, it was by no means the only force at work upon the Catholic Irish. In the days after emancipation the Catholic clergy and leading laymen gave vent, in public, to their hostility to the continuation of the system of tithes. The tithes were taxes in kind levied on the produce of the agricultural community for the benefit and upkeep of the clergy of the Established Church. Catholics naturally inferred that emancipation would give them equality with the Protestant establishment, but they were soon disappointed. Tithes were also regarded with disfavour by the Protestant nonconformists, though these on the whole stayed out of the extra-parliamentary agitation which occupied much of the attention of the Irish public in the years after emancipation, until a compromise was reached towards the end of the 1830s.

Refusal to pay tithes became general and it was organised as an underground resistance movement, like earlier agrarian agitations. But Catholic clergy and O'Connellite politicians alike watched it with concern. In a time of economic regression the cost was not inconsiderable to Catholics of replacing their ghetto-like mass-houses of the past by more prominently placed, if still modest, chapels. All the same, chapels were being erected throughout Ireland in the generation after emancipation, and it was not surprising, therefore, that Catholics should resent and refuse the continued payment of a tithe of their crops to Protestant clergymen who gave them no spiritual services and who often acted as hated government officials. During the tithe agitation collective resistance to the law was practised systematically over a great part of central and southern Ireland, and even some arbitration courts were organised for the solution of differences among the people. The whole situation bordered on war. The police, called in to protect the officials collecting the tithes of crops in the fields, were frequently to be reinforced by units of the army. In 1838 parliament finally agreed to substitute a fixed rent charge for the tithe, but by this time the Irish Catholic community had become accustomed to regarding the administration with contempt. Moreover, in certain circumstances it was clear that it could be defied with impunity.

Not surprisingly, O'Connell lost popularity for his apathy over the tithe war. Even for some of the Catholic clergy the position was rather embarrassing; many of them found it unpalatable to condemn illegal resistance to or combination against the tithe owner, who was usually a Protestant clergyman or one of his agents. Others among the second generation of Maynooth clergy, successors to those brought up by the Gallican *emigrés* of the French Revolution, turned to the people from whom they had sprung in sympathetic disapproval of the government. Ultimately, division among the Catholic clergy led to a new and less reticent attitude towards public affairs being adopted by the collective body of priests. In this they were influenced not merely by the tithe war, but also by the activities of the Orange Order, which had been established towards the end of the preceding century to resist the increased strength of Catholicism, particularly as regards the acquisition of property and power. Thus the Catholic clergy rejected the Protestant ascendancy of the Union and accepted instead association with O'Connell's movement for Repeal.

The success of O'Connell in winning the support of the clergy was not, however, a foregone conclusion. This conversion of the hierarchy to Repeal was only temporary. After the concession of emancipation the Irish bishops had publicly expressed their gratitude to the Duke of Wellington as the greatest living Irishman. The embarrassed Duke, who had been born in Dublin, is said to have commented that being born in a stable did not make you a horse. But in addressing Wellington the bishops were deliberately identifying themselves with the Union and with the United Kingdom, both because at first they did not wish to be linked with O'Connell's Repeal movement, and because, like many others, they romantically concluded that Catholic emancipation had brought the tyranny of Protestant ascendancy to an end. The continuation of the same régime in Dublin Castle and the experiences of the tithe war led them to think otherwise.

There was also substantial evidence that English clergy might be preferred to Irish for important Irish bishoprics if pro-British influence at Rome, encouraged by the Austrian chancellor, Metternich, were able to win a secret veto for the British government. It became known that Archbishop Curtis of Armagh and other bishops had been promoted because of their friendship with the Duke of Wellington. Ultimately, under pressure from Ireland, the Roman authorities took up a less committed position towards nominations allegedly approved by the British government. However, at the instance of the British government, whose wishes were conveyed to Rome by Metternich, the church authorities condemned the participation of clergy in the Repeal movement as an interference in politics. This only earned them a rebuke from Archbishop MacHale of Tuam and other bishops that the matter was one of religion and not of politics.

It was under O'Connell's influence that MacHale and a growing majority of the bishops attacked the undenominational system of education in Ireland and forced Rome into endorsing their action. Edward Stanley, (later Earl of Derby and Prime Minister) had, as Chief Secretary for Ireland in Grey's government, introduced a scheme for free public primary education in 1831. This was an important step towards dealing with the problem of Irish poverty, which had been substantially aggravated by a population explosion in the preceding fifty years. But denominational rivalries impeded Stanley's plans from the beginning, and eventually Irish public education was reorganised largely on denominational lines. The Catholic clergy were thus conditioned into thinking of their Irish co-religionists as separate from other elements.

In the United Kingdom politics was the first consideration in relation to Ireland. Reformers almost inevitably provoked

12

counter-reformers; or traditionally accepted reformers, such as Lord Grey or Stanley, became content to rest upon the laurels to which they felt entitled after their first modest achievements. After Grey's resignation in 1834, a more satisfactory situation prevailed for a short time under the government of Lord Melbourne, although the House of Lords could still obstruct Irish measures with impunity. Then the excitable William IV allowed himself to be inveigled into dismissing Melbourne towards the end of 1834. Sir Robert Peel, however, who succeeded him as Prime Minister, failed to improve his position at a general election. He was driven out of power and replaced by Melbourne and the Whigs in April 1835 as a result of some very astute parliamentary tactics which were worked out at opposition meetings at Lichfield House. These were attended by O'Connell. The Tories, and even some of the conservative Whigs, taunted the reform government with the 'Lichfield House compact', declaring Melbourne's new administration had been enslaved by O'Connell, and they organised further resistance to Irish demands on a national and sectarian basis. O'Connell was undoubtedly a great political bastion for Melbourne. On more than one occasion he kept the government in power through his influence on its English radical allies in parliament, which far exceeded that of the aristocratic Whigs. But British public opinion was so hostile to O'Connell that Ministers avoided being seen with him in public, and some, like the relatively radical Lord John Russell, even denied the existence of the Lichfield House compact.

In fact, however, O'Connell had agreed to use all his influence to support Melbourne, provided that justice was done to Ireland and the Protestant Ascendancy compelled to share administrative offices with Catholics. Reforms were introduced to give Catholics equal privileges in municipal government, and some progress was also made in organising in Ireland a better standard of living. The alternative was repeal of the Union, which O'Connell declared from time to time was the only effective cure for Irish malaise. But he was prepared to put the Repeal cause in cold storage and avoid embarrassing the government on this question. In any event, only a handful of British politicians were prepared to consider it favourably.

The change of government which had put Peel and the Tories in office for a few months in 1834–35 was not without advantage. It provided the élite of the Tories with first-hand knowledge of the way in which reforms were operating in practice in Ireland. Extreme conservatives had been hoping for a full-scale reversal of policy. In this they were sorely disappointed. It is true that the Tory government had to proceed warily and was continually experiencing defeats in the House of Commons. But it is equally true that Peel was anxious to attract dissident Whigs, including Stanley who had resigned from Grey's cabinet rather than agree to the appropriation of the revenues of the Church of Ireland for secular uses. Peel was a statesman who knew when to give way to the wishes of the British people. Even if he was coldly indifferent to the majority of Irishmen, and virtually incapable of agreement with O'Connell on anything, he was not prepared to put himself into the hands of reactionaries. He accepted the legislative changes of his Whig predecessors and avoided wholesale alterations in personnel and policy in Dublin Castle. Even after Melbourne's return to office in 1835 Peel exercised a moderating influence on William IV. In opposition, his attitude to Ireland was simply to try to limit the extent of reform measures and prevent the growth of an O'Connellite ascendancy. He accepted the principle that the greater number of closed Irish boroughs should be defranchised, but resisted every attempt to democratise them by lowering the voting qualification. He also opposed proposals for using church revenues for educational purposes.

As long as the Whigs could be maintained in office, O'Connell was ready to co-operate with them. He supported their policy of appointing Catholics to key positions so enthusiastically and so frequently that he exposed himself to accusations of jobbery and corruption. In Dublin the Whig administration after 1835, notably Thomas Drummond, the Under-Secretary for Ireland, had considerable success in imposing a fair-minded attitude on the police and magistrates and altering the accepted attitude among minor officials that all Catholics were disloyal. The ultra-conservatives in the House of Lords subsequently forced an investigation into Drummond's administration, but he was triumphantly vindicated.

Of another Whig innovation, the introduction of the Poor Law into Ireland, O'Connell was critical and unconvinced. He considered that the workhouse system would do much to pauperise people. This was undeniable, but at least it afforded some elementary administrative machinery for an unprepared government when a new and unforeseen potato blight led to the disastrous famine of the 1840s. Allowing for the cold reservation of the English governing class towards all things Irish, it is understandable that nothing more burdensome on the taxpayer was attempted than this poor law, whose operating costs fell on the local ratepayers. But to O'Connell the introduction of the ruinous poor law seemed to justify his turning away from improving British administration in Ireland towards Repeal of the Union and the restoration of the independent Irish parliament. He was careful however to do no more than take the first few cautious steps as long as Melbourne had the slightest chance of remaining in office.

The Repeal movement might be described as the revival of the nation idea of Grattan and the Protestant Volunteers of 1782. But O'Connell had to accept it that his movement was based upon an entirely different element in Irish society. O'Connell did so only reluctantly, because while denouncing revolutionaries, he subscribed to the United Irish idea of substituting the name of Irishman for those of Catholic and Protestant. But it was clear, from the first rejection of O'Connell's advances by Dublin Protestants in 1830, that Repeal of the Union was becoming so closely identified with him as to cause its repudiation by virtually all Protestants

concerned with the religious issue and fearful of expropriation by a Catholic majority. O'Connell carried few of the
colonial nationalists with him once he had become the
tribune of the emancipated natives. With some unwillingness
he accepted the patronage of Archbishop MacHale, fearing
that without him Repeal would never succeed. But
O'Connell only took up the Repeal cause in earnest, insisting
that real justice was being denied to Ireland, when Peel again
became Prime Minister in 1841. He got little support at
first, and it was Archbishop MacHale's public addresses to
his flock in Connaught which saved the movement.
O'Connell's achievement, apart from creating a new attitude
to the rule of law and to forcing the concession of emancipation, was to stimulate the masses to collective meetings,
described as being of a monstrous size, which took up the
cause of Irish nationalism under the guise of a movement for
the restoration of the independent Irish parliament.

In 1842 a new newspaper, *The Nation*, was established in
Dublin by a group of young men who were influenced by the
doctrines of Mazzini, and who were anxious to develop the
idea of Irish nationalism as a matter of principle and not
merely in support of the practical issues advocated by
O'Connell. The Young Irelanders, as they came to be called,
applied the principles of Grattan and of Tone to virtually
every political, cultural and social activity in Ireland. Their
paper set out to comprehend all Irish traditions, Norman and
Gaelic, Jacobite and Williamite, colonial and native, Orange
and Green. It avowed with enthusiasm the object of the
United Irishmen to substitute for Protestant, Catholic and
Dissenter the common name of Irishman. It praised Irish
heroes, popularised Irish history, proclaimed the need for
national art and music, craftsmanship and design. It moral-
ised for Ireland on the classical defenders of liberty, described
the contemporary movement for unity of Germany and Italy
and denounced Russian imperialism in Poland. It applied to
Ireland the contemporary attributes of nationalism and even
urged, or one of its editors at least, Thomas Davis, did, the

necessity for the educated upper classes to study the Irish language. Included among the Young Irelanders were a few middle-class Protestants, such as Davis, who were sympathetic to the doctrines of Wolfe Tone, though they carefully presented them in a constitutional framework.

So far as O'Connell was concerned, *The Nation* newspaper was a valuable ally, although on the political objective of Repeal it exercised a youthful disposition to be more extreme than O'Connell. The doctrines of *The Nation's* editors, Thomas Davis and Charles Gavan Duffy, might be a useful affirmation of ideals, but O'Connell was quick to resent their attempts to interpret the need for exclusive concern with Ireland as a bar to his re-allying with the Whigs, just when it appeared likely that an Irish-Whig combination would defeat the Tory administration of Sir Robert Peel, which had successfully ousted that of Melbourne in 1841. The Young Irelanders hoped that their influence would lead to a greater participation of Protestants in the national movement, but O'Connell took exception to their intervention in matters like public education as obstructing his struggle against Tory government. Under the influence of his tactless and talentless son, John, O'Connell was even to go to the length of outwitting the Young Irelanders with cunning and forcing them out of the Repeal organisation when they sought to prevent a new Irish-Whig alliance after Peel's fall in 1846. It might be said, in fact, that in the 1840s O'Connell was making such an issue of Repeal that it took priority over everything else while the Tories were in power.

Sir Robert Peel, Prime Minister once again from 1841 to 1846, had learnt considerably from the progress of politics in the United Kingdom. From his position of partiality towards Protestants while Chief Secretary for Ireland in 1812-18, he had come to the point where he was prepared to appoint Catholics and even Whigs to office in Ireland, provided they were not associated with Repeal. The incompatibility between the English and Irish leaders was unfortunate at any time, and to O'Connell Peel always remained 'Orange Peel'.

This was particularly deplorable as it led O'Connell to conclude that proposals by Peel to extend the government
subvention to Maynooth, to establish colleges for the middle
classes at Belfast, Cork and Galway and to set up a charitable
donations commission to facilitate Catholic bequests, was
part of a malignant conspiracy to enslave the Catholics of
Ireland. O'Connell's successful denunciations of Peel's ideas
destroyed the chances of real co-operation between most
Irish Catholics and a Tory government.

After the election of 1841 Peel's parliamentary predomi-
nance was assured. Since O'Connell had reached the end
of his parliamentary tether, he descended on the countryside
with his Repeal movement. Monster meetings commenced
as a petitioning movement to the queen, and they became a
series of spectacular demonstrations of Irish discontent. They
displayed the remarkable disciplinary control of O'Connell,
but they involved increasingly the language of defiance of
the government, and defiance might lead to rebellion. In
1843 O'Connell made the mistake of predicting victory
before the end of the year. The culminating meeting, at
Clontarf near Dublin, would have recalled the eleventh-
century defeat of the foreigners by Brian Boru. Peel intervened and prohibited the meeting. O'Connell obeyed and
his supporters turned back the converging thousands. The
government proceeded to put the organisers, including
O'Connell, on trial. But this saved the O'Connellites from
the revolutionaries, whose rebellious intentions might have
gained force had O'Connell been free and open to pressure
by them to go further, as extremists in the cabinet would
have preferred. The moderates in the cabinet, however,
prevailed over those who favoured giving the Repealers
enough rope to hang themselves. Thus O'Connell and others
went to prison only to be released on appeal to the House of
Lords where a Whig majority of the law lords reversed the
verdict. But Repeal was finished, and O'Connell had lost
all his partiality for monster meetings. Then there followed
the great famine.

The onset of potato disease was first reported in the autumn of 1845. Peel, the prime minister, geared himself for the ordeal. Everyone knew that the weakness of the Irish economy was that so many cottiers were dependent for food on a potato crop of variable productivity from the least reliable of the lands reclaimed on the mountains and on the bogs. So Peel coolly took precautions. He organised the stocking of redundant naval biscuits at strategic points, quietly arranged that the government would have the necessary local medical information, and so was able to restrict the worst incidents of the potato destruction which threatened the food supply and the livelihood of a majority of the population. Being Peel, he had to convince the British people that his actions for the Irish were personally distasteful, so he balanced the anti-famine arrangements with a coercion bill.

Unfortunately, Peel had already alienated the Tory landlords, some of the strongest supporters of his government. Ever since 1815 landlords had been able to maintain the prosperity of their estates only through the corn laws which imposed a tariff on foreign corn to keep up the price of English-grown corn. This was opposed by industrial interests at all levels of society. In the Irish crisis, the prime minister proposed to suspend the corn laws, and declared that he did not favour their reimposition after the emergency had passed. On this he was prepared to stake his future career, secure in the realisation that Russell and the Whigs would support him. What he did not expect was that an active Tory rural element would revolt against the abandonment of protection and force him out of office. But this was what they did, by allying with the O'Connellites and the Whigs on the issue of the coercion bill.

Thus in June 1846 the Whigs returned to power with Lord John Russell as prime minister. The Irish situation under Russell became much more serious when the potato crop was unexpectedly blighted for the second successive year. Unlike earlier crop failures, this blight came from a fungus carried from America by steamships. It was experienced generally in western Europe; crop failures took place in Great Britain too. But it was only in Ireland, where a large cottier population depended exclusively on the potato, that the consequences were catastrophic. Famine conditions got out of hand and fever extended throughout the country with disastrous results.

In repealing the corn laws the Tory Prime Minister had been primarily considering the needs of industrial Britain. To O'Connell the closure of the ports and the conservation of food in Ireland would have been a more practical policy. But the dominant economic theory was *laissez-faire,* and in pursuing it Peel felt constrained to provide for the first year's food shortage secretly lest government action would interfere with private enterprise and the delicate balance of commercial interests be upset. But these were the interests of capitalistic England and not of rural Ireland. So far as the history of Ireland was concerned in the community of Britain, the decision of Russell's government to treat the potato catastrophe as a local Irish question was the first clear indication that the resources of the United Kingdom as a whole would not be conscripted to meet the urgent needs of one area which was likely to affect unduly the well-being of the whole. The famine destroyed more than a quarter of the Irish population, led to the migration of another quarter and ultimately brought about its reduction from nearly nine millions to a little over four.

Early in the 1840s the financial difficulties of many Irish estates had already led to government proposals to facilitate their sale in the hope of replacing improvident landlords. This policy was pressed forward as a result of the famine, which left many landlords greatly in debt. There was no question of improving the tenantry. It was an age before government had become accustomed to planning the distribution of food in times of crisis. The situation in a country where more than a quarter of the agricultural population was usually without food in the summer months, except what could be secured by begging, was therefore particularly irritating to economists who were concerned with calculating the full potentialities of the industrial revolution. Reaction to the wretched poor relief system, which imposed on landed proprietors the responsibility for a rate-in-aid to relieve poverty, provoked among landlords during the famine a policy of clearances by eviction, to get rid of what was described as the redundant population, since their relief would inflate the rates.

The grimmest consequence of the famine in Ireland was the destruction of the poverty-stricken element of the population both by migration and by death. Among a long-memoried people, this was remembered against the evicting landlords. The Irish landlords system, protected by England and predominantly Protestant in its upholders was held, not without reason, to have been the direct cause of the unbalanced social and economic situation in the country. Two other matters must also be taken into account, however. The government, unaccustomed to administering relief on a national scale and reorganising resources, might not have succeeded in controlling the famine, even had Sir Robert Peel remained in office. Peel, despite his remarkable genius, had shown himself particularly blind to evidence of an earlier catastrophe in 1817. Secondly the situation was one in which lack of knowledge of the cause of the potato disease made it impossible to make plans. No one anticipated a recurrence of the nation-wide rotting of the roots of the crops in successive years after 1845.

In 1848 revolution broke out in most of the capital cities of Europe. This rarely led to profound consequences, except in France, where the monarchy was finally disestablished. Among the Young Irelanders the outbreak of this new revolution in France caused high excitement. The *laissez-faire* policy of the government and the death of O'Connell in 1847, powerless to avert the famine, had created an attitude of revolt among their sympathisers. The Young Irelanders sought help from France, in the belief that a revolution through a new independent parliament might arrest the rot and terminate the famine. The French revolutionaries, however, were to depend on the goodwill of England. Meanwhile the views of the Young Irelanders created popular excitement, and under the influence of France they abandoned the constitutionalism of O'Connell and adopted the republican policy of Wolfe Tone and the United Irishmen. Because of the famine, they were also concerned with prevailing doctrines about land. The idea of popular sovereignty over land, as a substitute for feudal notions of crown property, were canvassed by John Mitchel, the outstanding Young Irelander since Davis's death, and by James Fintan Lalor, who was himself no repealer, but theoretically a republican more socialist than Tone had been.

In his paper, *The Irishman,* Mitchel declared that the moment to rise would be when he himself was arrested. He was arrested, found guilty and transported, but nobody rose. William Smith O'Brien, another Protestant Young Irelander and an eccentric landlord of aristocratic background, attempted to rouse the country. But the rebellion was rapidly suppressed, as none of the leaders possessed military gifts, and everywhere the influence of the Catholic clergy was directed against them. Withdrawing from Dublin, the rebels were quickly overwhelmed in the country. Once more government and clergy had allied against revolution and, perhaps because of the famine, the rebels seem to have secured only negligible support among the people.

In one sense it was no more than a rebellion of pamphleteers and journalists, most of whom were transported abroad and used their subsequent leisure to popularise their ideas of Irish nationalism. The government wisely avoided the temptation to extreme measures and the rebels were without martyrs. The abortive revolution discredited the movement for self-government for over a decade. After 1849 the famine crisis passed, but only after the population had been seriously depleted through starvation, fever and emigration. Among the emigrants to the United States, the myth of

England's responsibility for the famine became generally accepted; conditions of horror in emigrant ships, of death and destitution at ports of arrival, were linked in the exiles' hostility to Britain to the supposed supineness of the government and the calculated complacency of its administrators. For some ten years, however, the men of 1848 had little influence at home. Repeal itself collapsed. Economic and social questions, rather than national issues, became the principal concern. From the ruins of Repeal, Duffy and other Young Irelanders formed an Irish land reform, or tenant right group, sometimes called the first independent Irish parliamentary party. By 1860 it had petered out, but it was an attempt to begin a national movement transcending denominational boundaries and to lead to a permanent Irish party.

In the middle of the nineteenth century, the majority of the English middle class supported reformers who like the Scots and Protestant Irish, came to be described, however inaccurately, as Whigs. As long as Toryism rejected middle-class Catholics this element in Ireland was necessarily drawn to the Whigs, and few of them were converted to Repeal while O'Connell was launching that movement. The changes in the attitude of the clergy, however, gradually began to influence the middle-class, more particularly because in Ireland the choice lay really between Peel and O'Connell. Once Peel had been rejected by the Irish hierarchy, the possibility of an alliance with the Tories became remote for middle-class Catholics.

Perhaps even more positive in its effect was the realignment of parties on new principles during the 1850s. This so transformed the old ideas of Tory and Liberal that the organisation in Ireland of a tenant party was hardly more unusual than one in England for protection. In both countries these parties were associated with agricultural movements and in both instances they did not succeed in prevailing against the growing forces of industry and urban wealth. After the death of Peel in 1850 the remnant of his party, which had supported him over ending the corn laws, became identified in a very general way with tenant right members of parliament from Ireland.

The outbreak, however, of an unexpected popular anti-Catholic spasm in England gave rise to a new wave of Protestant hysteria, following the establishment by the pope of a new system of Catholic bishoprics in England. Protestant bigotry was so provoked as to lead the liberal Lord John Russell to pass a pusillanimous and unenforceable Ecclesiastical Titles Bill, imposing penalties on any Catholic bishops who took their titles from English localities. This created a permanent divergence between the two countries, which during the 1850s accentuated denominational questions in Ireland, almost to the exclusion of other issues.

The religious issue split the Irish movement for tenant right. Archbishop Cullen of Dublin attempted to withdraw the clergy completely from politics, if only to satisfy Rome that their political-mindedness was now a thing of the past. Cullen's action, however, was misinterpreted, mainly by Young Irelanders, many of whom resented his interference with the new Catholic University of Ireland. This had been founded in 1854 by the bishops, after they had condemned the provincial colleges projected by Peel and set up under Russell, in the foundation of the Queen's University of Ireland. The first rector of the Catholic University was the famous John Henry Newman. He encouraged Irish scholarship, and made little of the dangers of Irish patriotism.

In Ulster, Protestant land reformers, notably William Sharman Crawford, were unable to make headway at elections against the landlord interest. A Catholic defence organisation was also launched in the country, and it sought support among members of parliament. But the attempt to build up in parliament a disciplined tenant right party overlooked the attractiveness of office for Irish M.P.s under favourable British governments.

The 1860s, in the wake of the Crimean war and the unification of Italy, saw a revival of international interest in military activity. The American civil war had involved many Irish exiles, some of whom decided to organise a new political movement to free Ireland. It was called the Fenian movement in recollection of the legendary Irish military class, whose romantic adventures were popularly presented to the public by John O'Mahony, founder of the new body. O'Mahony's Fenians expressed themselves in an American context, and were committed to the doctrines of Young Ireland and to the republican organisation of society on American lines. The Fenians' secret military organisation, the Irish Republican Brotherhood, was directed by James Stephens, and planned a rising in Ireland. The connection of Stephens with revolutionaries in Paris convinced Archbishop Cullen and Bishop Moriarty of Kerry that atheistic freemasons and Italian *carbonari* were at the bottom of Irish sedition. The *carbonari* had taken part in the revolution in Rome in 1848, when Pius IX was driven from his city and some of the principal ecclesiastical buildings only saved from destruction because Cullen, who was then living in Rome, was able to secure their protection by American naval units. Accordingly, from its inception in Ireland, Fenianism found a deadly enemy in Archbishop Cullen. He saw to it that it was condemned by ecclesiastical authorities in Ireland and ultimately by the pope. Cullen, however, was a man of deep, if inarticulate, patriotic feeling; he was simply anxious to avoid a recurrence of outbreaks like that of the United Irishmen in 1798, when his own uncle had been hanged.

After the collapse of the tenant right movement in the late 1850s, Cullen lent his support to a Catholic organisation, the National Association, which was set up in 1864. Superficially, his act ran counter to his earlier antipathy to the involvement of priests in politics. But Cullen had been disillusioned by British government partiality towards the Piedmontese attack on the Papal States and by the government's refusal to recognise the Catholic University. It was for these reasons that he revised his views on keeping the clergy out of politics. Cullen lent his support discreetly to the National Association to divert popular interest in Fenianism. This new body intended to pressurise parliament into improving the conditions of tenant-farmers as regards tenure, rent and sale. It also set out to secure the disestablishment of the Protestant Episcopalian Church in Ireland and win government endowment for the Catholic University, which was slowly dying from lack of official support.

Cullen's Association did not excite the public. Even if the people were too fickle to risk destruction in rebellion they were sufficiently romantic to attend in vast numbers the funerals of deceased patriots like Terence Bellew MacManus, a survivor of 1848. When the Fenians began to organise themselves for the establishment of their republic, and prepare the countryside for revolt through their newspaper the *Irish People*, the clergy supported the government, and in some cases even helped prosecutions of those suspected of preaching Fenianism. As a result, Cullen's popularity dropped steeply. Even many of the younger clergy, particularly in the west, became identified with the revolutionary movement. In 1867, after an abortive rising which was defeated by a combination of bad organisation, bad weather and unfavourable clergy, the Fenians rose in popular estimation in Ireland. This was particularly because of the execution in Manchester of three of their number, Allen, Larkin and O'Brien, for the accidental killing of a policeman when they were attempting to rescue comrades from a police van. The 'Manchester Martyrs', as they were known in Ireland, provided the heroic element in a hopeless struggle.

The Fenian crisis convinced Gladstone, the leading Liberal statesman in England, that the Irish question required immediate action. Gladstone strove to convert the policy of Cullen's Association to the purposes of his own party. In turn, Cullen and most of the bishops deserted Disraeli and the Conservative party for Gladstone and the Liberals, in order to achieve their own programme. In 1868 Gladstone took office and attempted to settle the Irish question within the framework of the United Kingdom. By 1870 he had carried two of his objects, by conceding a reformed land bill and disestablishing the Irish Episcopalian Church. On the third, university education, he was to fail in 1874. But with his success in 1870 there came to an end the three centuries old association of Protestant episcopalianism with the state in Ireland and the equally long monopoly of landed interest by the upper classes. The absolute ownership of land by the old proprietors was transferred into a conditional one, if only for a generation; feudalism had been given notice by the law.

The Union had again been saved. In 1845 the price had been the abandonment of Protestant ascendancy by the government's refusal to assist landlords ruined by famine. In 1870 the price was equality before the law for Catholic, Episcopalian and Presbyterian, and for landlord and tenant. But it still remained for England to restate the terms of the relationship between the two countries. Repeal had failed. Fenianism was rejected. Would any Irish formula succeed in modifying the Union? A new one first mentioned in 1870 as a reaction against Gladstone provoked among Irish Tories a movement for Home Rule within the United Kingdom. Unexpectedly, it was to win new support for Irish nationalism.

7
Ireland in the Community of Britain:
Home Rule, 1870—1916

HOME RULE for Ireland within the United Kingdom was a constitutional solution unembarrassed by associations with O'Connell's Repeal movement. The idea began to become popular from about 1870, and it attracted considerable support in Ireland. Ultimately it was adopted by the British Liberal party and a Home Rule Act was passed, though suspended, at the beginning of the Great War in 1914. The period of Home Rule properly ended by the time the case for modification of the Union had been accepted by the United Kingdom parliament. This was the situation in 1916, but the idea of implementing Home Rule collapsed in the aftermath of the Irish rebellion in that year. All future negotiations between the two countries were based on a general acceptance that a new situation had been created. The nationalist community of Ireland came to be moved by plans to repeal the Union, and even to establish Ireland as a self-governing dominion in the British Commonwealth, or as a separate republic. From the standpoint of the ordinary citizen of the United Kingdom in 1870, however, such developments out of Home Rule were quite unforeseeable.

The period from 1870 to the Great War has been described as one in which revolution spread from Europe to the world at large. At the beginning of the period the commune took control in Paris after the defeat of Napoleon III by Prussia, but its success was short-lived. Less transient was Bismarck's establishment of the German empire under the Hohenzollern dynasty of Prussia. It survived until 1918. The imperial and

13

colonial ambitions of European states led to considerable expansion overseas, in Asia, Australia and Africa, but reactions also showed themselves during these years. Revolution had begun nearly a century earlier in America; and European projects to aid Spain and Portugal to recover their lost American colonies, together with new colonial threats from France and Russia, led to the enunciation by the United States of its Munroe doctrine, which threatened retaliation against European countries attempting to recover lost American possessions as early as in 1823. Plans for retaliation on Europe had particularly touched the United Kingdom; and British sympathy for the confederate states in the American civil war gave rise to the schemes of Irish-American Fenians to win Canada and Ireland from England.

The Home Rule movement in Ireland began among a few Irish Tories as a protest against Gladstone's prescription for justice in the country: disestablishment, dual land ownership and extended university education. Home Rule at first was essentially a movement among the Dublin Protestant intelligentsia; and in 1866 neither Gladstone nor Cardinal Cullen, as the Archbishop of Dublin was to become, believed it had any political future. However, dissatisfaction with the Liberal Prime Minister's Irish policy, as it worked out in practice, quickly extended among Liberals in Ireland; and the majority of them unexpectedly adopted Home Rule as a political policy at the election of 1874. The result was that out of 105 Irish members elected to parliament in that year, some 60 supported the idea of Home Rule.

The defeat in 1873 of his Irish Universities Bill had left Gladstone resentful and regretful of his involvement with Irish affairs. Gladstone and Cullen were both cynical with regard to Home Rule, but Gladstone's government developed serious reservations about Cullen and the Irish bishops. The defeat of the Irish Universities Bill was particularly irritating, since a number of Irish Liberal Catholic MPs went into the lobby against the government, which had been assured that the bill would satisfy the hierarchy. In the

1870s Gladstone was not prepared to go beyond committing British liberalism to justice for Ireland. Self-government in its various phases, federal Home Rule, devolution of certain powers to an Irish body of some kind, or independence was only to be taken seriously by British parties after 1880.

The defeat of Gladstone in the general election of 1874 permanently weakened the position of the Irish Catholic clergy in politics. They retained considerable influence as auxiliaries and advisers to Irish members and Irish parties, but this influence was subordinate to that of the idea of Home Rule and that of organisations working to achieve self-government. However, the adoption of Home Rule by Catholic nationalists during the election impelled suspicious Protestants to condemn the project in spite of Cullen's disapproval and declare that 'Home Rule means Rome Rule'.

Isaac Butt, the leader of the Irish Home Rule movement and a former Tory politician, was primarily concerned to work out a compromise between republican Fenians and English liberal reformers. Besides a number of disgruntled Liberals and Conservatives, his followers included some old-fashioned constitutional nationalists who looked back to the 1840s, some supporters of land reform, some mellowed Fenians and some who were campaigning for an amnesty of the prisoners of 1865–67. Butt himself was an eccentric barrister who had opposed O'Connell on Repeal but had defended the Fenians in the treason prosecutions of the 1860s. He had become involved in the amnesty movement, which sought the release of Fenians sentenced to long-term servitude. He was also interested in the movement for tenant right, and was the author of an able pamphlet which was believed to have influenced Gladstone in favour of adopting dual ownership of land by tenant and landlord as the basis of the Land Act of 1870.

Butt proposed that Ireland be given a legislature for domestic affairs. Unlike the pre-Union Irish parliament it would be subordinate to Westminster; 'Home Rule', therefore, implied abandoning Repeal. Fenian extremists after 1870 found Butt's plan attractive, both because Cardinal Cullen opposed it and because it was preferable to Cullen's National Association, which appeared to them to be aiming at a Catholic national party for Ireland, similar to the one which already existed in Belgium. Accordingly, both Cullen's clerical nationalism and Gladstone's liberalism were rejected as inadequate by adherents of Butt's movement. Some moderate Fenians, or members of the Irish Republican Brotherhood as they were beginning to be known in Ireland, gave Butt their qualified support. The revolutionaries, or nationalists as they liked to call themselves in support of their exclusive claims to that name, agreed not to stand in the way of Home Rule for some three or four years, in the expectation that Butt's belief in the English parliament would be fulfilled. Butt argued that Tories as well as Whigs would give way if the case for an Irish parliament under that of the United Kingdom were cogently and rationally presented at Westminster.

The upholders of the old traditions of Irish self-government, revolutionary and constitutional, were united only in an uneasy truce, however. Furthermore, the Home Rulers in the election of 1874 agreed to keep the question of land reform separate, so as to avoid any commitment which might alienate the landlords in their movement. These men regarded the 1870 Land Act as a final settlement with tenant farmers, although Butt himself remained closely involved with the demand for tenant security, since many landlords could still evade the act and evict their tenants on technical breaches of the law. It was under Butt that the Home Rulers carried 60 seats in the election of 1874. They won several remarkable victories, notably in Kerry where their opponent was supported by the Catholic bishop, David Moriarty.

Disraeli's return to office after the election inaugurated a period of five years during which Irish affairs were given scant consideration. To his disappointment, Butt got no

British support either for Home Rule or a further advance on land reform. Gradually his party began to disintegrate and most of his supporters veered towards the Liberals. The land issue alienated the few Home Rule landlords and Butt himself ceased to be an effective leader. Only on the education question could the Irish party claim success, and that on a limited scale. The institution of a new examining body, the Royal University of Ireland, made it possible for the government indirectly to endow Catholic colleges, which could thus provide education leading to university degrees.

Butt's failure to achieve much success at Westminster provoked a number of radical nationalists to look elsewhere for leadership, and ultimately they settled on Charles Stuart Parnell. Parnell, a young Wicklow landowner, was one of a handful of Home Rule M.P.s who were actively obstructing parliamentary business. The ex-revolutionaries considered that he would prove more effective in the future, and possibly be easier to deal with, than the elderly Butt.

By this time the Irish revolutionaries had become divided. Some, influenced by the exiled John O'Leary, opposed any co-operation with constitutionalists. In America, however, a number of *emigré* Irish journalists, notably Patrick Ford, attacked the Irish landlords as being the most destructive element in Irish society. Another journalist, John Devoy, who had settled in America after his release from penal servitude for Fenian activities, set up the Clan na Gael organisation early in the 1870s, to provide a link with effective revolutionaries in Ireland. Devoy's intention was to acquire a group of Home Rulers as a constitutional front, and he came to the conclusion that Parnell was likely to be most influential for this purpose. Another amnestied Fenian resident in Ireland, Michael Davitt, was determined, like Ford, to uproot the landlords. Davitt believed that a land league led by some constitutionalists in parliament would give tenants effective security against any renewed threats of eviction. Devoy and Davitt came to work together, and later won Parnell for this 'new departure' in Irish politics.

In the 1870s bad weather and financial depression provoked a new agricultural crisis. To many tenant farmers it portended a repetition of the famine and another round of clearances by the landlords. In 1878 Butt, who had publicly admonished Parnell for obstructing parliamentary business in retaliation for the government's neglect of Ireland, had the mortification of seeing the more active man elected in his place as president of the Home Rule Confederation of Great Britain. In October 1878 Parnell was publicly offered support from America by John Devoy, on condition that a demand for self-government would substitute that for federalism or Home Rule. In addition, agitation would be started in favour of peasant ownership. Sectarian issues would be avoided and an aggressive policy would be pursued in parliament on all imperial and Home Rule issues. Struggling nationalities in the British Empire and elsewhere would be supported.

Parnell, however, was in no position to accept Devoy's terms, and he carefully avoided any public comment. Indeed he was so unpopular with the majority of the Home Rule party that he was lucky to survive a move to expel him from it altogether.

Meanwhile it was Davitt who took up the land question. In his native Mayo, in April 1879, a protest meeting on an estate administered by a priest successfully defeated the intended eviction of a tenant and secured reductions in rent. Archbishop MacHale, whose diocese was affected, condemned the decision to hold a further meeting in June at Westport, at which Parnell had agreed to speak. But Parnell honoured his obligation, and MacHale subsequently welcomed him at Tuam. Parnell, however, resisted pressure from Davitt during the summer of 1879 to join the Mayo Land League, a semi-socialist body which never got off the ground. But by October great public interest had been aroused and the National Land League was established, with Parnell as president and Davitt as secretary. This body decided to seek money from America in order to finance a campaign to win a permanent interest for tenants in their farms. Such a measure would have altered the structure of Irish land-holdings fundamentally. Parnell went to the United States on behalf of the National Land League in December, and he was careful to set up the American Land League as a distinct body and not to commit himself publicly to Devoy or any Fenian organisation. His tour was remarkably successful in terms of prestige and finance, and he had the almost unique honour for a visitor of addressing Congress.

There was a sprinkling of priests on the committee of the National Land League and Archbishop Croke of Cashel had privately indicated that he was favourable to it. Since Cullen's death in 1878 the monolithic structure of the Irish hierarchy had disintegrated. Equally invisible as Croke's support for the Land League was that of Clan na Gael, the Irish-American revolutionary organisation largely controlled by John Devoy. This alliance between parliamentarians and moderate revolutionaries, Irish and American, has been called the New Departure. Parnell, Davitt and Devoy were its three architects.

The dramatic circumstances of agricultural crisis in which the Land League was founded led Lord Beaconsfield, as Disraeli had become, in reward for having Queen Victoria proclaimed Empress of India, to dissolve parliament in March 1880. He raised the cry that the Union was being endangered by the Parnellite movement. Disraeli's words may have been prophetic, but they did not stir the British electors in 1880 into returning the Conservatives to office. In Ireland Home Rulers again won about sixty seats. Nominally the Land League took no part in the election; in fact, however, Parnellites fought and defeated some outstanding Home Rulers who were inimical to the League.

In Britain the election resulted in a defeat for the Conservatives. Gladstone made a comeback from retirement to campaign against Disraeli's imperialism, and he became Prime Minister once again in April 1880. But the problems of the empire seemed greatest at its eastern perimeter, and

Ireland occupied no space in the queen's speech to parliament, in which the new government's legislative programme was outlined.

Subsequent events demonstrated how remarkable was Parnell's political genius. Butt had died the previous year, and the Irish party was left leaderless. Parnell's supporters successfully postponed the election of a chairman of the Irish party for the new session of parliament until after Gladstone's policy was announced. Since the queen's speech seemed to indicate that the government had nothing new to offer on Ireland, Parnell arranged for the introduction of a bill dealing with the vital issue of compensation for evicted tenants. The debate on the Irish party's restricting landlords' rights of eviction convinced Gladstone that it should be taken up by the government. This won to Parnell's side the majority of the Home Rulers and he was elected sessional chairman of the party. It was Parnell's achievement that the Irish question should dominate not merely the beginning of that session but the whole of the 1880s, and end in the adoption of Home Rule by Gladstone himself.

After their defeat the Tories, relying on Liberal landlord support, reverted to the policy of the 1830s and overwhelmed Gladstone's land bill in the House of Lords. Parnell then launched a campaign to rouse Ireland and demonstrate the magnitude of the crisis in the tenant's precarious position. Within a year the Lords were forced to endorse a more drastic Land Act for Ireland, which established a judicial court for tenants by fixing their rents and guaranteeing them compensation for disturbance by landlords. This remarkable change in twelve months was brought about by Parnell's effective organising and disciplining of the Land League and by his use of public meetings to whip up Irish public opinion against the landlords.

Gladstone, however, was determined to coax his right wing by reintroducing coercion while mollifying his left and the Irish with his more comprehensive land measure. But his decision to revert to coercion was petty and short-sighted.

It paralysed Parnell's efforts to control extremists. The Land Act was more promising. It established a court to fix rents but, as Parnell saw, much depended on preventing a stampede of tenants into the court. He advised tenants to test the act, arguing that a few critical cases would result in the general acceptance of substantial reductions in rents by landlords. Gladstone decided that Parnell's advice was an incitement to intimidate the authorities. In October 1881 he gave way to Dublin Castle's advice and declared the Land League illegal, and imprisoned its supporters among the M.P.s Parnell himself was sent to Kilmainham jail.

Six months later, however, wisdom dictated a change of policy. In the Kilmainham Treaty, as it was euphemistically called, Parnell and Gladstone made an informal secret agreement: the one would drop coercion and the other agitation among the tenants. Unfortunately, the assassination of the new Chief Secretary, Lord Frederick Cavendish, and of the Under-Secretary, Thomas Burke, by an extremist group, in May 1882, led the government to reimpose coercion. Parnell, however, kept his side of the bargain and turned from the land question to the more general one of self-government. By the middle of the 1880s his following had grown substantially and his party secured the return of eighty-six M.P.s in the election of 1886.

Parnell had so extended his influence over the party as to make it the most effective political group at Westminster. Ultimately he was able to dictate to Gladstone and to Disraeli's successor as leader of the Conservatives, Lord Salisbury, the circumstances in which he would support or oppose them in the House of Commons. In 1885 he drove out Gladstone, largely over the Liberal government's attitude to coercion; in 1886 he did the same with Salisbury on the same issue.

Parnell next converted Gladstone to Home Rule, while the Liberals were in opposition. The Liberal leader, probably the most widely-read statesman in contemporary England, came to the conclusion that the future of England depended upon conceding self-government to Ireland, or at least self-government within the United Kingdom.

Gladstone's decision to campaign for Home Rule profoundly affected Anglo-Irish relations. The admission by one of Britain's greatest parliamentarians that justice demanded accepting the right of Ireland to self-government could have brought about a rapport between Britain and Ireland had Gladstone's opponents taken a similar view. Indeed, among the Conservatives there had always been some who were sympathetic towards Ireland. In 1885, when he became Prime Minister, Salisbury appointed Lord Carnarvon as the new Irish viceroy, and Carnarvon discussed with Parnell the possibility of governing Ireland without coercion and of granting the country a measure of self-government. But Carnarvon was the only Home Ruler in the cabinet. Conservatives in general tended to resist political structure; they were heirs to the seventeenth-century Tories, the party of the monarchy and of Anglicanism. They were also heirs to the Whigs, the party of the great landed proprietors of the early eighteenth century. The Liberals were heirs to another Whig element, concerned with reform of government and destruction of monopolies and corrupt vested interests. They also embraced the radicals, who were looking for a better England and greater prosperity. In a sense Gladstone's conversion to Home Rule was out of step with Liberal trends, since he was calling in question the validity of the existing state and so going against the Liberal role in world civilisation.

The defeat of Salisbury in the election of January 1886 returned Gladstone to power and provided him with the opportunity to introduce his Home Rule Bill later in that year. The measure was modest enough. It reserved certain services to the United Kingdom parliament and proposed to set up a domestic legislature for Ireland. Parnell accepted Gladstone's bill and thus undoubtedly set limits to the plans of the Irish leader who had hitherto avoided any definition of Home Rule. It seems that he would have been content with the federal proposals of Butt. Parnell had every reason to feel that a final settlement confined to domestic issues was as much as the community of Ireland could achieve, even assuming that Gladstone was able to convince the Westminster parliament. Moreover the Catholic clergy, with few exceptions, were prepared to support Home Rule, and even if extremists stood out in America, he was supported by a tolerably efficient organisation there under John Devoy, which regularly supplied him with the essential finances to keep his organisation in trim.

The debate on the Home Rule Bill in the House of Commons, however, revealed that in his anxiety to settle the Irish question, Gladstone had split his own party. The Conservative element under Lord Hartington and the prosperous radical wing under Joseph Chamberlain combined with Salisbury to oppose the bill and to defeat it. Hartington led the majority of the remaining Whig magnates who were against entrusting the control of Irish affairs to the Irish middle class. Chamberlain directed a group which feared the continued decline of Britain's commercial empire. He would have agreed to granting Ireland powers of local administration similar to those enjoyed by his native city of Birmingham, but not to setting up a parliament which would inevitably develop increasing powers of self-government, to the detriment of British prosperity.

Once the Conservatives had decided to oppose Home Rule it was easy for them to give in to the temptation to rouse Ulster, the only area of Conservative strength in Ireland. As the Home Rule party grew in Ireland it was from the Irish Liberals and not from the Conservatives that it won its electoral victories. But the Liberals also lost to the Conservatives in the appeals to old sectarian prejudices. That 'Home Rule is Rome Rule' might only be credible to simple-minded Ulster Protestants, but it certainly won for the Conservatives the votes of those who suspected Liberals of being contaminated with Romanist associations; and every Ulster Protestant knew that in any case the vast majority of Home Rulers were 'papishes'.

When Randolph Churchill declared, as part of the Conservative campaign against the bill: 'the Orange card will be the one to play' he was advising Irish Conservatives to lead from strength. Gladstone's case for Home Rule was that nothing else would satisfy the Irish, but the weakness of the argument, as Churchill appreciated, was the simplistic equation of Home Rulers with all the Irish.

There was another potential source of Conservative strength. After the Land Act of 1881 Lord Derby had observed that the last common ground for social discontent between Irish Protestants and Catholics had disappeared. The Act set up courts to which Ulster tenants, like those of any other province, could turn to fix their rents and establish their customary rights. After 1881 no organisation could have offered much more to the Ulster tenant-farmer; only a new material argument might have re-established the link of Sharman Crawford's day. The case against Home Rule seemed a strong one; so close were the industrial links between Ulster and Britain that Home Rule might well jeopardise Ulster's prosperity. Furthermore, after the Kilmainham Treaty the case for Home Rule was increasingly presented in terms of romantic nationalism, and it was easy to counter this in Belfast by 'playing the Orange card'.

The debate on the Home Rule Bill in the House of Commons was notable for some remarkable speeches, including Gladstone's. His colleague, W. V. Harcourt, pointed out that the strength of Irish exiles in America meant that it was unrealistic ever again to hope to crush Irish revolution at home. Randolph Churchill raised the issue of the Protestant community, particularly in Ulster. Stirringly he declared that Ulster would fight and Ulster would be right. Thereafter the Conservatives enlarged themselves into the Unionist party; they became committed against Home Rule and against the cause of Irish resistance to separation from Britain. Parnell, also in a memorable speech, accepted the bill as a final settlement, but even this failed to prevent its defeat in the Commons.

The defeat of Home Rule was followed by virtually twenty years of Unionist government, although the Liberal Unionists did not actually join the Conservatives in office until 1895. At first, Salisbury, as Prime Minister, and Arthur Balfour, as Chief Secretary, made efforts to intimidate the nationalists, by strict police activity and by prosecutions and imprisonment. The nationalists in turn brought the land tenants' issue back into play. A 'plan of campaign' was devised by which tenants were to be organised against landlords who resisted reductions in rent at a time when the fall in profits from the crop market was making it insupportable for tenants to pay approved rents. If tenants were refused reductions the plan was that they would pay the landlords nothing, and the agreed rent would be put into a fund until the matter was resolved. At least one section of the Irish parliamentary party, which, however, at first did not include Parnell, sponsored the campaign in order to secure effective improvements for the tenants from an unsympathetic government. This plan created centres of disturbance which the government found it difficult to suppress, and it resorted to coercion.

In addition to using coercion the government entered into secret negotiations with the Vatican in order to bring the Irish to heel. Through the Duke of Norfolk and other diplomatic representatives, the Vatican was induced to condemn the Plan of Campaign, and the practice of boycotting in particular. The views of Cardinal Manning of Westminster had for long been influential in Rome. Pro-Irish as he insisted he was, Manning did not favour any solution to Anglo-Irish problems which would remove the only Catholic representatives from Westminster. Manning, however, carried less weight at Rome than was generally believed. The appointment of William Walsh, President of Maynooth, to the archbishopric of Dublin in 1885, showed that the Holy See could accept an Irish recommendation against the known preferences of English interests for Patrick Francis Moran, Archbishop of Sydney, the cousin and former secretary of Cardinal Cullen. The pope's condemnation of the Plan of Campaign, however, created serious misapprehensions between clergy and people. After Gladstone's conversion to Home Rule many of the Irish clergy felt justified in identifying themselves publicly with the national cause. Rome's fulmination, therefore, came as a deep disappointment to them, and to Archbishops Croke and Walsh as well.

In 1887 the government became involved in a campaign against Parnell, which opened with a series of articles in the London *Times* entitled *Parnellism and Crime*. These articles were partly based on forged evidence provided by Richard Pigott, an ex-nationalist journalist, alleging that Parnell had agreed with the assassination of Burke and Cavendish in 1882. At this point, the government tried to bring about the fall of the Irish leader, but the enquiry which followed, and the sensational collapse and subsequent suicide of Pigott, only enhanced Parnell's reputation and helped to establish between Home Rulers and Liberals a 'union of hearts' which virtually made one party of the two. The Home Rule movement was thereafter regarded by most British Liberals as being undoubtedly law-abiding. Nevertheless suspicion of Parnell's and Davitt's association with extreme elements was not entirely unfounded, and the enquiry converted both men to a more moderate attitude, until Parnell, in his last years, turned once more towards the extremists, and became for Patrick Pearse in the next century a quasi-evangelist of Irish independence.

The negative policy of coercion and imprisonment taken up by Salisbury's government did not represent the total Conservative contribution to the maintenance of the Union. Under Balfour and later Chief Secretaries proposals for land purchase were carried through, so that early in the next century ownership of the overwhelming mass of land in Ireland was transferred to the tenants, and the landlord system, established more than two centuries earlier in the plantations by James 1 and by Cromwell, came to an end. The Unionists were also to introduce a measure of local government, in 1898, resulting in the establishment of county councils throughout the country. Finally, some of their supporters in Ireland, particularly Sir Horace Plunkett, organised a co-operative movement in agriculture towards the end of the century which proved extremely beneficial, particularly to the dairy industry.

To Nationalists, however, the Unionists could do no right, and Captain William O'Shea's initiation of divorce proceedings against his wife in 1890, in which Parnell was named as co-respondent, was attributed to Unionist machinations. This unlikely suspicion grew among Parnell's supporters, particularly after the Irish party split over the continuance of his leadership. Parnell found himself reduced to a handful of followers and opposed by the majority of his former lieutenants. The dethronement of the 'uncrowned King of Ireland', as Parnell's supporters liked to call him, created many crosscurrents in the political situation: Parnell attacked Gladstone for saying he was not prepared to continue leading the Liberals if he did not retire as Irish leader, and he challenged him to state the terms of a future Liberal Home Rule Bill.

From a Unionist viewpoint, Parnell's deposition diminished the difficulties of dealing with Home Rule. After his fall, the Irish concentrated on in-fighting with characteristic intensity. At Westminster they gave little trouble, and in America financial support for the Irish National League virtually dried up. In effect, the education of Irish nationalists in constitutional activity had sustained a reverse. Parnellism, defeated in the vast majority of elections, became linked with extremism. The Irish bishops, in throwing their weight against Parnell, deepened the division between the extreme nationalists and the clergy. This was to leave the Church in Ireland with scant influence on the forces of revolution in the twentieth century, a surprising development considering its important role in the nineteenth-century national movement.

After Parnell's death in 1891, exhausted in his titanic struggle against his enemies, the anti-Parnellite majority in the Irish party depended for survival on Gladstone and the bishops, and the question of whether the Irish party would have an independent future or become subordinate to the Liberals inevitably followed. Even if Gladstone succeeded in inducing the House of Commons to pass a second Home Rule Bill, it was not likely that the Lords would give way. When he returned to power in 1892, the aged Gladstone did introduce his second Home Rule Bill (1893), only to see it defeated as expected by the House of Lords. After Gladstone's retirement as leader of the Liberals the forces of imperialism seemed triumphant. His successor, Lord Rosebery, declared emphatically that he was in no way committed to Home Rule. This was a last effort to bring back to the Liberal party the conservative and radical wings which had defected from Gladstone in the preceding decade. Rosebery remained in office only for a brief period, and the Unionists returned to power in 1895, this time reinforced in the Cabinet by leading Liberal Unionists, and they remained in office for more than ten years.

With the Irish parliamentary party hopelessly divided, the future of an Irish political community seemed remote. But a variety of other interests developed, even before the reunion of the divided parliamentarians under John Redmond in 1900, and they added further dimensions to articulate Irish culture. The whole idea of an Irish renaissance, as W. B. Yeats wrote in one of his early works, was emerging in 'the unshaped image of reborn Ireland'. After 1900 these new movements transformed the various interpretations of cultural tradition, and out of them a new concept of the community developed.

The nineteenth century witnessed one remarkable change in the international position as far as Ireland was concerned. An Irish Race Convention was held in Dublin in 1896, and provided evidence, among many ephemeral indications of passing trivialities, of the belief of public opinion in the existence of Ireland as a cultural entity. A hundred years earlier such a convention would have been unthinkable.

Disillusionment with the Irish parliamentary party's squabbles over Parnell, and resentment at its assumed monopoly of national culture resulted in the growth of the literary renaissance. Yeats became its most notable figure, and he subsequently described it as his opportunity to be associated with the shaping of modern Ireland. The veteran Fenian, John O'Leary, also became one of the renaissance's foremost literary figures at the end of the nineteenth century, and he had a direct influence on the poetic development of the younger Yeats. James Joyce, in his writings, evoked the feeling for Parnell among some of the Dublin middle class who had a degree of sympathy for revolution and perhaps even for Fenianism.

The Gaelic League was started by Eoin MacNeill and Douglas Hyde in 1893. In the next two generations this organisation was to achieve much success in reviving popular interest in Gaelic culture and the Irish language. To MacNeill in particular it was an important step on the road to Irish self-government, since Gaelic literature and late eighteenth-century writings had immortalised the old Fenians. Moreover, recent German discoveries had shown that Irish was one of the oldest living languages in Europe, and this kind of information had a propagandist value in the political struggle over Home Rule and in the great debate about whether Ireland had any history before Britain came to civilise her. Other supporters of the Gaelic League, notably Hyde, were more concerned with Irish as the language still used by a substantial part of the peasantry in the West. They considered that their culture deserved to be rescued before it was destroyed by the insidious encroachment of English. The language movement with which the Gaelic League was particularly concerned attracted many who were repulsed by what they saw as a trend of vulgarity in modern life. These included some Catholic priests, who believed that the revival of Irish would act as a resistant force to foreign immoral influences.

The Gaelic movement was rejected by anglicised scholars

14

who sensed in it a discounting of their own cultural values. About the time of the Boer War a national controversy emerged over the educational value of Gaelic literature. The Gaelic League marshalled testimony for its case from international scholars and succeeded in defeating the effort to exclude Irish from the public examinations of secondary schools. Perhaps the most remarkable achievement of the Gaelic movement was on the eve of the Great War, when it carried its victory in the education controversy a step further, by having Irish made a compulsory subject for entrance to the new National University of Ireland.

Three significant elements in Irish society, the unionist, socialist and revolutionary, were affected by the expansion which was taking place in the idea of the community. Unionist opposition to Home Rule underwent a certain change, leading to an admission that Ireland was a separate cultural entity. Though some Unionists may have denied this, the historian Lecky had been attracted to nationalism in Isaac Butt's time. His *Leaders of Public Opinion in Ireland*, first published before the Fenian rising, was a survey of the movement for self-government in association with Britain from the beginning of the eighteenth century. To Lecky, the community of Ireland had endorsed the policies of four men in particular: Swift, Flood and Grattan in the eighteenth century, and O'Connell in the nineteenth. By 1870, when the second edition of his book appeared, Lecky's ideas were close to those of Butt. Lecky, however, never actually adopted Home Rule, and as one of the landed class was subsequently to deplore the association of the movement for Irish self-government with the Land League. Ultimately he emerged as a Unionist member of parliament. Another Unionist historian, Richard Bagwell, also favoured a view of some form of Irish distinctiveness. Lady Gregory and Eleanor Hull had similar outlooks, but they were more interested in culture than in politics.

The socialist approach to the Irish community was perhaps best represented in the writings of James Connolly, who in

1898 produced the first issue of his newspaper *The Workers'
Republic*. He later incorporated his Marxist views in his book
Labour in Ireland. Connolly fancied the notion that Gaelic
Ireland had been a Marxist Utopia. This idea was stimulated
by the Gaelic movement's propaganda, and much of its
investigation of Gaelic literature and history, but it was
effectively demolished by MacNeill's objective studies in
early Irish history.

The revolutionary element emerged from the underground
in time to influence the public celebrations of the centenary
of the Rising of 1798. 1898 saw simultaneous outbreaks of
imperialism and republicanism, the first in the rise of jingoist
feeling in Britain which culminated in the Boer War, the
second in the centenary celebrations of the rebellion.
Support for the Boer War among Unionists created, in
reaction, a substantial degree of support for Irish nationalism.
The spirit of republicanism began to take courage and revive,
to secure more following and popularity. The Parnellite split,
the appeal of the dying chief to the forces of revolution, the
savage attacks on his reputation by the respectable elements
in Irish society and by the enemies of revolution had together
created an atmosphere more favourable to extreme men. The
greater depth in Irish cultural investigation of the past, the
Gaelic League, the revival at home and abroad of an interest
in indigenous nationalism, the development of the Gaelic
Athletic Association, all helped to question and to challenge
the Tory contention that Ireland's grievances were essentially material and that the demand for self-government was
hypocritical and unreal.

The complex situation at the end of the nineteenth century
can also be regarded in terms of the appearance of compromisers between political rivals, particularly among the
nationalists. The compromisers between revolutionary and
parliamentary nationalism included the veteran Duffy of
Young Ireland, now Sir Charles Gavan Duffy, the retired
Australian statesman who had returned to Europe. His
literary works stimulated interest in the comparable period

which followed the death of that other great leader, O'Connell. The most notable of the compromisers, however, was Arthur Griffith, who in 1899, the year after the centenary of the '98 rebellion, published the first number of his news-paper the *United Irishman*. Griffith endeavoured to organise a new political group which would be more attached to the revolutionary tradition, while still remaining constitutional and perhaps even monarchical.

The compromisers between unionism and nationalism, such as Yeats and Hyde, were clearly looking to the living tradition of the community. But for some of them, particul-arly Yeats, there emerged a double allegiance, to Ireland as an entity and to Ireland in association with Britain.

Sir Horace Plunkett, the Unionist originator of the co-operative movement, published his book, *Ireland in the New Century*, in an attempt to work out a compromise gospel for a self-reliant Ireland detached from politics. Plunkett was critical of the excessive influence of the Roman Catholic clergy in the country. He was answered at length by Mon-signor Michael O'Riordan in another new nationalist periodical, *The Leader*, established by David Moran at the time of Redmond's election as leader of the reunited Irish parliamentary party in 1900.

The rule of Ireland by Conservative governments between 1895 and 1905, first under Salisbury and then under his nephew, Arthur Balfour, might have gone far to win Ireland from revolution. Stimulated by their Liberal Unionist allies, and particularly by Joseph Chamberlain, the Conservatives pressed forward with two measures of Irish reform, land purchase and local government, which were reluctantly accepted by Tories generally. Successive Unionist land purchase acts terminated the Irish experiment in dual landownership. Both in this and in the Local Government Act, the Unionist administration encouraged the remnants of the upper class to maintain a more realistic and entrenched position in Irish society. Except in the north, they were mainly unsuccessful. Coercion had done its work too well, for it permanently divided nationalists from unionists in Ireland. After the local government act of 1898 few Unionists were returned at local elections outside Ulster. Through the co-operative movement in dairy farming and other rural enter-prises, Plunkett tried to encourage self-sufficiency, but the results were disappointing.

Twenty years of virtually continuous Conservative firm government carried their own verdict when a Unionist project to devolve certain powers of local administration on an Irish body was condemned by their own party in 1904. Any suggestion of a central Irish democratic legislature, no matter how limited, could not be considered; the experience of the new system of local government had shown it would be used for the benefit of Home Rulers and Liberals. The end of the century saw a decline in constitutionalism. It had begun with Randolph Churchill's rousing of Ulster Protest-antism against Home Rule and the implied defiance of law and order by the Unionists. In the last years of Conservative government nationalist extremists began to turn to the same idea.

In the years before the return of the Liberals to power in 1905 Griffith's compromise movement, *Sinn Féin,* meaning 'ourselves', secured some attention from public opinion, largely because of the controversies in which Griffith became involved. His *Resurrection of Hungary,* published in 1904, argued in favour of a dual monarchy in the United Kingdom, on the analogy of the Austro-Hungarian empire in Central Europe. Griffith's object was also Home Rule, but he quarrelled with the parliamentary party's policy of alliance with the Liberals, allegedly as the Young Irelanders had dissociated themselves from O'Connell's alliance with the Whigs in the 1840s. Griffith's gospel of self-help and self-sufficiency stimulated more attention as potentially offering a practical alternative to the relatively moribund parlia-mentary party, which was virtually committed to supporting the Liberals even before their return to office. In the realm of real politics, however, no alternative to Redmond's party emerged. Redmond was sufficiently powerful to secure public endorsement for his view that the Liberals could be relied on to secure Home Rule if the government was given the chance to paralyse its opponents constitutionally. His party was well entrenched in the country, thanks to the operation of the Local Government Act and the success of its supporters at local elections. In 1905 the revolutionaries began to establish 'Dungannon Clubs' as a radical front for their treasonable activities, but their following in crude numbers was probably much below that of Griffith's organisation. Even this had ceased to be a serious political threat to Redmond after the defeat of a Sinn Féin candidate in a by-election in 1908.

It was only in matters of national pride that the extremists carried the day. A proposal to establish an Irish Council to co-ordinate Irish local counties' administration was put forward by the Liberal government of Campbell-Bannerman in 1907. It was rejected by a convention of Redmond's United Irish League in Dublin, despite the provisional approval of the proposal by the parliamentary party. This rejection followed the Unionist repudiation of Lord Dunraven's comparable scheme of devolution which had been proposed to Balfour's government three years earlier an as alternative to a Home Rule parliament. The Irish Unionist had rebuffed Dunraven's proposals as smacking too much of self-government. If the Liberals' Irish Councils' Bill smacked too much of mere devolution of local powers, it was also rejected because the party was sensitive to criticism by Griffith and the revolutionaries that to accept the measure would amount to a surrender of the claim for Home Rule.

The establishment of two universities in 1908 revealed the undertones of political rivalry in the names selected for the new institutions. In Belfast the foundation of the Queen's University was both a link with Peel's colleges of sixty years earlier and an anticipation of the political separation of Ireland in 1921. The National University of Ireland, on the other hand, derived its title from the determination of the parliamentary party to maintain its claim to monopolise Irish culture as well as avoiding the denominational implications associated with the name of the former Catholic University of Ireland with which Newman had been connected. As time would tell, however, it too was a recognition of the educational partition of Ireland into two spheres of influence, one predominantly Catholic and the other predominantly Protestant.

The years leading up to the Great War of 1914–18 witnessed the dramatic events which led to the collapse of the Home Rule nationalists and the emergence of a new situation after 1916. This period was the Indian Summer of Liberalism: for nearly ten years Unionism was deprived of its position of strength, and it seemed that self-government for Ireland would be achieved at last.

The victory of the Liberals in the election of 1906 had been so overwhelming that they were not dependent on Irish support at Westminster. At first the triumph of the Liberals proved disappointing to Home Rulers. With an overall majority, the governments policy as indicated by the Irish Councils' Bill of 1907 seemed more like the Liberalism of Rosebery than that of Gladstone, although the question of higher education was more satisfactorily resolved.

After Balfour had retired as leader of the Conservative party in 1911, the absence of an outstanding successor gave Irish Unionists the opportunity to organise an effective enclave within the party, and their leader, Edward Carson, trained them as a ginger group to stimulate it. Anticipating the decline of Liberalism under Asquith, who had replaced Campbell-Bannerman as Prime Minister in 1908, the Irish Unionists foresaw the re-emergence of Home Rule in the Liberal party's platform and made resistance to it an essential element in British Unionist strategy. Carson, a highly successful Dublin lawyer with a special talent for breaking down the morale of witnesses, devoted his time to studying the techniques of Parnell in his heyday. Ultimately he was to imitate Parnell and develop an extra-parliamentary, and therefore only quasi-constitutional, movement.

When Asquith's government embarked on a policy of public welfare for the aged, the sick and the unemployed, an increase in taxation became inevitable. The government decided to make provision in the budget for the extension of death duties, a decision which was attacked as allegedly calculated to cut across the capital investments of its opponents. The House of Lords maintained that it was entitled to throw out the budget, which it did, and the conflict between the two great British parties shifted from the issue of Ireland, where it has been fought out from 1886, to the United Kingdom as a whole. In the two general elections of 1910 the Unionist opponents of Home Rule carefully watched their position, fearing that their parliamentary strength would be seriously weakened if the House of Lords should lose its right to veto legislation. At each of these elections the Liberal position weakened preceptibly, so that their dependence on Irish nationalist support became more apparent. In 1911 the government decided to reduce the veto of the Lords on legislation from a permanent to a temporary one of two years. When the third Home Rule Bill was introduced in 1912 it was therefore greeted by the Irish party as the beginning of an irresistible advance to self-government.

In the meantime the Conservative opposition became transformed. The re-emergence of the Irish question provided them once more with an opportunity to appeal to popular Unionist opinion against the Liberals. If the Lords could merely prove a delaying force, it seemed justifiable to make an extra-parliamentary appeal to the forces of British Unionism. With the co-operation of the Conservative leader, Andrew Bonar Law, Carson organised a resistance movement in Ulster which evolved a formula described as the Solemn League and Covenant, in recollection of the Scottish resistance movement of 1638. This was solemnly signed by nearly half a million supporters towards the end of September 1912. British leaders of the Unionist party and upper-class English Unionists were also committed to supporting Ulster's resistance. The government, always slow to involve itself with such an unpopular issue with the British electorate as Ireland, was uneasy about quarrelling again with the Conservatives on a major constitutional issue, and it was easily intimidated by Carson.

An Ulster volunteer force, the first counter-revolutionary army in twentieth-century Europe, was established in 1913. A million pound fund was subscribed and arms were bought in Germany. The volunteer force appealed to tradition, especially to that of the resistance movement which in the 1770s and the 1780s had overawed the government into making concessions. British military association with the upper classes was sufficiently close to lead to the refusal of officers in the Curragh barracks in 1914 to coerce Ulster into accepting Home Rule. The second defeat of the Home Rule Bill by the Lords in 1913 did not worry Redmond's supporters, secure in their belief that the measure would ultimately be successful under the Parliament Act of 1911, which limited the Lords' powers to hold up legislation. More perceptive nationalists, however, aware of negotiations to divide Ireland between Unionists and nationalists, and worried about the fortunes of Home Rule, organised an Irish volunteer movement to counter Carson and to act as an extra-parliamentary support for Home Rule. Following the Ulster example, the nationalists' volunteers sought to import arms from abroad. In addition, in the aftermath of the failure of a great Dublin strike in 1913, trade unionists under Connolly set up an Irish Citizen Army. Thus on the eve of the Great War there existed in Ireland no less than three private armies committed to defending their views, if necessary by force.

Anticipating that Home Rule would be enacted at an early date, Carson decided to set up a Provisional Government of Ulster, which was to take over the province and prevent the transfer of services to the Home Rulers on the passage of the measure into law. To describe the situation in

Ireland as bordering on civil war is an understatement, if anything, to judge from the violent temper of political life: the probability was that civil war might extend to Britain as well.

A proposal to exclude certain counties from the operation of the Home Rule Act was at first rejected. But it secured the support of Asquith's most outstanding lieutenants, Lloyd George and Winston Churchill, after the Curragh mutiny had clearly indicated the opposition to the government which existed among the military class and in the War Office. Towards the end of July 1914 King George v intervened, and invited the Speaker of the House of Commons to organise a conference of rival interests at Buckingham Palace to ascertain the possibilities of compromise. By this time it was clear that the Irish Unionists would accept Home Rule outside of Ulster. But the existence of substantial nationalist majorities in at least three Ulster counties necessitated realistic discussions about possible re-grouping, if a Unionist entity of four or six counties was to be carved out of the province. Ultimately the conference broke down on the eve of the first World War, with everyone except the Redmondites convinced that the government would ultimately give way to Carson, and that his quasi-constitutional Ulster movement had succeeded in forcing partition to be adopted as a compromise to full Home Rule.

The outbreak of the war resulted in Carson's withdrawing the threat of the Ulster Volunteers against the government. This led Redmond to pledge his own volunteer supporters to the struggle against Germany and the central European powers. To Redmond the unexpected war situation was both mortifying, since it led to the postponement of Home Rule, and satisfactory, as it might permit a rapprochement between the rival volunteer forces in the protection of their common country from possible German invasion. Within a short time he successfully pressed the Prime Minister to enact Home Rule, though suspending it for the duration of the war or for one year, which, it was generally considered, was likely to be the longer period. In return, at a volunteer review at Woodenbridge, County Wicklow, he urged the volunteers to go to Flanders and fight for the defence of civilisation in the much denounced uniform of the British army. Almost inevitably his action split the volunteers. Though the vast majority supported him, about one-tenth reorganised under Eoin MacNeill, the originator of the force, who by this time was secretly supported by the revolutionary element led by Thomas Clarke and Patrick Pearse.

Redmond hoped that once the war was over there would be an end to the demand from Ulster counties to opt out of Home Rule. Early in 1915, however, he became seriously perturbed over the formation of a coalition government, involving leading organisers of Ulster Unionist resistance, including Carson himself. Redmond himself refused membership of the coalition ministry, realising that opinion in Ireland and among the Irish in America was becoming increasingly restive at his close co-operation with the old enemy. Nevertheless, the majority of his Irish supporters continued to rely on Redmond absolutely. The Dublin Castle administration, notably the Chief Secretary, Augustine Birrell, and the Under-Secretary Mathew Nathan, frequently consulted him, though both Redmond and his most prominent lieutenant, John Dillon, were careful to see to it that this was done as privately as possible. Their influence was particularly used to induce the government to ignore the provocative behavour of MacNeill's Irish Volunteers.

In the eighteen months which followed Redmond's speech at Woodenbridge, the rival nationalist volunteers openly quarrelled about their attitude to Germany. The minority were more influenced by Carson's attempt to win arms and support from Germany. Formerly they had been prepared to leave the question of war policy to Redmond, but now they insisted that he had no mandate to urge Irishmen to fight outside Ireland. Small as was the element which took this line, it was in the course of time to become extremely significant. Five months before the war broke out, the Irish Americans, and John Devoy in particular, had begun to take an interest in the nationalist volunteer movement. The occasion had been Pearse's visit to New York on a mission to secure funds for his Gaelic school, St Enda's. Devoy and others had persuaded Pearse to become associated with the I.R.B., some of whose members held key positions on the executive of MacNeill's volunteers. The revolutionaries were organising secretly in accordance with their traditional belief that England's involvement in an international war called for another Irish revolutionary outbreak. Devoy endorsed their decision to organise a rising before the war ended. Since he was already involved with Irish and German-Americans to keep the United States out of the war, missions were sent from Ireland to Germany with the assistance of the German Embassy at Washington, and arrangements were made for the transport by submarine of an adequate arms supply to make effective the revolutionary coup.

The views of the radical nationalists were mirrored in their paper *The Irish Volunteer,* which, in November 1914, looked forward to an alliance against Britain of Germany, France and the United States. The government's attempt to step up the war effort by introducing conscription was immediately attacked by the Irish Volunteers. In the summer months of 1915 the Redmondites began to lose with public opinion, which began to veer to the radical nationalists. The revolutionaries selected Pearse to publicise the programme of revolt as far as was possible. At the funeral of the veteran Fenian, Jeremiah O'Donovan Rossa, in August 1915, he defied the government to prohibit commemoration services for Fenian revolutionaries. Pearse's oration at Rossa's funeral was more than an unqualified denunciation of the British attitude towards Ireland; it was a declaration of war by the Irish revolutionaries against England. Pearse ignored Redmond and Home Rule, and asserted that the national tradition of freedom was that of Tone, Mitchel and Rossa; he declared that the Irish Volunteers had been rebaptised in the Fenian faith and concluded that 'Ireland unfree will never be at peace.' Thereafter, in a series of pamphlets, chiefly aimed at the nationalist intelligentsia, he argued the case for separatism, revolution and a sovereign independent state, democratic in organisation.

Tension in Ireland grew after the coalition government decided to introduce a conscription bill. This brought together some of the anti-Redmond forces which did not accept the Rossa funeral oration as representing more than the views of the Pearse element in the Irish Volunteers. In January 1916 Connolly's paper, the *Workers' Republic,* stressed the need for closer association between the Irish Citizen Army and the Irish Volunteers. In March 1915 Griffith's newspaper, *Scissors and Paste,* had been suppressed for reprinting foreign reviews of war conditions which were considered to be derogatory to the allied cause. His new paper, *Nationality,* came closer to the *Irish Volunteer,* which in June 1915 announced the determination of MacNeill's volunteers to resist conscription. From that date meetings against conscription became frequent and so embarrassed the Irish parliamentary party as to lead individual members, including John Dillon, increasingly to express hostility to conscription. The revelation in January 1916 that the conscription bill was not to be extended to Ireland was not enough to ease the situation. Connolly had given public notice of a new attitude and a new alliance linking the Citizen Army to the new purpose of the Irish Volunteers. This carried them both to the idea of expelling the British garrison, with whom they now identified those who had followed Redmond's advice and decided to fight for Ireland under the British flag and in the British uniform.

The revolutionaries in the volunteers tried to win over MacNeill in the hope that they would then have 20,000 men to rely on to rise. The revolutionaries problem, once they had decided on a rebellion, was how to commit the maximum number of volunteers to rise in revolt, without any reference to whether or not they favoured Home Rule, an Irish monarchy or a republic. Since the breach with Redmond after his Woodenbridge speech, MacNeill had moved a considerable distance from the position of merely holding the volunteers for the defence of Ireland. He had accepted it that conscription must be resisted. He had identified himself with the continual drilling and reviewing of the men. British acts of repression, the banning of 'seditious' papers, the arrest and deportation of prominent volunteers convinced the Irish Volunteer executive that the British authorities proposed to disarm their men. MacNeill agreed that this should be resisted, particularly as his friend, Roger Casement, was expected from Germany with the necessary guns for 20,000 men. That disarmament would be attempted was not unlikely, since Unionists were continually urging the suppression of disloyal elements. Redmond and Dillon, however, were influential enough to persuade Asquith and Birrell that there was no need for action; they certainly had no suspicions of any plans for a rising.

Accordingly when alleged plans to arrest and disarm the volunteers were revealed in April 1916, a defensive insurrection became a possibility. MacNeill was persuaded by Pearse and Thomas MacDonagh to sanction 'manoeuvres' coinciding with the expected arrival of the German rifles off the Kerry coast. On the interception of the German aid and the capture of Casement on 22 April, however, Mac-Neill finally countermanded the manoeuvres. But on the following day Connolly forced a decision from his fellow-revolutionaries to rise on Easter Monday, 24 April, on the practical grounds that the British would inevitably act at this juncture. Accordingly positions were taken up by about 1,000 volunteers at the General Post Office and at other strategic points in Dublin at noon on Easter Monday. The theory of a defensive insurrection, however, was abandoned. Instead, a republic was proclaimed in a document signed on behalf of the Provisional Government of Ireland, by Clarke,

Connolly, Eamon Kent, Sean MacDermott, MacDonagh, Pearse and Joseph Plunkett, who formed the military council of the advanced group.

Few Dubliners took much notice of the proclamation, which in any case was couched in a theoretical vein to which they were not accustomed. Fewer still believed that the rebels would win or that their cause could have any future. Rebellions were an anachronism to nationalists schooled for two generations to look for self-government by constitutional means. The occupied buildings in Dublin were held against British government forces for five days until Pearse, as commander-in-chief, ordered their surrender. Destruction by British shell fire had effectively terminated the rising.

The significance of the rising was the unexpected change it brought about in Irish nationalist thinking. A few romantically-minded Redmondites were quickly won over by their appreciation of the heroism of the occasion. But to the Irish party as a whole, and particularly to its political chiefs, it was a cruel blow to their hopes and aspirations. It seemed as if self-government was to be postponed indefinitely. The Irish Unionists were even more condemnatory; to them the rebellion was proof of the treacherousness of the native Irish, and a calculated attempt to defeat England in the greatest crisis of the war. At the beginning of May the War Office could announce that Dublin was quiet, but its representative, Sir John Maxwell, to whom all British authority had been made over, decided to institute military proceedings against his prisoners. Backed by Unionist opinion and, at first, by Redmond, Maxwell decided to try the ringleaders and execute the more prominent. This came more as a shock than as a surprise to nationalist Ireland. From 3 to 12 May fifteen executions were carried out, including all the signatories to the proclamation of the republic. Thereafter, the reaction in public opinion became discernible.

International reaction against imperialism and colonialism was about to emerge with the withdrawal of revolutionary Russia from the war and the entry of the United States into it on the side of Britain, France and their allies. As Europe stood on the brink of world revolution, Maxwell's action in Ireland made an example to many of the small revolutionary element. In Ireland the constitutional nationalist movement had sustained an almost irreversible loss. The methods of parliamentary agitation which had been first ridiculed by Carson had been outmoded by the revolutionaries. It was indeed parliamentarianism, as Dillon's protest against the executions in the House of Commons made clear, which had received its death sentence from the British military authorities. So far as nationalists were concerned, the patriotic leaders depicted by the historian Lecky were now replaced by the evangelists of Pearse, and by Pearse himself and his martyred comrades. After 1916, Home Rule within the United Kingdom would no longer satisfy an Irish majority. But it remained to be seen whether the Unionist minority would win Home Rule for themselves.

8

After 1916: making the world safe
for democracy

THE proclamation of the provisional government of the
Irish Republic contained nothing justifying the rising as a
defensive action by the volunteers, in the event of an attempt
by the British government to disarm them. The proclamation
defended a decision to take to arms primarily as a means to
secure representation for Ireland at the Peace Conference,
which, it was assumed, would be convened in the spring of
1916 by Germany and its supporters—Ireland's 'gallant
allies in Europe'. This was at a date when their victorious
armies seemed likely to terminate the Great War in a matter
of weeks. The volunteers by implication were expected to
hold Ireland, or at least Dublin, until that event.

The rising itself had not broken out until after complicated
negotiations had taken place among its proponents. Eoin
MacNeill was influenced in his decision not to participate in
it by the teaching of Catholic theologians against the law-
fulness of unprovoked rebellion. James Connolly, the Marxist leader of the Citizen Army, had entertained the belief
that England would never destroy the property of Dublin
capitalists and that therefore the volunteers would be in a
position to hold out. In this he was disillusioned, just as he
had been disillusioned at the beginning of the war when he
found workers prepared to fight their brother workers from
other countries at the instance of capitalist governments.
But Connolly's positive influence was to be seen in the proclamation's assertion of the claims of a sovereign people to
control the country's national resources, even if the actual

terminology of 'The Workers' Republic' was avoided.

At the news of the rising, nationalist Ireland on the whole recoiled in horror, with the exception of those who were committed to the extreme volunteer position. The majority of the people, no matter how indifferent to Redmond's campaign in support of recruiting for the British army, had no inkling of any reason for a rising. Nor would it appear, outside of the more uncritical disciples of revolutionary writers during the preceding two generations, that the insistence, in the proclamation, on the necessity to occupy strategic points forcibly, and disarm, if not drive out the British forces, was considered realistic. So far as ordinary Dubliners were concerned, many had neighbours and relatives fighting in Flanders, or perhaps in Gallipoli, and when the captured rebels were marched through the city on their way to prison in England, they were greeted in the streets with jeers and even with stones.

Nationalist Ireland, however, also recoiled at the callousness of the British military commander, Sir John Maxwell, who day after day ordered the executions of leading revolutionaries. The reaction was swift. A few days after the execution of Pearse on 3 May, the House of Commons was electrified by a speech from Redmond's lieutenant, John Dillon, who denounced the sentences and praised the courage of the rebels, who, he said, had inspired him with pride. Since Dillon was in no way connected with the movement, and, indeed, had not opposed Redmond on recruiting, his action was all the more sensational. His speech, however, was in no way emotional; it was instead a calculated effort to galvanise Asquith into stopping the executions. Dillon had every reason to believe that the fortunes of his party were deteriorating rapidly. He had sensed that the rebels were winning the confidence as well as the admiration of ordinary nationalists.

In the spring of 1915 Asquith had reorganised his cabinet, after the majority of Unionists had joined the government in the crisis of the war. In this coalition government Lloyd George was rapidly moving to the top. The great German offensive of 1916 provoked a feeling of grave insecurity on account of the serious losses sustained by the allies on the river Somme. A progressive group within the cabinet felt that it was essential to reinforce the depleted troops at all costs, including extending to Ireland the system of conscription which had just been enacted for England. However, in the atmosphere which developed after the rising and the executions, politicians of both parties quickly realised how difficult it would be even to maintain any recruiting in Ireland, let alone to resort to conscription. Accordingly, after visiting Dublin and Belfast in May 1916 Asquith authorised Lloyd George to conduct conversations with Irish Nationalist and Unionist leaders, including Redmond and Carson, to bring about a return to normal conditions as soon as possible, although in circumstances most conducive to the prosecution of the war.

In fact Lloyd George had already initiated the conversations, and believed it would be possible to get sufficient support to justify the immediate establishment of a Home Rule government, excluding only four Ulster counties. With Redmond as Prime Minister in a Home Rule parliament he hoped that Ireland could be preserved for the United Kingdom, the popularity of the revolutionaries could be arrested, and the campaign for recruiting re-established; perhaps, indeed, Redmond would be sufficiently in control to introduce conscription himself.

The success of Lloyd George in the first instance was remarkable. He won the agreement of Redmond and Carson. The Unionist leader went to Belfast and persuaded the Unionist council to accept the proposals. Redmond succeeded in imposing his views on a convention of his own supporters also at Belfast, though with greater difficulty. Then the unexpected happened. Unionist members of the coalition government declared that Lloyd George's scheme was inoperable, unless the existing military command of Sir John Maxwell were to be maintained, together with the controlling influence exercised over the country by the War Office through the Defence of the Realm Acts.

After these fresh proposals, Redmond withdrew and the scheme collapsed, but the damage to his party was already done. His open consent to partition worked havoc among nationalists of the north, not merely in the four counties to be excluded, but in Tyrone and Fermanagh, whose fate was also in some doubt. Nowhere was the indignation so great as among the northern Catholic clergy. They organised meetings establishing the Irish Nation League in an attempt to preserve the integrity of the thirty-two counties rather than agree to what they regarded as the handing over of the fortunes of Catholics in those areas to bigoted Protestants. As they saw it, Lloyd George's proposals would condemn them once again to the servitude which had existed before O'Connell's day when Ireland had been ruled by the Orange Order. In no part of the nationalist organisation was the Catholic Church so deeply entrenched as in the north, and thereafter Redmond's fortunes were seriously in doubt. He himself however appears to have remained unaware of this, resident as he was in England, and devoted to the progress of Britain's struggle for victory in Flanders, where his son and his brother were fighting against the Germans.

In the autumn of 1916 the Irish Nationalists at Westminster kept up their efforts to induce the government to restore the civil administration, if recruiting in Ireland was to continue. Some of them even urged an amnesty for rebels, or at least for those interned at Frongoch and other camps in Britain, and who had not actually been sentenced to imprisonment. Despite electoral setbacks, the Redmondites were gratified by an unexpected success in a by-election before the end of 1916. In the following year, however, their fortunes were seriously impaired by the successive losses of four seats to men associated with the Dublin rising. So concerned were the nationalist members of parliament at the war front that several of them, including Major W. K. Redmond, the party leader's brother, crossed to Westminster from Flanders to attempt even at that late date to win over the Unionists, particularly the Irish Unionists, to accepting Home Rule.

The subsequent deaths at the front, which included Major Redmond himself, did little to alter the situation, except that they weakened the initiative of the Irish parliamentary leader as the course of the war created greater and greater tensions. Early in 1917 the outbreak of revolution in Russia led to the defeat of her troops and the collapse of the eastern front. Not until the entry of America into the war in April did England and her allies, and the Irish constitutional nationalists, breathe easily again. The withdrawal of Russia and the entry of America enabled the western powers to pose as a democratic block against autocratic Germany and its imperial allies. But so far as the Irish domestic situation was concerned, democracy pointed more to the republican party than to the parliamentary nationalists. Thus election losses appeared for the parliamentary party to be the writing on the wall. Their displacement by the revolutionaries was thus forecasted.

At the same time as these events were taking place, David Lloyd George, who had replaced Asquith as Prime Minister in December 1916, proposed making one further effort to solve the question of Irish self-government, as a prelude to introducing conscription in the country. This was partly an attempt to sweeten the American situation for President T. Woodrow Wilson who, since the executions, was exposed to continual Irish lobbying against Britain in Washington. Accordingly, early in the summer of 1917 Lloyd George announced the establishment of a convention of Irishmen under the presidency of Sir Horace Plunkett. It was represented as an opportunity for Irishmen to settle their own affairs. The Prime Minister had already tried to secure more popularity than had been enjoyed by his predecessor, Asquith, by releasing the unsentenced prisoners and, as a gesture of goodwill for the Convention, he also agreed to release the prisoners serving terms of penal servitude.

The reaction in Ireland was to treat the releases as an endorsement of the policy of defiance; Britain, it was said, gave way only to threats. The third and fourth by-elections lost by the Redmondites were won for the revolutionaries by two of the released 1916 leaders who had been on long-term sentences: Eamon de Valera and William Cosgrave.

The revolutionaries now proposed to hold their own separate convention, supported by the semi-clerical Irish Nation League and by other semi-constitutional bodies critical of the Westminster nationalists, including Griffith's Sinn Féin. From this a new composite party emerged. As the rebellion in the preceding year had been generally, if inaccurately, described as the work of Sinn Féin, the convention party decided to adopt this name, and reorganised the Sinn Féin constitution substantially as a republican one, defiantly linking it to the principles of the proclamation of the rising of 1916. Sinn Féin, however, remained a constitutional body, though it was pledged to withdrawing Irish M.P.s from Westminster. Yet another popular convention, of reorganised national volunteers, was held, to bring together those who had taken part in the rising as well as those who had supported MacNeill or Redmond. At both of these popular conventions de Valera was elected as president. Thereafter the former revolutionary movement was provided with two constitutional facades. Later, when the War Office made the mistake of declaring them illegal, it added to the popular supporters of these new groups most of the recent converts to belief in British justice, now alienated by questionable government tactics. Ironically, such tactics only added to the strength of the extra-parliamentary nationalist movements which had now in de Valera a leader competent to challenge their Westminster rivals and to defeat them, particularly through his effectiveness in propaganda whenever an opportunity arose.

The Plunkett convention despite, or perhaps because of, its official origins, proved abortive. From the beginning it was handicapped by the refusal of either the Ulster Unionists or the new Sinn Féin party to become members of it. Its chance to settle the Irish question was lost when both northern nationalists and unionists opposed a plan for Home Rule for all Ireland which was put forward by Lord Midleton, a Unionist from the south and a former minister for war. His proposals did not contain adequate safeguards to suit either northern element. If Home Rule was not already dead, failure of the Plunkett convention killed the possibility of reviving it.

Immediately afterwards, at the instance of Lloyd George, the government introduced a conscription bill for Ireland. An anti-conscription movement was quickly organised. In April 1918 a conference held at the Mansion House in Dublin was attended by, among others, the parliamentary nationalists. They had left Westminster on the instructions of John Dillon, who had succeeded as party leader after Redmond's death earlier in the year. An appeal to President Wilson drafted by de Valera was preferred by the conference to drafts by former Westminster statesmen. The hierarchy at Maynooth endorsed resolutions against conscription which, according to the bishops, was not morally binding in that particular context. They too therefore agreed to be identified with the national resistance movement. Before the end of April 1918 a one-day strike took place in protest against conscription and was observed everywhere in Ireland except by Unionists. A pledge to resist the recently enacted measure of conscription followed closely the style of the 1912 Unionist pledge against Home Rule. It was subscribed to by more than a million nationalists and a Dublin Mansion House fund to assist resistance was opened. But the credit for the postponement of conscription, which in fact the government never again attempted to introduce, went entirely to de Valera and the Sinn Féiners.

The parliamentary party had begun to lose the confidence of the people over conscription and over its failure to keep Asquith and Lloyd George to a policy of self-government for the whole of Ireland. Theoretically the party still supported recruiting, but its influence continually diminished and the numbers joining the forces fell off. Inevitably Ireland was affected by the changes in Europe, where before the end of 1918 the central powers began to break up. Germany and her allies crumbled and they surrendered on 11 November. New republics were established as imperial governments abdicated and the imperial powers themselves fragmented under the impact of national resurgence. Partly under American and western European influences, the new states which came into existence in this way emerged at first as parliamenatry democracies.

Despite its unexpected successes in by-elections in 1918 the Irish Parliamentary Party faced the general election at the end of the year conscious of its doom. In fact it returned with only six M.P.s. By contrast, seventy-three seats were won by Sinn Féin and twenty-six by Unionists.

Thus, early in 1919 the community of Ireland contained few believers in sweet reasonableness. The general election had not merely destroyed the Irish constitutionalists at Westminster; it had apparently endorsed two extreme groups. In Ulster the Unionists secured more seats than previously; in the whole of Ireland the Sinn Féiners claimed the endorsement of a majority for their programme of establishing an independent Ireland, preferably as a republic.

In England the 1918 election was known as the 'Hang the Kaiser' election. Having won the war, to win the peace was the issue on which Lloyd George fought to continue in office. He was forced to give away many liberal seats to his Unionist allies and thereby became head of a new cabinet which was predominantly Unionist, but committed to the difficult task of solving the Irish question.

If Lloyd George's new coalition was to survive, therefore, the Unionists position in the north had to be safeguarded, preferably by providing a separate parliament for six counties of Ulster. The remainder of that province was to be included with the rest of Ireland in any revised parliamentary arrangements which might be brought forward to replace the abortive Home Rule Act of 1914. All this, however, was very much a matter for secret diplomacy when time would permit.

Just then the victorious allies were concerned with planning the peace conference. It would be dominated by President Wilson of the United States and the French premier, Georges Clemenceau. Wilson was known to favour an Irish settlement, although he personally had little favour for the Irish Catholic republicans, since they had in 1916 been busily arranging to carry their appeal to a peace conference of victorious German allies, as they were now attempting to do to that of the allies at Versailles. Clemenceau, for his part, could be relied on to regard Ireland as a domestic problem within the United Kingdom.

In the beginning of 1919 the Sinn Féin M.P.s arranged to summon a meeting of all members of parliament elected for Ireland at the Mansion House in Dublin. There they inaugurated a unicameral legislature called Dáil Éireann, the Parliament of Ireland. The Sinn Féiners, however, were the only representatives to attend the Dáil and, indeed, many of the members of the victorious party had been arrested the previous year, suspected of further negotiations with Germany, and were still awaiting trial or release. The Dáil undertook two immediate duties: to act as a constituent body for the elaboration of an Irish constitution, and to arrange for Ireland's representation at the Peace Conference.

The principles of the 1916 proclamation were reaffirmed by the Dáil, but, in order to leave matters reasonably free for negotiation, the Declaration of Independence which it adopted left the ratification of a republican form of government to the future. Later it was assumed that the republic was already in existence at that date, but this suggestion was only put forward after the Peace Conference had refused to admit Irish representatives. After an Association for the Recognition of the Irish Republic had been set up in America, it was decided to send de Valera, elected by the Dáil as president of its executive, to visit the United States. This was done after the successful organisation of his escape from a British prison. In America de Valera, almost imperceptibly, became known as President of the Irish Republic.

Coinciding with these activities was the continued censor-
ship of information by the British government in Ireland, and
the prosecution of nationalists acting in contempt of His
Majesty's Government. The Dáil, obliged to meet secretly,
began to treat the situation as one of war. British administrators and soldiers were declared to be illegally operating on
national territory. The volunteer organisation was transformed into the Irish Republican Army (I.R.A.) and
individual units clashed with British forces and police. In
their efforts to secure arms they even raided police barracks.
Over the greater part of the country British law and order
broke down, at first in a limited way, as had happened in the
1830s during the tithe war. Ultimately a limited number of
government departments of Dáil Éireann were organised,
some of which functioned very successfully. The Department
of Justice in particular ran a variety of courts of arbitration
under a Supreme Court of Appeal, in which professional
barristers were appointed judges.

In the north-east of Ireland the British government continued to function effectively. The Dáil government could
only do so spasmodically as the Protestant community in the
north would not co-operate with it and the Catholics were too
weak to do more than give it secret assistance occasionally.

Throughout the rest of the country tolerance for the Sinn
Féiners strengthened gradually, partly because of growing
resentment at British activities, notably those carried out by
undisciplined soldiers of the crown, and partly because the
troops more recently sent to Ireland were inclined to regard
anyone failing to fly the British colours as a rebel. On both
sides outrageous acts took place, but the propaganda machine
of the Republicans, admittedly on their own ground, was
infinitely superior to that of the English, whose crude efforts
to misrepresent their opponents were usually greeted with
ridicule, and were seen through, even by their own supporters
in Britain.

The war activities of the volunteers were gradually centralised under an effective Department of Defence of the Dáil

government. By the beginning of 1920, largely under the direction of Michael Collins, the I.R.A. was engaged in continual guerrilla warfare with British forces. Partly in order to control any professional criminals, the I.R.A. imposed on its members a compulsory oath of allegiance to the republic. It was this last oath which, after the signing of the treaty of 6 December 1921, appeared to justify the I.R.A. leaders in insisting on the army's right to vote on acceptance or rejection of the agreement.

The return of Ulster Unionists from active combat in the Great War, numerically inferior though they had been to the constitutional nationalists, provided Irish Unionists with an opportunity to build up, outside the British administration, a resistance to what they regarded as a renewed effort of a more treasonable and infamous nature to destroy the Union. In Belfast, which had a bad history of sectarian strife among workers, Protestant attacks upon Catholics escalated in the shipyards and factories. A concerted policy, first of restricting Belfast Catholics to limited areas within the city, and finally of driving them out of it 'to hell or to Connaught' created a situation bordering on civil war in the north-east. In these circumstances Lloyd George moved towards a solution of the Irish question which would ensure the dominance of the north by Ulster Unionists.

Meanwhile, President de Valera's mission to the United States proved extremely successful. For years Irish-American organisations had mainly spent money on their Irish activities at home, except for the occasional transmission to Ireland of funds urgently required by revolutionaries there. Under de Valera, most of the funds were diverted to Irish purposes, at first largely for the support of families of murdered patriots, as those executed were termed, and of families of interned prisoners. In this way, the virtually complete loss of American confidence in the Redmondite party had been publicly demonstrated. A national loan was established. Liberally and very quickly Americans invested in it. Apart, however, from establishing a personal ascen-

dancy comparable to that formerly exercised in America by
Parnell, de Valera was no more successful than his colleagues
had been at the Paris Peace Conference in pressurising
President Wilson into recognising the Irish republic. At a
later date the Irish-Americans, resentful of Wilson's failure
to co-operate with them, threw their weight against ratification of the peace treaty signed at Versailles, and so prevented America's entry into the League of Nations, the
international peace organisation which was Wilson's dream
to end world wars.

In 1920 the British cabinet, after several postponements
and parliamentary scenes in protest against outrages by
crown forces in Ireland, finally produced and passed an Act
for the Better Government of Ireland. Its reception in
Ireland was generally unfavourable: to the Sinn Féiners it
was inadequate, to the Unionists unwelcome. It proposed
to set up two subordinate legislatures in Ireland under the
Westminster parliament, one for Northern Ireland at
Belfast with a jurisdiction over six counties, one for 'Southern
Ireland' at Dublin with jurisdiction over the remaining
twenty-six, including Donegal, which was the most northerly
county in Ireland, but which was included in 'Southern
Ireland' since it had a strong nationalist majority. These
subordinate legislatures were to be entrusted with domestic
powers. It was proposed that the common interests of the
two parts of Ireland would be provided for in a 'Council of
Ireland'. Its powers however were minimal and would not
come into force without a joint agreement between northern
and southern governments. Each of these governments was
to be elected by a bicameral legislature, the lower house of
which was to consist of M.P.s elected by proportional representation and the upper house, or Senate, to be partly
elected and partly nominated. The ministry in each area
was to include heads of departments responsible for finance,
justice, home affairs and labour. Residuary powers were
reserved for the parliament of the United Kingdom at
Westminster, and a number of M.P.s from both parts of

Ireland would still be returned to it. It soon became apparent that, despite the continued protests of unionists from southern Ireland, their northern colleagues were prepared to accept the solution, at least in so far as setting up the northern government was concerned. Elections were held throughout Ireland in May 1921 for the new legislatures. In the twenty-six counties there were no contests. The Sinn Féiners nominated their representatives who were returned unopposed, together with four Unionists elected for Trinity College, Dublin.

In the north, nationalists contested the elections wherever feasible, but failed to return more representatives proportionately than they had secured in 1918. A few members of the old Irish Parliamentary Party at Westminster were successful, as also were a few Sinn Féiners already returned for southern constituencies. Sir Edward Carson, the Dublin-born hero of unionist resistance, did not go forward. His place was taken by James Craig, who early in the summer of 1921 became Prime Minister of Northern Ireland, after the northern parliament had been opened by King George v and a government duly constituted. In his speech on that occasion the King used some suggestions given to him by the South African leader, General Smuts, appealing to all Irishmen to come together in their common interests and restore peace to their country.

As a result of the King's declaration, Lloyd George proposed a truce to the leading Sinn Féin leaders. The southern parliament was not functioning since Sinn Féin had issued a public declaration that it would boycott it. There followed some long-drawn-out negotiations with de Valera and the Dáil government, which eventually decided to send negotiators to meet the British Prime Minister in order to arrive at an agreement regarding the future of Ireland. A period of truce was agreed on in July 1921. After considerable cross-correspondence reserving and preserving the jurisdictions and claims of the British and of the Dáil governments, Griffith, Collins and other plenipotentiaries accepted articles of agreement for a treaty between Great Britain and Ireland on 6 December 1921. By this instrument 'Southern Ireland' was to have the same constitutional status as the Dominion of Canada and was to be known as the Irish Free State. The position of Northern Ireland was safeguarded, but the implication of provisions for a Council of Ireland was that the integrity of the country as a political unit would be maintained. It was southern Ireland, however, without representation at Westminster, which was to be the launching pad for the new community.

Dáil Eireann ratified the treaty by a narrow majority early in 1922. The anti-treaty group, however, included de Valera, who resigned as President of the Dáil government and was replaced by Arthur Griffith. The parliament of the United Kingdom also endorsed the treaty, as did the parliament of Southern Ireland which was specially summoned for this purpose. It was on the authority of the latter body that a Provisional Government of Ireland was to be set up for the twenty-six counties under the chairmanship of Michael Collins. To this Britain formally transferred the civil departments at Dublin Castle and elsewhere which had previously come under the jurisdiction of the lord lieutenant. A general election in the twenty-six counties in June 1922 returned an increased majority for the treaty, and reduced its opponents appreciably.

In the debate on the treaty the issue of Republic versus Dominion had loomed largely in de Valera's cabinet and in the Dáil itself, as well as in the I.R.A. and among a substantial minority in the twenty-six counties. Supporters of the treaty were sensitive at being taxed with abandoning the independent republic, and devoted considerable attention to maintaining the forms established by the Dáil in 1919, in order to insist that they were being preserved and that the Irish Free State was the lawful successor to a native authority. Thus they hoped to ensure continuity for their claim to represent the whole of Ireland. Difficulties inevitably arose, as when it became necessary to exclude members elected to represent areas in Northern Ireland from meetings of the Dáil when the twenty-six county area became the recognised jurisdictional unit.

The question of popular sovereignty and where it rested became a lively subject of controversy which was aggravated by the inclusion in the treaty, and in the constitution of 1922, of an oath of allegiance to the King 'in virtue of his headship of the British Commonwealth of nations'. Thus a provision, in what was virtually a new dominion, for the observance of usages similar to those of Canada, became a cause of contention and division among former comrades. They divided respectively into upholders of the republic and defenders of the dominion. Canadian practices had been specified in the treaty as the exemplar for the powers exercisable by the Irish Free State, and might conceivably have provided the basis for an agreement between Craig and the Dublin leaders, calculated to meet the susceptibilities of northern Unionists about abandoning the constitutional position of the King.

De Valera had resigned as President of the Dáil ministry at the beginning of 1922 after the treaty had been ratified by the Dáil, and arguments followed, denying the right of a majority in the Dáil to substitute the Free State for the Republic. Despite the welcome given to the treaty by the Catholic hierarchy, amongst other bodies, controversy persisted as to the powers of the people to disestablish the republic in a general election. Insistence by volunteer I.R.A. conventions, which tended to be predominantly republican, as to their right to pronounce on the issues and to assert their independence of any constitutional authority, led to the decision of Collins to build up an army under the provisional government.

Some I.R.A. units were occupying strategic points in Dublin and others, allegedly with the connivance of Collins, were planning to resume hostilities in Northern Ireland, particularly on the border with southern Ireland where British units were still maintained. The assassination in London, in

June 1922, of Sir Henry Wilson, a former chief of the Imperial General Staff who was about to be employed as military adviser by Craig, threatened to precipitate a breakdown of relations between Dublin and the British government. The assassination was attributed to republican soldiers, and the Colonial Secretary, Winston Churchill, sent an ultimatum to the Provisional Government, ordering it to assert control over the headquarters of the republicans in Dublin, which were located at the Four Courts. Collins decided to act, since the republicans had begun to kidnap key officers of his new army and to requisition supplies by raiding stores, shops and banks. On the refusal of the republican garrison to evacuate, Collins, who feared a possible return of British forces, bombarded the Courts with guns borrowed from England. The civil war had begun. In the course of it, within a matter of months, Griffith was to die and Collins himself was to be shot in an ambush.

The leading anti-treaty members of the Dáil, including de Valera, meanwhile delegated their authority to the Irish Republican Army. But within nine months it was clear that the I.R.A. had not the popular support which it had won in its earlier struggle with British forces, and that it had failed to keep control of any substantial areas. Before the end of 1922 the Catholic hierarchy had condemned the republicans as lacking in popular authority. The bishops stigmatised republican actions in the civil war in the most opprobrious terms and excommunicated those who were actively disputing the legitimacy of the Provisional Government. To counter this, de Valera was subsequently persuaded to resume the title of President of the Republic. However, three years later, after a further election reduced the number of anti-treaty members of the Dáil, he abandoned it.

To a large extent the discussions in 1922 of the powers of the projected new Irish Free State concentrated on the extent of its independence from England and on whether the oath of allegiance to the King was real or only theoretical. The succession in August 1922 of President William Cosgrave to both Griffith and Collins, the deceased heads of the Dáil ministry and of the Provisional Government respectively, aroused little attention. Except for services specifically allocated to the six counties of Northern Ireland, the tendency of Britain to recognise the Irish Free State as successor to the jurisdiction exercised by the Viceroy and Chief Secretary before 1922 was hardly noticed either. The Free State régime formally came into force on 6 December 1922 and Cosgrave became president of its execuitve council, set up under a constitution in accordance with the treaty. The military victory of the Irish Free State government in Spring 1923 over its republican opponents, which brought the civil war to an end, did not relieve it from continued embarrassment. The republicans insisted in maintaining their own sequence of legitimate authorities from the Dáil of 1919, and even from the proclamation of 1916, allegedly to prevent the Irish republic from being destroyed by what they insisted was merely a new subordinate British authority.

War conditions in the twenty-six counties allowed the government of Northern Ireland to take control of the six counties without any of the comparable obstruction faced by the Provisional Government in Dublin. The northern government reinforced its authority by enacting a stringent coercion act. The civil war in the south enabled Sir James Craig, as the northern Prime Minister had become, to negotiate for increased power within his own area, which thus asserted even more positively its claims against any claims of the Irish Free State which might tend to subordinate the six counties under a common Irish government. The treaty of 1921 theoretically provided for the whole of Ireland but allowed for the continuance of Northern Ireland, perhaps on a temporary basis, subject to the setting up of a boundary commission. This commission would readjust the territories of the two political entities in the country, so as to bring them more into harmony with the desires of their communities than the existing division by counties did. The northern government, however, refused to co-operate

16

in this commission, and the governments of the United
Kingdom and of the Irish Free State finally agreed in 1925
to maintain the existing boundary after the report of a
substitute commission had pleased none of the parties
affected. Northern Ireland thus evaded the temporary status
implied for it in the 1921 treaty, perpetuating the position
provided for in 1920.

The two political units set up in 1921/22 were theoretically
to carry over the single parliamentary organisation which
had been envisaged in all the bills for the government of
Ireland that followed Gladstone's federal proposals of 1886.
But the Council of Ireland provided for in the 1920 Act never
came into being. The collapse of the boundary commission
in 1925 was used not only to confirm the existing border but
also to make a supplementary agreement abolishing the
projected council.

The abandonment of the proposed Council of Ireland
appeared for a period seriously to weaken the prestige of
President Cosgrave. De Valera, though still boycotting the
Free State Dáil, showed interest in the situation; his position
regarding the treaty, though doctrinaire, was never one of
absolute rejection. He was ready to accept a formula associ-
ating the republic with Britain, if Britain recognised the
events of 1919, in particular the foundation of the Dáil and
its reaffirmation of the 1916 Declaration of Independence.
He insisted that 'external association' of Ireland with the
Commonwealth would have secured everything Britain
justifiably required, including the exclusion of the forces of
enemy powers from Ireland. His proposals, however, would
have meant dispensing with the oath of allegiance to the
King. But in other respects de Valera's alternative was
comparable to the treaty, provided it was internationally
guaranteed. In 1925 a revival of such ideas seemed practicable.

Early in 1926 de Valera failed to carry a majority at a
convention of his Sinn Féin party for a resolution which he
had supported that they should re-enter the Dáil as a con-

stitutional opposition, with a view to securing revision of the treaty in accordance with the views he had previously expressed. On the defeat of this resolution he resigned from the presidency of Sinn Féin, and, by implication, of the republic, and established instead a new organisation—Fianna Fáil. This he led as president, contesting the next general election and entering the Dáil in 1927. Fianna Fáil won increasing success as a constitutional party and ultimately, after the general election of 1932, with the support of the Labour party, secured a majority in the Dáil for de Valera's election in succession to Cosgrave as president of the executive council.

The main lines of the contemporary republic of Ireland of today had already emerged by 1929. The revolution was at an end, but it had secured a parliamentary democracy for the Irish people. Despite the serious losses of the endemic warfare between 1919 and 1923 the country had not sustained any serious set-back. The defeat of the I.R.A. in the civil war had secured victory for constitutionalism and affirmed the right of the people to choose their own form of domestic government. If, because of the intransigence of Lloyd George, relations between the twenty-six counties and Britain had been established only on an impermanent basis, which lasted for some ten years, the arrangement had been sufficiently elastic to enable Irish statesmen to play a decisive part in the shaping of events at Commonwealth conferences. After the passage of the Statute of Westminster in 1931, the Irish Free State, Canada and other dominions were permitted to work out their own futures as self-governing states. It was as a result of these decisions that, between 1932 and 1938, de Valera was able to alter the constitution of the Free State and transform it virtually into an independent republic which was freely associated with the British Commonwealth and was also a full member of the League of Nations, over whose assembly at Geneva de Valera presided in 1937.

During sixteen years in office (1932–48) de Valera made

use of the existing machinery of government, sanctioned by the act of 1931, and by the constitution of 1922, to recast Ireland's relations with the United Kingdom. The most spectacular of these changes took place on the abdication of King Edward VIII in 1936. The powers of the monarchy, so far as the Irish Free State was concerned, were transferred by Irish statute to the Executive Council. The office of Governor General, who represented the King in Ireland as in other British dominions, was abolished at the end of 1937. A new constitution submitted to a popular referendum in the same year provided for Ireland's external association with Britain and the Commonwealth and altered the name of the Irish Free State to that of Éire (Ireland). The constitution carefully avoided the direct conflict that any reference to British power over the six counties of Northern Ireland would have provoked. It also established a new elective position, that of President of Ireland, but the powers of government were vested in a cabinet consisting of the Taoiseach (Prime Minister) and other ministers.

The constitution of 1938 still governs the twenty-six counties. It provides for its extension to the whole of the 'national territory' should future agreement make such a course practicable. As such, unlike the northern government, it claims some relation to the community of Ireland as a whole. Politically speaking, however, the government of the twenty-six counties has rarely tried to act on this basis, although the claims recorded in the constitution may have influenced the British government during the second world war against attempting to enforce conscription in Northern Ireland. However, it cannot be said today that the government of the twenty-six counties is regarded by any specific political element in Northern Ireland as deserving of recognition as their sovereign political authority. This is not to deny that a theoretical belief in Irish political unity persists, but merely to point out that, after two generations, the political division of the country has become sufficiently strengthened to establish habits of thought which automatically resist any claims by the present government to speak for the whole community of Ireland. Thus even if two separate elements can be discerned in the northern community, it cannot be said that the government of the twenty-six counties today is any closer than it was in 1923 to representing the Irish community as a whole.

The position of the government of Northern Ireland in relation to the community might appear irrelevant. The slogan 'Ulster is British' has tended to emphasise the attitude that developments there were maintained *pari passu* with those in Britain. The degree of self-government exercised by Northern Ireland has corresponded in many respects to that exercised by the whole country under the constitution of 1782, qualified by Northern Ireland's dependence on a substantial British subsidy and the presence of its twelve M.P.s at Westminster.

The community of Ireland then, since 1922, may well be regarded as a controversial or at least a complex concept. However, the events connected with the major political area in the island need to be taken note of, both because of the policy-assumptions of its rulers and because of the increasing tendency to identify the concept of 'Irishness' with them.

The government of the Irish Free State had secured its admission to the League of Nations in 1923, thereby strengthening its case for sovereign independence. This was subsequently guaranteed by the United Kingdom, by implication at least, when the Statute of Westminster was enacted in 1931. Since the succession to power of Fianna Fáil in 1932 these guarantees have been tested, particularly by the neutrality of the twenty-six counties during the second world war which the government maintained successfully, and by the country's admission, somewhat tardily, to the United Nations in 1955.

The constitutional alterations in Anglo-Irish relations reduced to a minimum any social or economic revolution visualised by the signatories of the 1916 proclamation. Ironically, the social revolution has come to Northern Ireland first, as a result of its continued connection with the United Kingdom. Few of the old administrators left the Free State or moved to Northern Ireland in 1921/22, apart from members of the British military and police forces. The policy of imposing tests in the use of the Irish language became the only real restriction on entry to the civil service, and this was just as liable to exclude the ill-equipped among nationalists as among ex-unionists. For the rest, the traditions of the British Treasury and its administrative system were maintained. Socially this put a limit on revolutionary reorganisation. Above all it retarded the development of an egalitarian society, which might have emerged if the state had taken responsibility for education and public health.

After the end of the first world war the strains and stresses of revolution led many states to concentrate more on their internal affairs and to take steps to arrest radical change. Northern Ireland, from its establishment in 1921, had set limits to democratic principles, the honouring of which might in time have given majority control to the nationalists, who favoured unity with the Irish Free State and, later, with the Irish Republic. The principles of a fascist state which subsequently emerged in Italy were to be seen here in embryo. The virtual restriction to one party of cabinet positions, higher administrative offices, the control of the police, the doctrine that 'Ulster was a Protestant state with a Protestant people' dominated by an extra-parliamentary body, the Orange Order, all helped the parallel development. The trade unions were subordinated to this principle and pressurised to dissociate themselves from national labour bodies. The barring of nationalists from all key offices, their exclusion from most opportunities for social and economic advancement, proceeded on similar lines. Similar developments took place in the 1930s in Spain and in Japan where a more militaristic reorganisation of politics and social affairs affirmed the monopolistic control of the ruling military classes. The case of Northern Ireland was not so obvious because when the counter-revolution had become established, it was essentially negative in its attitude to foreign affairs. These had been reserved to the United Kingdom government which successfully used its influence to prevent any attempt by the government of Northern Ireland to exploit extra-territorial questions, particularly in the Irish Free State, to its own advantage.

It was perhaps fortunate that for the first ten years of its existence the Irish Free State was not in the hands of the republican party. It was also important for the future of parliamentary democracy in the Free State that its first government, in contending with a powerful opposition, at first outside Dáil Eireann, and from 1927 within as well, was obliged to emphasise its own adherence to democratic parliamentary principles. It is significant that the electorate in 1922 and in subsequent general elections confirmed the supporters of the treaty in power as long as majority rule was challenged by the I.R.A. and their supporters. It may not be accidental that the defeat of Cosgrave's party followed his government's adoption of a coercion policy which could be represented as anti-democratic, and even as capable of transforming the government into a fascist régime. The preservation of parliamentary democracy after the victory of de Valera was assisted by various factors which imposed on his Fianna Fáil party, whose very name had militaristic overtones, the necessity for assuming and maintaining a constitutional role. Among these factors was the need to convince the electorate that Fianna Fáil supporters had abandoned their intransigent doctrinaire and absolutist tendencies of the 1922–25 period. The maintenance of propaganda against the quasi-totalitarian régime in Northern Ireland undoubtedly required that Fianna Fáil establish its *bona fides* vis-à-vis parliamentary democracy. The reorganisation of Cosgrave's party as Fine Gael, shortly after its defeat in 1932, certainly assisted de Valera in maintaining this role. Fine Gael's Army Comrades Association, nicknamed 'the Blueshirts' after the colour of its members' quasi-military uniform, undoubtedly played into the hands of de Valera.

From its early days an economic policy of industrial protection was virtually dictated to the Free State, if only out of loyalty to the Sinn Féin policy laid down at the beginning of the century by Arthur Griffith. In the building up of new industries the government increasingly resorted to discrimination against imported goods, and this, of course, particularly affected relations with Northern Ireland and Great Britain. When the question of partition was first canvassed a favourite economic argument was that a divided Ireland could not be economically viable. Unionists, however, had always argued that a Home Rule Ireland, virtually committed to a policy of protection, would bring about the bankruptcy of Belfast, since the major city in Ulster would be cut off from its traditional connections in the neighbouring island. The policy of protection was deliberately followed in the Free State under Fianna Fáil, and accentuated mutual resentments north and south of the border. Gradually, therefore, the development of prosperous industries in the twenty-six counties seemed to strengthen the divisions between the two parts of the island, the industrial rivalries appearing to grow as insuperable as all others. Inevitably, however, entry into the European Common Market will tend to diminish this.

After the outbreak of an economic war between Britain and the Free State, when de Valera was in office, relations between the two countries deteriorated. The dispute arose in the first instance over the question of whether the Free State was still bound to pay land annuities to the British Treasury, particularly as the northern government had been exempted from any liability for lands purchased since the sale of estates early in the century. De Valera was fortunate in being able to represent the British government as resorting to coercive tactics when it imposed sanctions in retaliation for his decision not to repay the land annuities. The economic war, however, proved to be the occasion for a new confrontation between old antagonists of the civil war. The Blueshirts in particular provoked anxieties at a period when many countries in Europe were experiencing the activities of private armies. They also voiced the resentment of large farmers, chiefly in the south, whose cattle-selling interests suffered losses in the economic war. Ultimately de Valera's party, which in its early years had emphasised its urban industrial policy, adjusted itself to agricultural demands, and more recently has derived much of its strength from the rural community.

In 1938, a new Anglo-Irish agreement was negotiated between de Valera and the British Prime Minister, Neville Chamberlain. This ended the dispute over the annuities by an agreement for the payment of a capital sum to Britain in lieu of the land annuities and for the transfer to the government of Éire, as the Irish Free State had been renamed the previous year, of the strategic ports reserved for defence purposes to the United Kingdom in the treaty of 1921. This agreement, as far as the ports were concerned, was subsequently the subject of bitter comment and resentment by Chamberlain's successor as Prime Minister, Winston Churchill, largely because it enabled de Valera to maintain the neutrality of the state in the second world war.

This international war was in a sense the last European bid for world dominance. From Germany's point of view it was at first an attempt to reverse the decision of the Great War by reimposing the legendary teutonic hegemony over central and south-eastern Europe. Initial German successes extended the theatre of war, until the counter-revolutionary powers seemed likely to control all western Europe. The decision of Hitler to attack Russia was based on his conviction that Germany's military preparedness would give it sufficient advantage to achieve victory and, with the assistance of Japan, to contain and ultimately defeat the United States. Thus the conflict became another world war, and one with enormous significance for Europe's former colonies in Africa, Asia and other continents.

The decision of de Valera's government to remain neutral was perhaps inevitable in a country still smarting at the

maintenance of partition, which to many was the result of
Britain's treacherous instigation of the Carsonite movement
and its continued support of the Craig régime. Admittedly
sympathy for Britain was widespread, but, as in the Great
War, the pro-German element in Ireland was not contemptible, and a policy of neutrality with an obviously benevolent
attitude towards Britain and America was virtually imposed
on de Valera. The neutrality which de Valera maintained
with masterly exactness observed the spirit of his 1938 agreement with Britain by neglecting no undertaking necessary to
prevent the use of Irish territory by an enemy of England.
Churchill's resentment, however, persisted, particularly after
de Valera protested at the use of bases in Northern Ireland by
American troops, after the entry of the United States into the
war late in 1941. The strength of Dublin's government
position seemed evident when it appeared that Britain would
not extend conscription to Northern Ireland in this war. For
this de Valera secured the credit as he had been able to do for
the whole island in 1918. In May 1945 Churchill wisely
avoided replying to de Valera, who effectively answered the
great British Premier's unfair reflections on Irish neutrality in
his victory speech on the defeat of Germany. Since the war,
relations between Irish and British governments have become
increasingly harmonious, although this was hardly noticeable
while Fianna Fáil was out of office between 1948 and 1951.

The war also made it clear to Ireland that the sovereignty
of the state was no longer absolute. The theory behind the
demands for independence during the preceding century had
been based on absolutist notions of jurisprudence. But mutual
dependence of nations, the extreme dangers of any policy of
isolation or neutrality, the difficulties of maintaining essential
supplies or of procuring adequate defence weapons made it
evident during the early 1940s that nineteenth-century
notions of the self-sufficient state were no longer valid. The
war also revealed the vast difference in resources between the
minor powers and the super-states, Russia, the United States
and China. The movement towards a closer integration of

Europe gathered momentum and support.

De Valera was defeated at the election of 1948, a defeat which was perhaps analogous with that of Churchill in the first British post-war election, and could be attributed to a general feeling that a change was overdue. Yet sixteen years of government under de Valera, following ten years of less intensively protected industrialisation under Cosgrave, had certainly brought about a remarkable difference in Irish society. Between the conclusion of the first world war and the conclusion of the second, Ireland as a whole had, on the face of it, become more prosperous than a century earlier, in town and in country. The eradiction of the landlord class by the land purchase acts had transformed the large farmers into a thriving element in the community. The policy of economic self-sufficiency had built up substantial industries behind tariff barriers. Problems of emigration and acute poverty, however, had not been faced. Nor is it clear that this prosperity would not have been greater had Ireland remained in the United Kingdom.

A coalition government of all parties opposed to de Valera took office in 1948 under John A. Costello, a leading member of the Fine Gael party. This, the main opposition party built up by Cosgrave and his supporters, had come to be regarded as the Commonwealth party. It was ironic then that Costello's coalition ministry should sever the connection with the British Commonwealth and declare Ireland a republic in April 1949. Since then the state has been known as the Republic of Ireland.

The decision to issue the declaration was virtually dictated to a coalition which included members of the Labour party which, perhaps out of sensitivity at its own abandonment of Connolly's policy of creating a Workers' Republic, had for years been accusing de Valera's government of hypocrisy in continuing to recognise the nominal superiority of the British monarch as head of the Commonwealth. Through de Valera's pursuance of the policy of 'External Association' Ireland was still nominally associated with it. The Repeal of the External Relations Act ending 'External Association', however, boomeranged on the coalition. Many believers in the traditional connection with Britain were shocked by the action of a government which included the Commonwealth party, and later transferred their allegiance to de Valera, if only because he apparently cold-shouldered clerical politicians. De Valera also out-manœuvred a new republican party, Clann na Poblachta, led by Sean MacBride, Minister for External Affairs in Costello's government. By reviving the issue of partition de Valera provoked the government into making its own attempt to direct international attention to the question, which was unsuccessful. But it was on the issue of introducing a modified form of the welfare state, which was concurrently in operation in the United Kingdom, that the coalition ministry disintegrated. Under criticism from the Catholic hierarchy, the government abandoned proposals for an enlarged health scheme under public control, after the resignation of the minister concerned with the project. In the ensuing general election of 1951 Fianna Fáil gained sufficient support to return to office, where it has remained ever since except for one further three year interval between 1954 and 1957.

A second coalition government, also led by Costello, ruled the republic for that period. It initiated Irish military involvements on behalf of the United Nations, though these did not entail actual foreign commitments until after Fianna Fáil's return to office. Troops were sent to Lebanon in 1958, to the Congo in 1960 and to Cyprus in 1964. In these instances its new role in international affairs contributed substantially to the maturing of the Irish state, if only because it was being realised that Ireland's struggle against imperialism led to her being regarded as uncommitted in a world increasingly hostile to colonialism. The Republic of Ireland, it could be said, came of age and ceased to be preoccupied with its own affairs and with the more controversial aspects of its relations with its neighbour. Concurrently it found itself involved in a new relationship with the descendants of Irish emigrants in the new world. For the first time they, and particularly the American-Irish, came to regard themselves as aliens in Ireland, since the foreign policies of their countries could differ.

After more than thirty years of self-government in which the material well-being of the people obviously appreciated, an economic crisis arose in 1956 which was probably responsible for the electorate's withdrawal of confidence from the Costello government in the following year. Undue pessimism over Ireland's position in a critically sensitive international situation may have added to the government's unpopularity. Certainly, after the middle 1950s economic questions became an overriding priority in government planning. Under Seán Lemass, who succeeded de Valera as head of the government in 1959, official policy began to show signs of change as external affairs, and particularly the question of closer relations with the United Kingdom and western Europe, made their impact. As Minister for Industry and Commerce for many years Lemass had been concerned with building up Irish manufactures and, after he became head of government, a programme of economic expansion was adopted. Its success in doubling national productivity appeared to justify Ireland's application for entry into the European Economic Community in 1961. Inevitably such a decision created misgivings, not merely among new manufacturers who faced the likelihood of substantial tariff reductions at an early date, but also among those who feared unpredictable consequences of E.E.C. membership for agriculture. Recollection of the aftermath of Ireland's association with a wealthier state in the Union of 1800 provoked considerable anxiety. The successful increase in productivity and increased experience in state planning led the government in 1963 to decide that a second economic programme was needed. Its subsequent failure to maintain the rate of productivity increased doubts as to whether the state was sufficiently equipped to meet international commitments in the event of ultimate success with its application to the E.E.C. A free trade agreement with

Britain and Northern Ireland, signed in December 1965, appeared to be a more justifiable risk, though even here the consequences for recent industrial growth appeared to be so serious that only a Fianna Fáil government seemed likely to secure popular approval, with industries established in consequence of the party's own policy. In November 1966 Mr Jack Lynch was elected Taoiseach in succession to Lemass. His endorsement, mainly by rural constituencies, in the 1969 election placed him advantageously for the future.

The inauguration in the 1960s of an economic survey of education was another demonstration of the state's growing maturity and sense of responsibility. For more than a century interdenominational rivalry had led government departments to take an irresponsible attitude to education. To describe state educational provisions as being comparable to the worst in western Europe even as late as the beginning of the 1960s would hardly be an exaggeration. Economic progress urgently dictated a substantial increase in government expenditure on education at all levels; this could well justify more deliberation in future agreements with other communities. If Irish emigration persisted at a comparable rate to what it had been over the last century, it should at least influence a more adequate instruction and intellectual equipment of Irish people seeking employment outside the state. Such an improved policy could also terminate those demographic movements of the past in which masses of emigrant unskilled Irish workers were exploited and even provoked to racial rivalry with comparably uneducated peoples in America and Britain.

Relations between governments north and south improved quietly in the last two decades, particularly since all constitutional parties in the republic condemned any efforts to bring about Irish reunion by force, and in particular the activities against the northern government initiated by a revived I.R.A. For the first time agreements between the Belfast and Dublin governments were made on several minor issues, notably on river drainage and fisheries. The first of these was negotiated in 1950 under Costello's government. In 1965 the Fianna Fáil Taoiseach, Seán Lemass, visited Captain Terence O'Neill, the northern Prime Minister, in Belfast, and the visit was returned. Improved relations between the two governments since Captain O'Neill's visit to Dublin were not popular with more extreme Ulster unionists. They organised, under Dr Ian Paisley, a Presbyterian minister of a minor denomination, and raised the banner of alarm that Protestant Ulster was being endangered by the combined forces of republicanism and popery in a conspiracy to amalgamate with the south. They were sufficiently strong in 1969 to secure the replacement of O'Neill by Major James Chichester Clark. More recently, in 1971, under the stress of increased threats by the I.R.A., not without some support in the republic, Clark has had to give way to a broader Protestant administration led by Brian Faulkner. But since O'Neill's time British government's influence has favoured political and social reforms in Northern Ireland.

The apparent stalemate over partition provoked new thinking about the nature of the state and the community. The distinction between the nation and the state had already been stressed in some historical articles written subsequent to the treaty by Professor Eoin MacNeill, who had been associated with the foundation of the Gaelic League and of the Irish Volunteers, and who acted on the Boundary Commission of 1925 for the Irish Free State, partly because of his specialised knowledge as an Ulster man. The idea which he expressed of a community linked culturally rather than politically is particularly associated with dispersed peoples like the Jews. In the context of the Irish literary renaissance persons with affiliations on both sides of the Irish Sea, such as Yeats and Lady Gregory, had no difficulty in distinguishing between the historic Irish nation and the political states established in 1921/22. At the same time, identification of the nation with the state is, of course, common. In Ireland, it had clearly existed in the thinking of Henry Grattan, who greeted the independent legislature of the 1780s as that of a newly-established nation. This nation, he considered, was in turn extinguished in 1800 by the Act of Union. To Thomas Davis in the 1840s the possibility of Ireland emerging 'a nation once again' had seemed to depend upon winning Repeal. In America today the association of the word state with the former colonies of New England, enshrined in the name United States, has led Americans to equate 'nation' with their whole territorial area. The same confusion is found in the League of Nations, inspired by President Wilson, and in its replacement, the United Nations, which was set up by the victorious allies at the end of the second world war.

The concept of the cultural community, then, so far as Ireland is concerned, is more of an intellectual one than the ordinary man's customary political notion of the community. In the sphere of religion the historic territory of the whole of Ireland has been maintained as the unit by Christian denominations, Anglican (Church of Ireland), Presbyterian and Roman Catholic. In some forms of athletics the older traditions have also been preserved. In the realm of scholarship the Royal Irish Academy and similar organisations continue to function for the thirty-two counties. And for professional historical purposes the International Committee of Historical Sciences, which is organised by countries, admitted Ireland to membership as a cultural unit in 1938.

The assumption of the Irish community as a cultural unit tends to be linked more with manifestations throughout the politically-divided thirty-two counties rather than with its association with Britain, which might well be considered more intimate. In their emphasis on distinctive Irish attributes, nationalists since the Young Irelanders have tended increasingly to stress the significance of the survival of the Irish language. The movement for its preservation in the twentieth century almost inevitably led the Free State authorities to accept as an obligation not merely to encourage its use but also to enforce the compulsory use of Irish in teaching. This had already been done by many schools since the language was imposed in 1913 as a compulsory subject for students entering the National University of Ireland. In the reorganisation of administration after 1922 this cultural demand had the advantage in its favour that a knowledge of Irish rather than membership of a political or party allegiance became the only essential requirement for appointment in the civil service. But in the arguments put forward in the twenty-six counties for unifying the community politically, the policy of compulsory Irish obviously creates a problem for the future.

'The British Isles' as a term has also been increasingly favoured, since the seventeenth century, to describe a political unit. After the unification of Scotland and England the term 'British' was used to describe the compound 'English-Scottish'. Since the Union of 1800 it has not secured the same favour as a compound to include 'Irish', though more recently the governing party in Northern Ireland, in an effort to cement its connection with Britain, has employed it rather loosely to include 'Ulster', or at least the six counties of the province which constitute the area of its jurisdiction. In the same way 'English' is loosely taken to include the Welsh and the Scots, if not the inhabitants of Northern Ireland. Culturally the term 'British' has been accepted in Ireland, even in the twenty-six counties, mainly and almost only by the remnants of the upper class with long affiliations in the imperial services, administrative, military and religious. The term remains opprobrious to radical nationalists, partly in recollection of its employment in allegiance tests during the struggle with England. Culturally the devising, after 1800, of a flag of the United Kingdom known as the Union Jack, consisting of the heraldic crosses of St George, St Andrew and St Patrick, would not on the surface have appeared objectionable. But the use of the emblem by Unionist forces, particularly in a period of stress, converted it into an irritant. Its more recent association with the Unionists of north-east Ireland poses a problem, apparently as insoluble as the linguistic one of Irish, in schemes for reunification.

17

The struggle for Irish independence from the United Kingdom over the last two centuries passed from one for the preservation of political powers in both components of a dual monarchy to that for upholding an independent republic, rejecting all association with the United Kingdom. Since the recognition of the independent republic by the British government in 1948, the political demands for sovereign independence of more radical Irish nationalists could be said to have been fully realised, apart from the question of partition. More recently, in 1965, the agreement negotiated between the British government and that of the republic aimed at closer association in economic policy. This achievement has not, perhaps, attracted sufficient attention as bringing together the common interests of the two islands as well as of the two political divisions within Ireland. Even if Ireland does not enter the Common Market, should the United Kingdom do so, it will involve at the very least 'external association' with the European community and particularly with Britain and Northern Ireland.

Since 1896, international conventions have occasionally been held of persons claiming to be of Irish descent. These include many inhabitants of Great Britain, the United States, the British Commonwealth, and even Europeans and South Americans possessing recognisably Irish names. The idea of a cultural unit comprising this heterogeneous combination may, perhaps, seem ridiculous. But from the standpoint of propaganda its value was obvious in the movements to encourage Irish independence. Down to 1922 people of Irish descent in the New World, particularly in the United States, maintained a critical attitude towards the United Kingdom's government. Indeed they partly attributed their own migration to its allegedly anti-Irish policies. In this way persons calling themselves 'American-Irish' romantically maintained some community feeling with the 'ould sod!'

Since 1922, however, the establishment of the Irish state at Dublin with dominion status has tended to break the abstract connection. This can be explained partly by the impact of habitual thinking in a world where political units exact a monopoly of allegiance from their citizens, who are normally expected to renounce citizenship rights elsewhere, at least for purposes such as the issuing of passports and other diplomatic credentials. It would be difficult today to locate any substantial collection of national groups arguing the case for regarding the 'Irish race' as a cultural unit.

The decision of the Costello government to proclaim a republic and the subsequent adoption of an independent role in international controversies at the United Nations differing from that of Britain and of the United States has also served to emphasise the new distinctions. Emigrants who had become American citizens came to regard themselves as aliens in Ireland. Politics assisted in bringing reality to Irish thinking. An attitude on international affairs based on the history of Ireland's struggle against Britain was being replaced by one based on the role of a small nation in a revolutionary world emerging from colonisation. Ireland in the last century has made a modest contribution to the diffusion of Christian civilisation over the English-speaking world. The history of those missions has usually been affected by the fortunes of the British Empire. Today these missions are confronted by situations in which European influence has clearly weakened. Their future largely depends upon the limited possibility of readjustment within the new nations and particularly on their relations with the new super-states. In the world since 1945 there have been great changes transforming, and in a certain sense creating, the belief in a new Africa and a new Asia. Just as the world wars impinged upon Ireland, so these changes are likely to modify Ireland's outlook, particularly in regard to the influence of the superstates over these new countries, the reaction to absolute ideas of nationalism, the role of revolution, the backlash of racism, the problems of population and the dangers of atomic warfare.

Since the existence of the Roman Empire more than 1,500 years ago, and particularly of the Roman Empire in the west, similar historical traditions have tended to preserve relations between adjacent territories occupied by different political units. The common elements, of course, included the use of Latin as a medium of communication. This marked off the later western empire from that of the east, which tended to employ Greek in a similar way. The extension of Christianity beyond the traditional confines of the Roman Empire widened the European cultural area. This was subsequently strengthened by the establishment of the Holy Roman Empire and its persistence, however hypothetically, for a thousand years after the year 800. Over the same territory the influence of the Roman Catholic Church has also been associated with the concept of western Europe as a cultural unit. Even the break-up at the Reformation did not wholly destroy this influence. More recently the emergence of the European Economic Community has revived and strengthened this cultural assumption, although serious political rivalries and the territorial extensions of the Community, including those projected for the near future, may lead to an alteration in this concept. The association of Ireland with it was at first very much marginal, just as in its past history its adjustment to the imperial norms of the Roman Church has been noticeably slow. In the future Ireland's connection with the European Community may still remain peripheral; but the concept of the cultural community of western Europe needs to be considered, if only because to the historian of the future the writing of an Irish history may well emerge as an anachronistic enterprise. For we cannot even be sure that at the beginning of the second milennium there will still be a public interested in a study such as this of the history of Ireland.

Epilogue: the writing of the word

HISTORY in Ireland has been written by every generation according to its own predilections. For centuries the presentation of history has been a professional occupation in which men of one generation wrote very much like one another. But in the middle of the twentieth century we have come to the point when the written word is beginning to lose that pre-eminence in communication which it has enjoyed for so long. The public today listens more to the mass media, all of them basically oral.

Writing was first known in Ireland about the fourth century A.D. It was then a country in which there was a long oral tradition of history. The guardians of that oral knowledge transmitted it faithfully from one generation to the next with strict adherence to the literal wording, so that writing down the old stories led to unexpected alterations in folk memory.

The knowledge of writing is pre-Christian, but the earliest form in Ireland, ogham, based upon the Latin alphabet, appears to have been confined to inscriptions. The consistent use of writing was brought to Ireland by the Christians who established their own communities, separate from the pagan people among whom they developed. The Christians used the Latin language and in their religious rites employed Latin service books. They were also concerned with recording important matters about their own religious communities. Special reference can be made to their knowledge and use of the Bible and of some of the writings of early fathers of the

Church. The rest of knowledge they considered profane, something not to be entertained by the most devout.

At this period it could be said that Ireland was divided into two separate communities with different ways of life. The Latin religious group must have been very restricted in numbers for the first two or three centuries, until it expanded during the golden age of Irish monasticism and extended from Ireland into Scotland, the north of England and even into Merovingian Gaul. Meanwhile the Celtic inhabitants of Ireland were becoming more and more aware of their Christian neighbours, particularly as these increasingly drew their converts from among the natives. The Celts had played a remarkable part in the history of western Europe, apart altogether from their earlier impingement upon east-central Europe and Asia Minor. In Britain and in Ireland they destroyed all vestiges of an earlier history, by compelling those they conquered to abandon their language and customs and become assimilated to the Celts. Part of the process of assimilation involved their acceptance of the skilled craftsmen of those they conquered as an honoured element in their society. The Celts justified their destructive actions towards their predecessors by claiming to be the children of the gods. But the very force which assisted in destroying their predecessors contributed to the deformation of their own history by the Christian historians, who looked with horror on anything associated with the false gods. Thus when the Christians began to record the history of the Celts they distorted the record by suppressing any reference to the gods or any supernatural connections of the pagan Celts. Where formerly a king was traced back to some deity, it became increasingly accepted that an effort should be made to relate the royal lines to identifiable biblical figures. Thus the work of the historian today involves making allowances for those elements in the early Christian recording of ancient Ireland which ignored pagan mythology or claimed for it a biblical justification.

The ecclesiastical tendency to be interested in the secular history of people in Ireland intensified after the raiding attacks of the Scandinavian Vikings. These raiders learned at an early date that the Christian communities were centres of wealth, and incapable of systematic resistance. By contrast, the militaristic secular communities were able to defend themselves more effectively than the Anglo-Saxons had been able to do in Britain, with the result that the Church was only preserved by securing the close alliance of the state. It has been remarked that, like the Celts, the Romans were effective destroyers of the tradition of those they conquered. But it is remarkable that among the Celtic people the literature surviving from Gaelic Irish areas is much richer than that which survived from areas dominated by the Romans. It was in this context that an acculturation became possible between the Christian missionaries and the Irish. Nothing like that, however, except in a limited way, took place in areas where the Scandinavians successfully established themselves in Ireland. Their own traditions continued to be associated with their place of origin and rarely rooted themselves in the area they colonised.

In the face of this external attack the monastic historians and the secular professional writers of the Irish used their position and their control of writing to strengthen the tendencies towards unity in tradition. Thus early Irish history begins to assume a form of proto-nationalism, which is seen only on the surface once the record is subjected to detailed analysis. The success of the professional historians in this matter was substantially assisted by their ability to move freely from one *tuath* (as the population groups were termed) to another. The professional class, in fact, was using its position to bring about a form of national unity in the teeth of the Scandinavian invasions. Their very success marks off the period since the sixth century as being different from what had gone before. No longer was it possible to destroy the record of a defeated people. The Scandinavian communities in Ireland might have little interest in the literary traditions of their predecessors, but the victors were never able to wipe the slate clean. With the arrival of the Anglo-

Normans and their absorption of the Scandinavians, two distinct ways of life, Gaelic and English, became perpetuated, and a mutual policy of excluding the other community ensured that each would be concerned with a different Ireland.

Maintaining existing conventions of recording events from year to year in what were called annals, the Gaelic Irish virtually ignored the presence of the Anglo-Normans and described them as foreigners, the *gaill*. The term is all the more suggestive because it implies that the Celts themselves were not the earliest Irish speakers and that to the pre-Celtic population these first invaders from Gaul were never really accepted as indigenous.

Many of the ancient Irish collections of legends and stories have come down to us in different versions dating from the tenth to the seventeenth century. The longevity of this record is not solely due to the fact that later versions survived the destruction of the earlier. It also represents something of the history of contemporary public interest, and here we come to something of vital importance over more than fifteen centuries of Irish history. The architects of the rebellion in 1916 were very concerned to inculcate devotion to the earliest heroic stories and particularly to the deeds of the youthful Cuchulain. Patrick Pearse in his school, St Enda's, educated his pupils on these lines, and he was determined to make the best use of something which had come back into Irish recollection almost in his own life time, during the last quarter of the nineteenth and the first quarter of the twentieth century. Cuchulain was the outstanding personality of hero tales connected with a great conflict between the men of Ulster and the men of Connacht. (This may perhaps explain why, after the defeat of Ulster and its division among peoples claiming descent from those of Connacht, Cuchulain was almost forgotten.) As the story comes down to us it depicts the boy hero who intimidates and indeed defeats the forces of the western peoples who could not, even with the best offices of the literary class, continue to enjoy the story of those they had defeated. By contrast to Cuchulain, right through the Middle

Ages, the popularity of stories about the Fianna is represented by many versions which survived for century after century, particularly among the military class of society. The writers of these legends, such as later Irish chroniclers of the seventeenth century, Geoffrey Keating and the Four Masters, looked on them as part of history and continued to ignore as far as possible the Anglo-Norman tradition. Individual Normans were brought into the record only when they were essential to the narrative of the fortunes of the Irish kings and their communities.

A new type of writing emerged in Ireland in the twelfth century when Giraldus Cambrensis, Gerald the Welshman, presented a justification for the Anglo-Norman conquest and the story of the conquerors, in two remarkable works. Cambrensis ushered in a new phase, in part because he sought to justify his heroes by depicting the moral imperfections of the Irish and partly by making it virtually a Christian obligation for Henry II to use crusader tactics to defeat them. From Giraldus Cambrensis in the twelfth century to the Tudor historians in the sixteenth, the history of the Anglo-Norman way of life in Ireland was represented as a conflict between civilisation and barbarism. The fact that a reforming pope was identified with Henry II's Irish enterprise served to strengthen the association of the foreigners with the cause of religion and the natives with the forces of darkness.

The story of the English in Ireland became all the more associated with religious reform in the sixteenth century, when Tudor adoption of Protestantism and the conservative Irish preference for Catholicism brought Ireland into the clash between the two forms of Christianity in western Europe, which contributed more than any other force to the great wars of the sixteenth and seventeenth centuries. But the divorce of the papacy from English government led in Ireland to an alliance between the forces of the Counter-Reformation and the native tradition. Thus it can be said that in the age of the dynastic nation England became confronted in Ireland with the international papacy and with national elements unwilling to be assimilated to the expanding English nationalism. Thus the record began to change: history in Ireland began to be written with the outlook of a foreigner in the sixteenth century.

In the seventeenth century most of those who wrote Irish history were concerned only with the victory of a Protestant England, but once again an unexpected element entered the picture. The Protestant writers were hardly professional historians; they compare poorly with professional writers on the continent. The wars which gave victory to Tudor England in Ireland drove a substantial number of members of professional families out of the country into Spain and France, the Low Countries and the Papal States. Abroad they entered on an ecclesiastical or a military career. A few of these, as well as some of their fellow exiles who had no traditional learning, devoted part of their time to preserving the history of their defeated nation, either by collecting its literary remains or by representing it in a seventeenth-century context, usually in deep hostility to England. Thus, at the very time that Protestant historians in Ireland were presenting the country's history as an integral part of the struggle against popery, superstition, obscurantism and barbarism under a patriotic Protestant prince, there was growing up abroad the interpretation of the recent history of Ireland as a struggle for faith and fatherland, for Catholicism and nationalism, against ruthless foreign conquerors.

Both these interpretations had in common a concern for presenting a unified impression of Irish history, in which communities unworthy to be recorded were regarded as inferior and somehow not Irish, whether they were conquered or foreigners, Papists or Protestants. This is the background to the writing of history in colonial Ireland in which the protagonists of legislative independence welcomed the birth of a new Irish nation. This was first conceived in the tradition of the English revolution of 1689, by William Molyneux and Jonathan Swift.

Concurrent with the claim for the new nation being made

by Grattan and his fellow patriots of the Irish parliament in 1780 the systematic publication of the records of Ireland before the English conquest was beginning. The first interpretations of ancient Ireland by Charles O'Conor and others were uncritical, but they were at least indicative of O'Conor's awareness of the need to present ancient Irish history in a form palatable to the eighteenth-century rationalistic mind. In this instance, it was perhaps more successful than it deserved as the national struggle involved calling into question political traditions introduced from England. If the Irish had no original contribution to make to political life, how could they be worthy of self-government?

The end of the eighteenth century saw the challenge to the national monarchy in France and elsewhere by the forces of revolution which destroyed the past and replaced its tradition by the principles of enlightened government. If historical writers did not thrive in this atmosphere, at least in countries where revolutionaries sought public endorsement the past was still conscripted to justify the new doctrines. Thus the United Irishmen attempted to build up a case for an independent Ireland by referring to former glories, even though these could not always be justified in relation to the more democratic principles of the French revolution.

After legislative union had been enacted in 1800, as part of the effort to organise resistance to the conquering French armies of liberation, a new interpretation of Irish history commenced. The forces of nationalism regrouped themselves in order to preserve the old traditions, much as exiled writers had done in the seventeenth century. The glories of the past were soon used by the critics of the Union to contrast the failure of that amalgamation to secure justice for Ireland. The delay in conceding Catholic emancipation brought the Roman Church in Ireland into conflict with the government, to which its Irish prelates had sworn eternal allegiance as the price of avoiding the penalties of the anti-Catholic laws. Thus Catholic emancipation transformed a public organisation for religious freedom into a national one for independence. The leader, O'Connell, who brought this about, not merely weakened the case for maintenance of the Union but established the norms of patriotic historical writing for more than a century to come. The history of Ireland became a history of struggle against England for religious toleration, for parliamentary reform, and for political freedom which would ultimately secure once more an independent nation. As O'Connell presented this, using the infringements of the treaty of Limerick of 1691 as a justification for challenging the social contract between the rulers of Ireland and the Irish people, Ireland's history was represented as an illustration of democratic development, though still in the English tradition of such freedom fighters as Hampden, Pym, Locke and Paine, and very different from such revolutionaries as Cromwell and the United Irishmen. Dimly, O'Connell perceived that his interpretation of Irish history was based upon the English traditions of Grattan, and he never treated seriously the claims that a democratic Ireland had existed before the English.

It was the doctrinaire thinkers among O'Connell's contemporaries who sought to establish an independent Ireland on absolute principles, with the result that exponents of a simply utilitarian justification for Irish self-government could not seek a monopoly of the national mandate to destroy the Union. Thomas Davis, Charles Gavan Duffy, John Mitchel and James Fintan Lalor created the Young Ireland interpretation of the past as an absolute justification for an independent nation. If they failed in the political sphere and dragged the O'Connell movement for Repeal down from the pedestal of public endorsement, so that Irish national politics was without a respectable cause for a quarter of a century, at least they stimulated successive generations to support their abstract case for political nationhood. Their writing of history may have been as much dominated by their unhistorical ideas as was O'Connell's by the argument against the Treaty of Limerick, but they presented their view in the romantic atmosphere which was so appealing to a Europe in which France put Louis Napoleon on the Bonapartist throne of his immortal uncle.

The late nineteenth century witnessed an increasing cleavage between the historians who favoured Union and progress and those who rejected as un-Irish any sense of community which was not in tune with the Irish tradition. Even within the Catholic Church in Ireland there are distinct signs of a division among clerical writers of history, between those who looked back to past glories and those who looked forward to converting the Empire to Catholicism. In the realm of politics, the acceptance by the English Liberal Party of Ireland's right to self-government gave authority to one interpretation of Ireland's past. The rejection of the same claim by the Unionists in turn justified the other interpretation of the past which left little room for any culture which had not been imported from Britain.

Concurrently two external influences operated on Irish historiography. German philological scholars laid the foundations for the study of early Irish literature, and their labours were brought into service by the nationalists, to preserve and secure the rightful independence of the oldest nation in Europe. Thus the literary movement which threw up Yeats, Lady Gregory and Joyce became a prelude to revolution by 1916. Simultaneously Irish exiles in America, where they had emigrated in increasing numbers after the famine, began to present their interpretation of the Irish story as worthy of comparison with that of the inhabitants of the land of the free and the nation of the future. Even the experience of life in a British dominion was not without its lessons for the writers of Irish history. From Australia, both Sir Charles Gavan Duffy and Cardinal P.F. Moran increasingly emphasised the rightfulness of the Irish case for self-government and the association of the Catholic Church with that fight for freedom. By the end of the nineteenth century an English writer on Ireland's history would normally accept it that politics, meaning pro-unionism or pro-nationalism, coloured one's approach to the past.

It is hardly necessary to say much of the interpretation of Irish history in the twentieth century before the concession of self-government in 1921. Connolly's *Labour in Irish History* was a condemnation of the English conquest as the source of the evils of capitalism and colonialism, in contrast to the communist paradise which he claimed existed in Ireland before the English. The interpretation adopted by Pearse in his political writings is not incompatible with Connolly's, save that Pearse more categorically asserted the monopoly of expounding the national gospel for leaders in the revolutionary tradition, and rejected constitutional heroes as compromisers with the mammon of iniquitous imperialism. Perhaps the outstanding contribution of Pearse in non-political as well as in political writings, was to conscript the Christian message to justify Irish revolution. It was, perhaps, understandable in an age which saw the causes of conflicting protagonists in the first world war defended by their respective Christian leaders. It also followed the affirmation of the righteousness of the Protestant opponents of Home Rule in the Ireland of 1912 by leading Anglican, Presbyterian and Methodist pastors. Thus Ireland was involved in the first so-called struggle against world barbarism in circumstances which made it difficult to claim to be an Irish patriot without being involved in anti-British politics.

With the establishment in 1921–22 of independent self-governing Irish states, north as well as south, there really emerged the first opportunity of an objective approach to the history of Ireland. Nevertheless the abandonment of the anti-British interpretation did not follow more quickly than it had in the America of post-revolutionary days. The re-emergence of a professional body of Irish historians during the last half century has materially assisted the development of a greater objectivity, though it has also created two new dangers: an over-consciousness of the need to 'bend over backwards' in dealing with past British iniquities and an obsequiousness towards modern Irish government north as well as south. Perhaps one may conclude with the consolation that the vast extension in source material available will, in the long run, prove more effective in establishing historical thinking, though there is a danger that the slowness with which documentation is absorbed will seriously retard any over-all reinterpretation.

It should not go without comment that a history of Ireland such as this one is unlikely to appeal to future generations, which will no longer be dependent on the written word, which, after centuries of critical discipline, had been accepted with more reverence than are the new media of communication respected today. Perhaps when these mature, in their own still unpredictable ways, they will evolve a more responsible attitude to professional studies.

The writers of history, in the nineteenth and in the twentieth centuries, have established the modern profession of historian. In any historical consideration of the community of Ireland, one must take account of how that profession has developed in western civilisation. The research methods of the historians, and their attitudes to the sources upon which they rely, inevitably shape their historical writings.

The profession of historian has emerged chiefly from university teaching, where critical standards of other disciplines have imposed the methods of the scientist on the historian, even if the latter sometimes likes to regard the exposition of his material as an art. The scientific method has led to exclusive reliance on historical objects and documents. In turn this has led to a reappraisal of the pre-scientific writers, who were often accepted as authorities for other reasons than for the facts they contributed from a limited use of original sources. In writing on Ireland much documentary work has still to be accomplished. The most immediate task is that of saving the monuments and papers as well as the oral traditions of our people from destruction if the full history of the community is to be written.

And there are still newer challenges which the professional historian faces, challenges which stem from the interests of a society which is concerned for an expanding world, but which is also devoting more attention to the development of individual groups. In this situation sources are subjected to a different type of analysis. The integral archives of an organisation come to be considered as essential to the reconstruction of its administration. The source methods of the sociologist and the statistician must also be studied by the historian.

In the age of the computer, the community of Ireland, regarded historically, will be presented in a still newer way; but it will take some time before the historians have disciplined themselves to asking the computer the right questions having regard to the data submitted. And it will be even more essential than ever to remember the purposes for which the sources were compiled, to study the contexts of the communications media in which the sources appear, and to assess the processing of the information by precision instruments with reference to achievements where their accuracy has already been tested. Meanwhile this short history of Ireland may help us to think ourselves more effectively out of the past into a more mechanised future.

Index